DEATH

Confronting the Reality

William E. Phipps

John Knox Press
ATLANTA

Acknowledgment is made for permission to quote from the following sources:

To Concern for Dying for the Living Will and for excerpts from the Concern for Dying Newsletter. Reprinted with permission of: Concern for Dying, 250 West 57th Street, Suite 831, New York, NY 10107/(212) 246-6962.

To Macmillan: Reprinted with permission of Macmillan Publishing Company from *On Death and Dying* by Elisabeth Kübler-Ross. Copyright © 1969 by Elisabeth Kübler-Ross.

To Mayfield for graph and excerpts from Lynne Anne De-Spelder and Albert Lee Strickland, *The Last Dance: Encountering Death and Dying*, copyright 1983 Mayfield; and for excerpts from Edwin S. Shneidman, *Death: Current Perspectives*, copyright 1984 Mayfield; reprinted with permission.

To Merrill for excerpts from DEATH, SOCIETY, AND HUMAN EXPERIENCE, SECOND EDITION by Robert J. Kastenbaum, copyright 1981 C. V. Mosby Co., © copyright 1985 Merrill Publishing Co., Columbus, Ohio.

Library of Congress Cataloging-in-Publication Data

Phipps, William E., 1930–
  Death : confronting the reality.

  1. Death. I. Title.
BD444.P49 1987   306.9   86-45405
ISBN 0-8042-0487-X

To Carroll Tyree Pool

(1949–1985)

my artistic and witty nephew, who died at the full flowering of life. In Henry Wadsworth Longfellow's poignant words:

> There is a Reaper, whose name is Death,
> And, with his sickle keen,
> He reaps the bearded grain at a breath,
> And the flowers that grow between.

(*The Reaper and the Flowers*, lines 1–4)

PREFACE

Early this century H. L. Mencken commented in *Smart Set*, "Go to any public library and look under 'Death: Human' in the card index, and you will be surprised to find how few books there are on the subject." That dearth of death literature has now been remedied. More books have been written in the past generation about death from psychological, sociological, anthropological, biological, medical, historical, religious, and philosophical perspectives than had been written in the previous century. At the same time thousands of colleges and high schools, churches and synagogues have introduced courses in death education. Not only are scholarly studies being pursued vigorously, but also the popular media are giving attention to death as never before. In June 1971 Edwin Shneidman analyzed results from a death questionnaire *Psychology Today* had issued to its readers (pp. 43–45, 74–80). The magazine's editors were flabbergasted when more than thirty thousand responses were received, fifty percent more than for a sex questionnaire—the largest previous response. (Appendix A.1, "Death Probe," is a questionnaire of this type.)

One factor which has stimulated inquiry in a discipline now called thanatology is the possibility, for the first time in human memory, of total annihilation. The reaction of some to the threat of atomic destruction is captured in this popular slogan: "Live fast, die young, and have a good-looking corpse." But the bleak prophecy of nuclear winter motivates more responsible persons to explore the human fascination with slaughtering other members of their own species and to learn strategies for averting individual and mass killing. Another causative factor is medical advancements which impose novel life-extension dilemmas. For example, the Baby Doe and Barney Clark cases have drawn national attention to the problems created when technology threatens to become a master rather than a servant. The resurgence of interest in death also illustrates the pendulum principle: intelligent adults tend to swing in the opposite direction from rigid early conditioning. Structuring primary experiences of death out of children's environment motivates some to draw back the veil when they come of age and investigate what has been mysteriously concealed.

From classroom discussions I have learned of the awe-ful/awful ambivalence toward death in human consciousness. As an old maxim puts it, "Death and the sun are two things not to be looked on with a steady eye." Attraction and repulsion characterize both. Exploration of these sensitive and taboo areas may help us avoid becoming traumatized by future personal experience with death.

Although the chapters of this text may be studied in any order, there is some logic for the sequence given. The first chapter attempts to blend an introspective probe with objective data and thereby establish an affective/cognitive balance that will be pursued throughout the book. Chapter 2 is devoted to clarifying the meaning of the key concept *death* by juxtaposing it with the term *life*. Socrates long ago called attention to the time wasted when people in search of wisdom use abstract nouns without agreeing on definitions. The third chapter looks at demography with respect to mortality and ponders why some have more quantity and/or quality of life than others. The chapters on terminal illness, suicide, and violence describe ways of dying in America and wrestle with moral issues raised by particular kinds of death. The body disposal and bereavement chapters focus on how survivors can best deal with after-death situations. The study ends with a consideration of immortality theories in world cultures.

The appendices provide a variety of materials for developing personal positions on life-and-death matters. The questionnaires and worksheets can be used to establish a tentative stance on issues relevant to the subject matter of a particular chapter. The differing perspectives encountered in the chapter may then prompt more internal and external dialogue. The appendices also provide a sampling of what several early leaders of world religions have said about death. Realizing that individual interest in Sakyamuni the Buddha, Jesus the Christ, and Paul the Apostle varies, their extended viewpoints are placed there to heighten the versatility of the text. The appendices contain many seminal ideas for reflection and discussion that should not be overlooked.

My research and writing on the topic of death have been facilitated by two institutions. I am grateful to Davis and Elkins College, where I have served as Professor of Religion and Philosophy since 1956, for granting me a sabbatical leave in 1985. Thanks to an appointment to the faculty of Boston University as Special Researcher, I have had the resources of excellent libraries at my disposal.

I acknowledge also my indebtedness to the hundreds of students in college, church, and prison settings. They have stimulated me during the fifteen years I have taught a course entitled "Death and Dying," and their interests are reflected in the choice of topics in this book. It has delighted me that some students have been frank enough to share with me different perspectives from those I advocate. My thanatology students have ranged widely in age and in experience. Many have been teenagers making their first inquiry into the subject, but some have been nurses with years of exposure to dying patients. From these students I have collected responses to questionnaires similar to those found in the appendices, and their collective viewpoints are occasionally echoed in this text.

The responses received from the death-related articles I have written for the *New York Times* and a number of professional journals have also enabled me to reevaluate information and reassess positions taken. I am interested in receiving readers' criticism of points of view expressed in this book.

Bill Phipps
Elkins, WV 26241

CONTENTS

1

FACING UP TO DEATH

My death education began more than fifty years ago. Granny instructed me in death and dying by both word and example. After her husband died in 1930, in the same house where I was born and during the year of my birth, my family continued to live with her for nine formative years of my life. Caring for one another was the main responsibility that Granny and I were given. Following the established expectation in Virginia that elderly widows mourn for the rest of their lives, Granny always wore long black dresses. She occupied the choice bedroom in our large house because her crippled condition made it difficult for her to move about. As she could not climb stairs, she always stayed at home.

My grandmother told me stories of death. She had been a girl about my age, living on a slaveholding plantation near one of the last battlefields of America's most costly war. She shared with me horrible seventy-year-old memories of the "War Between the States." When I asked her about the sword that hung over our fireplace, she related her husband's terrible experience of fighting Yankees at Piedmont with a hundred other boys and of being imprisoned in Delaware. While I sat beside her rocking chair, she also scared me with the story of a wolf with big teeth eating up Red Riding Hood's grandmother. I was not relieved when she told me that bears, but not wolves, lived in the nearby Blue Ridge Mountains.

Granny could read only with the help of a magnifying glass, and because of this difficulty she limited her reading to the Bible. I recall being fascinated by the 4004 B.C. date printed alongside the opening words of her Bible. I wondered how anything could be so old. Granny was the most ancient thing I knew, and she was not even four hundred years old. When I encountered balls of dust under her high bed, I thought of one of her Bible stories. She had explained that Adam and Eve returned to dust because they had been caught stealing fruit. Sometimes Granny expressed herself in biblical language: "There's a time and a place for everything, Billy; there's a time to live and laugh, and a time to weep and die."

Granny talked frankly about her approaching death. Because she had grown up with gruesome tales of being buried alive, written by Edgar Allan Poe and other nineteenth-century authors, she insisted that a physician should check carefully for signs of life before pronouncing her dead. Also, my grandmother verbally declared her last will to our family. The possessions she had to divide were few because the Great Depression had depleted her inheritance. I asked her to give me the metal pitcher which perspired as I did on a hot day. After she graciously arranged for me to have her silver service, I willingly kept it polished.

We shared pleasant and unpleasant experiences. My oldest sister chose Granny's wedding day for her own marriage, and I brought in flowering branches from our yard for Granny to arrange in the living room where the ceremony would be conducted. Not long after this joyous event, she slipped and further injured her hip. I had removed the rubber tip from the cane on which she depended, and this resulted in Granny's being bedridden for weeks. She forgave me after I agreed to thread needles for her and keep my toys out of her path.

Granny had a stroke at the age of eighty-three. The physician who was called in said he did not think she would "rally"—whatever that meant. Shortly afterwards, close friends came by to make their farewells, and her labored breathing ceased. It seemed fitting that

she died on the "Sabbath"—the name her Presbyterian heritage had
taught her for the weekly holy day. As a witness to her death, I was
curious but not shocked. She had taught me that what was going to
happen to her was the inevitable way of all flesh. Soon after her death
her jaws were tied shut with a strip of cloth. After rigor mortis set
in, her mouth remained closed without being bound.

My parents directed the funeral. They selected pallbearers: active
ones for carrying the casket and honorary ones for carrying the floral
tributes. Mother wrote the obituary, but even before the local newspaper published it, word of Granny's death had spread widely by the
telephone party line. The neighborhood had also been notified of
death's incursion by a wreath bound with a white satin bow placed
by the side of our front door. Father talked with Granny's pastor in
Waynesboro about her favorite Scripture passages, from which appropriate readings would be selected for the funeral ceremony. A
musician was asked to play the out-of-tune piano on which I practiced and to lead the worshipers in singing a cherished hymn of Granny's which begins,

> Rock of Ages, cleft for me,
> Let me hide myself in Thee.

Friends were helpful: some brought food, some cleaned the house,
and some greeted the callers. Granny's casket was brought from the
funeral home and placed in our unheated parlor beyond the living
room. I helped carry in the extra chairs supplied by the funeral home.

The day after Granny died I went to school as usual. During a
school recess my teacher put a hand on my shoulder and expressed
her sympathy. She asked why I had not told her about the loss. Until
then I had not realized that she had any concern for my family or
would ever touch a pupil affectionately. Screwing up my courage, I
asked to be excused from attending school the next afternoon in order
to attend Granny's funeral. Since I felt obliged to go to school even
when sick, I was relieved when my teacher suggested I stay home all
the next day.

That evening after everyone else had gone upstairs, I decided I
would give Granny a good-bye kiss. On raising the veil covering
what appeared to be a large open trunk, I noticed that the rouge on

her face was different from any cosmetic she had ever worn. I was also offended by a strong perfume which did not smell like Granny. When I touched her face I recoiled, certain that the person whom I loved was not in the fancy box. I had expected the warmth I had always received when I cuddled closely, but what I felt was hard and chilling.

On the morning of the funeral I noticed that the flowers in the wreath outside the door had frozen stiff. When the undertaker later removed them, they were thawed but ugly. What happened to those cut flowers symbolized well what had happened to Granny's body. The flowers had been arranged for an impressive show, but only a sentimentalist would forget that they were severed from their source of vitality and would necessarily disintegrate.

The funeral service was reassuring. Sitting with my sisters on the stairs in the center of our house, I could see and participate fully. I had not realized before that many people I did not even know were also sad. After seeing my strong father cry for the first time ever, I did not feel embarrassed by my own tears. When the minister read the Twenty-third Psalm, one Granny had me memorize, I recalled her comment on "Yea, though I walk through the valley of the shadow of death, I will fear no evil: for Thou art with me" (vs.4 KJV). She had said, "God doesn't protect us from death but dwells with us forever in spite of death."

The service was concluded in the cemetery where I had often visited. Each summer I went there with my father to trim around the gravestones of the family plot while he used the lawnmower. An older brother and my grandfather were buried there. When the minister said we are all dust-to-dust creatures, I thought of Granny's favorite Genesis story. She had prepared me for the hallowedness and hollowness I felt when her body was lowered into the grave.

My experiences with Granny seem quaint in comparison with the typical death and dying circumstances of contemporary America as described in this book. Although death customs are generally the cultural institution most resistant to change, this century has seen a major shift concerning where and with whom people die and where and how funerals are conducted. The only features of my testimony which do not now seem old-fashioned are the age of death, the cause of death, and the method of body disposal. There is nothing atypical today about an octogenarian dying of a cerebral hemorrhage or about using a casket to inter the remains.

But the multigenerational family structure has virtually disappeared during this century. Only about ten percent of American widows now live with their married children. Houses are constructed with fewer bedrooms, so there is usually no room even if there is a desire to accommodate a widow or a widower. Widows who were never employed but were married to Social Security participants now have retirement benefits, and widows who were employed may have additional benefits as well. Neither of these economic advantages enabling independent living was available to Granny. After a husband's death now, a widow who does not care to remain in their house alone may obtain a smaller retirement apartment, perhaps in a more suitable climate. In today's circumstances, readjustment after death is quite different from what it was in a multigenerational home. My mother, who was never employed outside the home, considered homemaking to be her career and genuinely appreciated the opportunity to care for Granny in return for the earlier kindnesses of the mother who had adopted her. By contrast, the typical pattern today is one of occasional contact between a widow and her progeny, and a long-distance call is the usual way for them to learn about her eventual death.

As the acids of modernity erode the extended family, personal exposure to death correspondingly lessens. On the average, there is only one death every two decades in the shrunken family. In American culture today, few experience an untreated corpse firsthand. Whenever a death occurs, the body is quickly covered and made to disappear. One might conclude that unless it was whisked away a plague would strike or the body would immediately reek. America's great faith in medicine impels our health-care professionals to seal off from us direct exposure to any evidence that all illnesses are not curable.

I belong to the last generation of Americans not oriented to hospitals for the birthing and dying processes. As were all seven of my brothers and sisters, I was born at home, and my parents died in the same house where my grandmother died. Centered in the home were the main rites of passage: births, marriages, and deaths. Today only about twenty percent of American deaths occur at home, and even fewer births, weddings, or funerals occur there. A dying person is now more likely to be surrounded by members of a health-care institution than by members of his or her family.

My emotional life would have been greatly diminished had I not been a full mourning partner with the older members of my family. My association with Granny had been closer than most of theirs, for I was the only one who had spent all my years with her. She was not the only grandparent that my siblings could remember, but she was the only one I ever knew. I felt as though I was the chief mourner, and consequently the memory of her life and death is deeply and vividly etched in my psyche.

The role of funeral homes has also changed. We thought of them principally as places to purchase caskets, not places to visit the dead or worship God. My conservative southern town had not been affected by the reintroduction of neo-Egyptian mortuary chapels, already stylish in urban areas. Funerals were customarily conducted from homes or from churches. The latter were especially convenient when homes were not large enough to accommodate the expected mourners. The undertaker—as we always called the mortician—was secondary in importance to the officiating clergy. This was symbolized by the order of the vehicles in the funeral procession. The minister's car led, followed by the undertaker's hearse.

As a child I attended dozens of funerals, mainly because I enjoyed the companionship of my father, who was a rural pastor. The funeral service for a pillar of the church attracted overflow crowds to the sanctuary. Such an occasion was one of the few times when visitors from other denominations were present. After the service at a church or home, I rode with Father, who led the slow procession to the cemetery. I imagined myself to be a parade marshal, attracting the attention of all we passed and causing traffic to stop and men to remove their hats in respect. Black-suited undertakers, trying to appear sad, assisted the pallbearers at the cemetery. After the committal service I sometimes helped the sexton fill in the grave with loose dirt piled nearby.

Children are now often segregated from death experiences, both before and after. Due to hospital rules, they usually do not visit with dying family members. A child commonly has no personal experience of a family death throughout the formative years of growth. Robert Kavanaugh's study of American college students reveals that only eight percent have witnessed a person dying and only twenty-two percent have encountered a corpse closely.[1]

I have found that many young adults have never attended a single funeral. Sociologist Robert Fulton, director of Minnesota's Center for Death Education, has commented, "This present generation in America can be said to be the first 'death-insulated' generation in the history of the world."[2] He believes that this situation is robbing both the young and the aged of an important dimension of life.

In a brilliant essay entitled "The Pornography of Death," British sociologist Geoffrey Gorer contrasts the Victorian generation, of which Granny was a part, with our own day. He describes "a shift in prudery": "Whereas copulation has become more and more 'mentionable' . . . death has become more and more 'unmentionable. . . . The natural processes of corruption and decay have become . . . as disgusting as the natural processes of birth and copulation were a century ago. . . . The ugly facts are relentlessly hidden; the art of the embalmers is an art of complete denial."[3]

We now reveal the facts of life but conceal the facts of death. Formerly children were told that they were brought by a stork, yet they were exposed to frank scenes of death. Granny responded only with a blush when I asked her to tell me the meaning of the term *gestation* that I had read or to explain why my married sister looked as if she had swallowed a watermelon. Explicit sex education is now commonplace, but children are likely to be told that those who have "passed away" now rest in lovely gardens. The very word *death* is suppressed. A study of sympathy cards shows that only three percent mention the forbidden word.[4] "Leave-taking" or "called upstairs" are among the fig leaves used to cover the four-letter word *dead*. In contrast to the weather, dying is what everyone does and no one talks about. In fact, "Never say die" is one of our most common sayings. Like superstitious primitives, some believe that anything never mentioned will disappear.

Some remaining sexual taboos, however, are analogous to death attitudes. Death is like masturbation: people do it, but it is considered obscene to talk about. Or, death is like an incurable venereal disease: it is too embarrassing to discuss with one's family, and only reluctantly does one consult about it with a physician.

In surveying American high school seniors, Hannelore Wass found that thirty-nine percent never talked about death at home and an additional twenty-six percent talked about it only when it was absolutely necessary.[5] Reinforcing her findings, a Los Angeles study found only one-quarter of those surveyed, regardless of age or gender, had ever had a serious conversation about death.[6] Even though hundreds die every hour in the United States, David Hendin labels it "un-American" and says, "Its inevitability is an affront to our inalienable rights of 'life, liberty, and the pursuit of happiness.'"[7] In *The Immortalist*, Alan Harrington defiantly asserts, "Death is an imposition on the human race, and no longer acceptable."[8] Americans want to forget that no one gets out of this world alive!

"Nothing [is] certain, but death and taxes," Benjamin Franklin quipped in a 1789 letter. Actually, death has an infinitely higher degree of certainty than taxes. Some clever, crooked, and poor people have intentionally or unintentionally managed to avoid taxes. Nothing can be more certainly predicted of our future than death. One hundred out of every 100 people die, and 150 years from now everyone currently living will have died.

Some Americans are beginning to face up to their anxieties over death and are distinguishing between realistic, rational fears and neurotic, irrational fears. Thanatophobia, the fear of death, is positive when it causes people to take safety precautions. It is both unreasonable and self-deceptive to claim to have no fear of death. In his novel *Julie*, French philosopher Rousseau states: "He who pretends to look on death without fear lies. All men are afraid of dying; this is the great law of sentient beings, without which the entire human species would soon be destroyed." Fear of death is like fear of darkness. The fear of being on a street at night is reasonable in many areas because more vehicular accidents, stealing, and personal violence occur then. But some have a phobia of darkness that stems from childhood nightmares of boogeymen. Mental health can be jeopardized when irrational superstitions are not exorcised by the light of reason.

When a sample of college students was given a list of fifty possible causes of fear, death of a family member ranked as the single most upsetting event imaginable.[9] There is a rational as well as an irrational basis for death anxiety leading the list. The loss of a family member may be for many students the loss of the one who encourages them to do their best or who accepts them in spite of failures or who provides the funding for their education. But neurotic fears regarding what might happen before and after death lurk. These need to be dredged up from the subconscious, examined carefully, and discarded. It is hoped that this text will facilitate an in-depth personal examination.

Some wise people in the modern world encourage us to engage in the painful exploration before us. Before his accidental death while negotiating peace in Africa, the Secretary General for the United Nations, Dag Hammarskjöld, recorded this insight: "In the last analysis, it is our conception of death which decides our answers to all the questions that life puts to us."[10] Consider also the reflection of philosopher George Santayana: "To see life, and to value it, from the point of view of death is to see and value it truly. . . . It is far better to live in the light of the tragic fact, rather than to forget or deny it, and build everything on a fundamental lie."[11]

2

DEFINING DEATH
AND LIFE

Defining Death

Throughout history it has been, in most instances, not difficult to ascertain when a person ceases to live. However, in every generation there are some cases where erroneous judgments have been made on this crucial matter, with results that have been either potentially or actually ghastly.

In the ancient Roman era it was reported that a girl was being carried out on a bier to be buried when she was awakened by the touch of a Pythagorean named Apollonius. Witnesses could not decide whether "he detected some spark of life in her, which those who were nursing her had not noticed . . . or whether life was really extinct and restored it by the warmth of his touch."[1] This account is similar to one told about Jesus' traveling in Galilee as a physician (Luke 4:23; 5:31). He came to visit Jairus' daughter because he had been told she was seriously ill. On arriving at her home he found her family wailing because they assumed she had just died. When Jesus said, "She is not dead but sleeping," the mourners "laughed at him, knowing that she was dead" (Luke 8:52–53). The girl then showed vital signs when Jesus took her by the hand and spoke to her. After the resuscitation he advised her startled parents to give her food (vss. 54–55). Assuming these stories of Apollonius and Jesus are true, the miracle may have been the understanding that the girls were in a deathlike coma.

A vigil custom became widespread in Europe, in part to avoid premature burial or cremation. During the night after death kith and kin gathered around the body to mourn and to make sure the body showed no signs of life. What was called a *vigil* in Latin countries was referred to as a *wake* in Western Europe. Both words meant staying awake to watch over what appeared to be dead.

Spooky tales about mistaken death determination are told in every generation. A few centuries ago Margaret Erskine was buried in a Scottish churchyard, wearing valuable jewelry. The sexton who was left to cover the grave opened her coffin to steal the jewelry. She groaned when he tried to cut off her ring finger. He fled in panic, but others found her breathing.[2] In eighteenth-century France, Antoine Louis, a professor of medical jurisprudence, published an account of a monk who was asked to watch over the body of a young woman who had just "died." He had intercourse with her, and nine months later she gave birth.[3] A century ago a reputable British medical journal reported cases of premature burial. For example, when the supposed remains of an Australian citizen were about to be lowered into the grave, a grieving son demanded that he see his father one last time. When the coffin was opened its inmate was found to be alive.[4] These stories cause one to wonder if coffin asphyxiation has been for many people the real cause of death. When tombs are opened, the position of an occasional skeleton suggests that the person was buried alive.

In the late nineteenth century before embalming became widespread, there was an epidemic of phobia over premature burial. Some of this may have been triggered by writings such as *One Thousand Buried Alive by Their Best Friends*. Inventors patented elaborate alarms that could be triggered by the slightest movement of those who had been wrongly encoffined. In 1890 a physician won a handsome prize for arguing that putrefaction was the only foolproof sign of death and that therefore public policy should require bodies to lie in morgues until they began to rot.[5]

Mistaken death certification has by no means ended in the present day. Newspapers frequently carry stories of people judged dead, then found alive. In New York a funeral home attendant heard low moans beneath the sheet covering a person who had been declared dead from a heart ailment four hours earlier. One wonders if the shock of learning what had happened caused a fatal cardiac arrest later! Charles Herrell was found alive in West Virginia because a mortician unzipped a body bag before pushing his body into a cooler. Herrell suffered from hypoglycemia which caused a blackout when his blood sugar dropped too low. After recovering from this ordeal he made this grisly comment: "It makes me think how many people have been embalmed who weren't dead." A woman in Illinois was pronounced dead after being found lying motionless and cold on the floor of her apartment. Detectives left the body there for two hours as they investigated the scene for a possible crime. When it was then placed on a morgue table for an autopsy, a police officer heard the "corpse" swallow and gasp for breath. It was discovered that the woman had passed out from a combination of alcohol and drugs which had caused her temperature, her breathing, and her pulse rate to drop sharply, producing a hibernation-like condition.[6]

These contemporary stories of wrong death pronouncements occurred in the United States, where standards for the practice of medicine may be the highest in the world. Mistakes in life and death assessment are likely to be even more common in other nations, although this embarrassment to the medical establishment may not be publicized where the press has little freedom.

The reason that morticians have rushed some people appearing to be dead into an early grave may be in part that physicians have received little training in how to determine the death of a patient. Several doctors examined dozens of medical school textbooks and surveyed graduates from fifteen medical schools to ascertain if physicians were adequately educated in ways of accurately diagnosing death. They found that the subject was discussed in only one of the texts and that none of the medical practitioners could recall receiving instruction in this area. This study, published in a November 1968 issue of the *Journal of the American Medical Association*, points out that revival of those prepared for burial is no longer possible because "the twentieth-century practice of embalming all persons pronounced dead has served to remove any mistakes from public view." This study shows that virtually everyone assumes that a death certificate is required before embalming is permitted but that this has not been the case. The lack of adequate medical safeguards against determining death has resulted in the rational fear of premature embalming replacing for Americans the former fear of premature burial.[7]

It is not the responsibility of morticians to search for life indicators, and they have vested interests in presuming they are handling dead bodies. One embalming manual reassures morticians that cadavers may simulate life signs such as gasps and muscular contractions when fluid is injected to replace the blood but that these will soon go away. Morticians embalm bodies as soon as possible after receiving them since tissues are easier to manipulate before rigor mortis sets in several hours after death.

Modern life-support technology, administered by persons or machines, has made defining death more difficult. There is, for instance, the case of an Oregon baby who fell into a swimming pool and was under water so long that he was presumed to have drowned. Even so, a rescue crew using mouth-to-mouth artificial respiration revived the "essentially dead" child. Again, when a "cadaver" was left attached to a mechanical respirator for removal of donated vital organs, a cough alerted a medical technician that the drunken accident victim was still alive. There is an amazing account of a Wisconsin boy who was trapped for fifty minutes under ice. When he was taken out of the creek he was pronounced dead, for he had no pulse and his body was cold. Even so, he recovered because a phenomenon called "mammalian diving reflex" had cut off circulation to his arms and legs but kept the blood flowing to his brain where it was most needed to preserve life.[8]

It is apparent from these exceptional cases that the common ways of determining death are not comprehensive enough. The traditional view that equates the extinction of life with the cessation of breathing and heartbeat is defective. Due to the impact of religious and romantic writings from earliest times onward, the throbbing heart has been popularly exalted as the main organ for revealing the crucial signs of life. In reality the human personality, including intellect and emotions, is primarily the product of the brain rather than the muscle which pumps blood through the body.

During the past generation a more sophisticated definition of death has supplemented the cardiopulmonary standard. For the majority of cases the criteria of no beat of the heart and no respiration of the lungs are still useful. However, as we have seen, in a number of cases the traditional signs of death are invalid. By the old standard, about fifteen percent of comatose patients in American hospitals are dead because their breathing is not spontaneous. Many of them will regain consciousness, so it is confusing to refer to them as "clinically dead."

In 1970 Kansas became the first state to establish a legal test that was more refined than the common law definition of death. It adopted the standards developed in 1968 by a Harvard Medical School committee. The committee identified four essential criteria of an irreversible coma: (1) a complete lack of patient response to external stimuli; (2) an absence of spontaneous breathing and muscular movement; (3) no observable eye, nose, or mouth reflexes; and (4) a flat electroencephalogram (EEG) to confirm that there is no brain activity. These tests must be repeated for twenty-four consecutive hours without changes being detected before the patient is declared dead and life-sustaining equipment is removed. The Harvard committee recognized that hypothermia (when the body temperature is below ninety degrees Fahrenheit) and the presence of depressants—such as barbiturates—are two conditions in which a flat EEG does not necessarily signify death.[9] The National Institute of Neurological Diseases maintains that the Harvard criteria are too conservative because a flat EEG printout for more than thirty minutes shows an irrevocably dead brain, except in cases of hypothermia or drug overdose.[10]

Most states have now passed statutes for determining death which give primary focus to the brain rather than to other organs. The Harvard criteria, endorsed by both the American Medical Association and the American Bar Association, have been widely used as a legislative guideline. They are in accord with the Uniform Determination of Death Act which was proposed in 1981 by a United States government commission. That model law states that "an individual who has sustained either (1) irreversible cessation of circulatory and respiratory functions or (2) irreversible cessation of all functions of the entire brain, including the brain stem, is dead."[11] A uniform national standard is needed since it is still possible for the same body to be "alive" in one state and "dead" in another.

An important by-product of the brain-death statutes has been the harvesting of certain body parts for transplantation before they deteriorate. The rapidly developing technology of organ transplantation depends on the availability of a large group of potential donors and on ventilating the cadaver to preserve the needed organs until the operation on the recipient can be arranged. In most states there is now no question that a patient who is entirely dependent on a mechanical respirator and whose brain stem is permanently destroyed can be declared dead.

Even though cardiac stoppage usually occurs in a few days, the heartbeat in such bodies can continue indefinitely. In 1983 a brain-dead pregnant woman was kept on a respirator in Virginia for a record eighty-four days until a normal child was delivered by cesarean section. That same year a similarly brain-dead Japanese woman gave natural birth to a live baby.[12]

The current brain-dead statutes do not deal with the absence of cerebral functions, which are the first to cease. The cerebrum is that portion of the brain where memories, identity, and consciousness are located. Even though there is an irreversible loss of consciousness, an EEG may register some activity—because the lower brain stem is regulating breathing and blood circulation. For a decade Karen Quinlan breathed without the aid of a respirator in a nursing home, and her brain gave off sporadic EEG signals. Yet her cerebral cortex irreversibly died in 1975 for lack of oxygen. Although certain of Quinlan's involuntary bodily processes operated spontaneously, she remained in a vegetative state, receiving food through a nasogastric tube and excreting wastes through another tube. Her once lovely body shriveled to about half its normal weight and curled in a fetal position. Was the person Karen Quinlan in the emaciated body that could never think, speak, or move again?

The Quinlan case is similar to that of a less publicized person who has been called "the six-million-dollar-woman." As the result of a concussion sustained at the age of twenty-seven, the Illinois woman was continually unconscious until her death eighteen years later in 1974.[13] At astronomical expense she received tube feedings, catheterization, antibiotics, and extensive skin care because her deluded parents believed they were extending the life of a human. Large sums were paid to neurologists even though they agreed that her chances for the recovery of cognitive functions were zero.

Biological life can be determined by blood pressure and respiration, but essential personhood implies conscious interaction with one's environment and with other humans. Robert Veatch, a Hastings Center associate with a background in science and theology, maintains that a definition of death should include this primary element: "A person will be considered dead if in the announced opinion of a physician, based on ordinary standards of medical practice, he has experienced an irreversible cessation of spontaneous cerebral functions."[14] Should nourishment be withdrawn from one whose mind has degenerated to a persistent vegetative state? An extraordinary emotional and financial hardship is often imposed on the family or other support groups by a hopeless patient. Also, advanced medical resources are misallocated when used for this purpose. Although the cases cited above are rare in that they involve years of spontaneous breathing in a comatose body, there are hundreds of cases each month in the United States in which bodies are maintained on artificial support systems when only the brain stem is alive. In 1986 it was estimated that there were about ten thousand patients in a "permanent vegetative state" in the United States.[15]

Near-death Experiences

Establishing a comprehensive definition of death provides a perspective from which to evaluate stories of personal encounters with death that have captured much public attention as well as the interest of some scientific investigators. In 1975 psychiatrist Raymond Moody reported in *Life After Life* on interviews with dozens of persons who had close brushes with death. He found a number of common elements in many of their experiences. By piecing together recurring characteristics, he formed this fascinating composite picture:

> A man is dying and, as he reaches the point of greatest physical distress, he hears himself pronounced dead by his doctor. He begins to hear an uncomfortable noise, a loud ringing or buzzing, and at the same time feels himself moving very rapidly through a long dark tunnel. After this, he suddenly finds himself outside of his own physical body, but still in the immediate physical environment, and he sees his own body from a distance, as though he is a spectator. He watches the resuscitation attempt from this unusual vantage point and is in a state of emotional upheaval.
>
> After a while, he collects himself and becomes more accustomed to his odd condition. He notices that he still has a "body," but one of a very different nature and with very different powers from the physical body he has left behind. Soon other things begin to happen. Others come to meet and to help him. He glimpses the spirits of relatives and friends who have already died, and a loving, warm spirit of a kind he has never encountered before—a being of light—appears before him. This being asks him a question, nonverbally, to make him evaluate his life and helps him along by showing him a panoramic, instantaneous playback of the major events of his life. At some point he finds himself approaching some sort of barrier or border, apparently representing the limit between earthly life and the next life. Yet, he finds that he must go back to the earth, that the time for his death has not yet come. At this point he resists, for by now he is taken up with his experiences in the afterlife and does not want to return. He is overwhelmed by intense feelings of joy, love, and peace. Despite his attitude, though, he somehow reunites with his physical body and lives.[16]

Moody's bestseller has challenged other researchers to make similar investigations. Psychologist Kenneth Ring interviewed many who had recovered from life-threatening medical crises. About one-third reported out-of-body experiences and one-fifth told of going through a dark tunnel and seeing a bright light at its end.[17] Other psychologists have found that respondents give horrible as well as pleasant accounts of their almost deathbeds.[18] Michael Sabom, a professor of cardiology, found that forty-three percent of the near-death survivors he interviewed reported "Moody-like" experiences.[19] These and other studies leave little room for doubting that a large percentage of resuscitated patients have had altered states of consciousness with recurring themes. Pollster George Gallup estimates that several million Americans have had such experiences.[20] Age, gender, race, educational level, and occupation seem not to be factors in these near-death encounters.

As to the meaning of the descriptive data that investigators have uncovered, there is a wide difference among evaluators. For purposes of analysis these may be divided into the psychological, religious, and physiological interpretations. Russell Noyes and others in the mental health field have advanced a psychological explanation. Patients tend to escape into wishful thoughts of peace and well-being when facing impending death. When annihilation of the self is threatened, impressions stored in the memory flash by at a frenzied pace. Unable to tolerate the traumatic present, the patients nostalgically relive happy scenes from the past. Noyes accounts for separation-from-the-body experiences as "projections that the brain makes to negate death, to pretend we are only witnessing it as a spectator."[21] This interpretation is based on a discovery of Sigmund Freud during World War I which he published in "Thoughts for the Times on War and Death": "It is indeed impossible to imagine our own death; and whenever we attempt to do so we perceive that we are in fact still present as spectators. . . . In the unconscious every one of us is convinced of his own immortality."[22] Even as those who attempt to imagine their own funerals generally picture themselves as observers rather than as stiffs in a coffin, so similar defense mechanisms may be stimulated by being wheeled into an operating or emergency room.

Those who believe in the immortality of the soul may interpret the out-of-body experiences as true glimpses of a reality beyond space and time. The commonly experienced light could be pleasant or painful, depending on one's religious conditioning. A woman who had a vision of light when death seemed imminent said, "Since my experience I am constantly reminded of Jesus' words, 'I am the light.'" Those who have been nurtured on hellfire religion may interpret the light as a foretaste of a place of fiery torment awaiting the damned at the end of a descending tunnel. One patient told of being frightened on coming into the presence of a grotesque giant who was surrounded by moaning sufferers. On the other hand, those who are confident that their souls will ascend to a peaceful paradise when they die are not likely to report hellish vistas. Dina Ingber suggests that "the threat of death causes people to grasp unconsciously at the last straws of comfort offered by biblical stories taught them when they were young." [23]

Over against these interpretations is a hard-nosed physiological explanation. There is about a six-minute lapse between the cessation of blood circulation and brain death. Brain cells quickly die when they are deprived of the oxygen carried by the bloodstream. The first effect of cerebral anoxia, lack of oxygen, is a hallucination of tranquility. When an anesthetic is administered, the rising level of carbon dioxide in the brain can bring on vivid dreams. Moreover, a brain under stress releases painkilling chemicals called endorphins, which trigger a floating sensation. [24] An understanding of these neural response mechanisms helps to explain why some patients relate experiences that fit the Moody pattern even though they had no prior awareness of their lives being in jeopardy. For example, a patient who reports such experiences may have had a heart attack during a simple surgical procedure which he or she entered with no dread of possible death.

Probably no one explanation fully accounts for the difficult-to-label experiences under consideration. Psychological, religious, and neurological perspectives are needed to understand these complex phenomena. Moody coined the "near-death experience" phrase to refer to the cases he studied, and this designation has been so widely accepted that it is often abbreviated NDE. It is important to realize that being *near* to death does not imply that one has entered the state of death and then returned. There appears to be such a yearning for evidence of an afterlife, however, that NDE testimonies are often believed by the tellers and the hearers—including Moody—as proof of life beyond death.

By current definition, a dead person is one who cannot be resuscitated because his or her condition is irreversible. Only when brain damage is irreparable can a body be considered dead. Reports of fabulous mental phenomena in NDE cases demonstrate cerebral cortex activity. The testimonies which frequently appear in popular journals of persons who allege they once were "dead" are plausible only to those who continue to accept the traditional cardiopulmonary definition of death. It would be impossible for anyone accepting the generally endorsed Uniform Determination of Death Act to presume that those who have Moody-like experiences have really died before being revived.

Defining Life

There is as much difficulty in determining precisely when a human life begins as when it ceases, even though many have presumed that this is an easy judgment to make. Again, complex physiological, psychological, and religious considerations surface, especially when abortion is debated. Different influential perspectives on when human life begins can be found in history.

Judaism generally assumed that human life begins when a fetus is viable, that is, when it can live apart from the uterus. Jews find support for their position in the Garden of Eden story which tells of man becoming a living person when breathing began. They have also interpreted a law attributed to Moses as distinguishing between a prenatal organism and a breathing person. According to Exodus 21:22–23, if a miscarriage results from a man fighting with a pregnant woman, a fine should be imposed, but if the woman dies, it is a capital offense. Categorically different penalties are given feticide and homicide because the fetus is considered an organic part of the mother's body until separated by birth. Rabbinic authorities did not consider abortion of a nonviable fetus as murder. They permitted it when a mother's life was endangered by the continuation of pregnancy and even in some situations when her life was not threatened.[25]

In Western civilization the Jewish interpretation of Scriptures pertaining to the beginning of human life has had a weighty impact on Christian viewpoints and on civil laws. For example, a committee appointed by Presbyterians to study abortion arrived at a conclusion similar to the prevalent outlook of Judaism. The biblical interpretation on the question of when human life begins which the 1973 General Assembly of the Presbyterian Church, U.S. distributed for study is probably representative of mainline American Protestantism. It states: "Genesis 2 suggests that individual human life begins when the presence of the breath of life causes one to become a 'living being'. . . . Strictly speaking the fetus is not fully a human being."[26]

The question of when human life begins is not directly addressed in the New Testament. Attention is given there to conditions accompanying spiritual rebirth but not to conditions defining physical life. Consequently the Christian church refrained from making an authoritative ruling on the matter for many centuries.

It was only after the philosophy of Aristotle influenced Christian theologians in the Middle Ages that a consensus was reached on when human life begins. Thomas Aquinas, one of the most venerated of Catholic theologians, agreed with the Greek philosopher that the embryonic matter is ensouled and thereby humanized some weeks after conception.[27] Aquinas held that there is an essential difference between what is potential and what is actual in living organisms. It is therefore as reasonable to differentiate between an embryo and a human life as to distinguish between a nut and the tree it can become. To eat a walnut is to consume what might have developed into a tree, but it would be ludicrous to suggest that a tree was swallowed. Likewise, to abort an embryo is not to kill a person since it has not been infused by God with a human form. On the basis of appearance it would be difficult to differentiate between an embryo from a human and one from another animal. At the Vienne Council in 1312 the Catholic Church officially adopted the viewpoint of Aquinas. As a result, the baptizing of miscarriages that lacked a human shape was prohibited.

In 1869 Pope Pius IX shifted the position of Roman Catholicism regarding when human life begins by declaring that the soul enters the fertilized ovum at conception. Consequently, for the past century the church has not only automatically excommunicated members who procure abortions but also has urged governments to outlaw the murderous act. In addition, the Catholic Church has based its doctrine of the sinfulness of contraception on the assumption that human life is wasted when fertilization is made impossible.

It should be realized, however, that there are many Catholics who do not accept their church's present position on this controversial matter. In 1970 Jesuit Joseph Donceel, a Fordham University philosopher, argued for a return to Aquinas' ensoulment doctrine, which the church had accepted for centuries. Donceel asserts, "I feel certain that there is no human soul, hence no human person . . . during the early stages of pregnancy and that, consequently, it is not immoral to terminate pregnancy during this time, provided there are serious reasons for such an intervention."[28] Donceel commends the medieval Catholics who permitted abortions before "quickening," the time when the first fetal movement is felt by a woman during the third month of her pregnancy.

In 1981 a bill was introduced in Congress which declared, "Human life shall be deemed to exist from conception." Its sponsors presumed that if this bill could be enacted into law, then every fertilized ovum of an American woman would be a citizen protected by the United States Constitution. If the law was not successfully challenged as unconstitutional, it would in effect annul the 1973 Supreme Court decision which legalized abortion.

At the Senate hearing on this Human Life Bill, Dr. George Ryan, president of the American College of Obstetricians and Gynecologists, was called on to give expert testimony on behalf of his professional organization and was asked, "Do you believe life begins at conception?" He responded: "Biological life, yes; human beings, no. . . . There is no question that a cell is living. . . . When life should be considered human is not a scientific question. It is philosophical, moral, and theological. All these years we have said a human is entitled to all rights of the Constitution at birth. This has worked pretty well so far."[29]

Although the Senate Judiciary Subcommittee passed the Human Life Bill, it fell far short of obtaining full congressional support; therefore, no law has challenged the Supreme Court's *Roe versus Wade* abortion judgment. That landmark decision did not attempt to specify exactly when human life begins but did affirm that a person has full legal rights only after birth. It was pointed out that "the unborn have never been recognized in the law as persons in the whole sense."[30] Since a fetus is usually viable around six months after conception, the high court permitted states to restrict severely or even to prohibit abortion after the second trimester. This much-debated court ruling is in harmony with the biblical interpretations which we reviewed.

A large and vocal minority of Americans, non-Catholics and Catholics alike, object to this ruling of the Supreme Court. These people generally believe that human life begins with conception. Such a doctrine logically leads to some curious consequences. The microscopic one-celled fertilized egg, called a zygote, has about a one in four chance of spontaneous expulsion during the first week of its life after coming down the fallopian tubes and before implantation in the uterine wall. Thus by this minority judgment thousands of dead humans are monthly released in menstruation by women who did not even know they were pregnant. Along with the more developed miscarriages the humans are usually disposed of without death certificate or funeral ceremony. The millions of American women who use the intrauterine "loop" should be charged with homicide, for this birth control device functions to prevent the zygote from adhering to the uterus. In the case of identical twins, one human soul multiplies when the ovum splits at an early stage of pregnancy. The implications of the doctrine that human life begins at conception are absurd.

There have been some in the past and are some in the present who believe that human life begins even before conception. It was traditionally believed in Europe that human organisms were like plant organisms in that the vitality is found in the *sperma*, the Greek term for seed, before it was planted in a container. Accordingly, the uterus provided only the receptacle and the nourishment for the male's preexisting baby.[31] All that made up the defining characteristics of a human person was generated in the testicles. The discovery of ovulation in the nineteenth century resulted in a scientific recognition that the female contributes to conception an ovum with twenty-three chromosomes, to combine with an equal number of chromosomes received from the male. However, on the folk level, parents often still explain human reproduction in an androcentric and unscientific manner, saying that Mommy grows the seeds that Daddy sows.

The erroneous identification of what is still misnamed *spermatozoa* with human life has resulted in some historical sanctions against some expressions of male sexuality. Homosexuality has been considered a crime in many nations because miniature human lives were allegedly destroyed when "seed" was not sown in vaginas.[32] Likewise, male masturbation has been condemned because "seed is spilled." The first-century Latin writer Martial, who introduced into our vocabulary the word *masturbation* (from *manus*, hand, and *stuprare*, to defile), warns, "What you are losing between your fingers is a human being."[33] Puritan clergyman Richard Capel, who called masturbation "a secret kinde of murther,"[34] illustrates the way in which the infection of Martial's idea entered the mainstream of Christianity.

The traditional outlook on semen has influenced recent discussions on human insemination. For example, in 1983 a Frenchman who had made a deposit in a sperm bank died. His widow asked to withdraw it for implantation, but the bank refused on grounds that no instructions were left for its disposal. In court the state prosecutor agreed, arguing that it was part of the deceased body even though separated from it. Since the corpse has a right to physical integrity, he reasoned, the widow has no more right to her husband's sperm than to his ears. In the end the court agreed with the wife, ruling that this "secretion contained the seeds of life." The expected offspring would be heir to that part of his father's estate which law assigns to an "issue." After giving this account of a bewildering problem that has resulted from the new breeding technology, Otto Friedrich concludes, "There are elements of absurdity in such a controversy, and yet it derives quite directly from a broader question that is not absurd at all: When does human life begin?"[35]

Some who endorse the view that human death can best be measured by a flat EEG reason that the beginning of human life can correspondingly be measured by a jagged EEG. Those in search of a mechanical confirmation of the dawn of humanness grasp at the fact that an embryo begins to have brain waves at about eight weeks. Fearing this logical implication, an organization called People Concerned for the Unborn Child has opposed brain-dead legislation. Those anti-abortionists take this position: " 'As pro-lifers, we hold what science has proven: that human life begins at fertilization. A definition of death which refers to brain function is anti-life because in the early stages of human development there is no brain.' "[36]

Some argue that the determination of human life should be delayed until postnatal observations can be made. Some fetuses are extremely deformed physically and/or mentally when they are born.

A newborn is able to breathe when the lower brain is functioning, but because the higher brain is diseased or absent, it may have little or no reason or memory capabilities. Since such capabilities are necessary for even marginal human interaction with the environment, some think the organism should be allowed to die. Regarding newborns who have virtually no potential for mental development, pathologist W. S. Albrink has said, "The fact that an infant has the genetic makeup of the human species doesn't necessarily mean that the infant is a person."[37]

Apropos here is an adjective used in the 1973 Supreme Court decision which declares that life is more than breathing. The Court defined viability as the capability "of *meaningful* life outside the mother's womb."[38] Consider the case of a newborn who had a heart or lung abnormality, a deformed left side including no eye or ear, and a damaged windpipe. The lack of reflex response to being touched displayed severe brain damage. Because of these multiple defects the parents requested that nothing be done to prolong life. Some physicians, however, believed that windpipe corrective surgery was warranted to enable oral feeding. When the case was brought before a Maine court in 1974, the judge ordered surgery, ruling that "at the moment of live birth there does exist a human being." In the opinion of that judge, all newborns are entitled to medical procedures which would ordinarily be given to other citizens. In spite of the surgery the newborn died a day later.[39]

Debate on public policy with respect to abortion and newborns has often been confused by the failure to distinguish between the beginning of organic life and the beginning of *human* life. It is scientifically beyond doubt that an organism begins to live at conception. The fertilized egg has at that time the genetic package that will guide unique development. However, genetic inheritance alone does not determine the individual who is produced. Even identical twins are different individuals at birth because their nervous systems have responded to stimuli received in their different uterine locations. The infant is therefore a product of both genes and prenatal environment.

The problem of determining when individual life begins is parallel to the problem of declaring when primate animality becomes human animality in historical evolution. Both involve a gradual process which confounds those who maintain that there is an exact point when humanness begins. One needs no classification expertise to realize that a dog or another species in our mammalian branch of the tree of life is not human and to know that a school child is human. But paleontologists sometimes uncover data about animals who walked upright millions of years ago that do not fall neatly into either a human or nonhuman classification. Likewise, an obstetrician may deliver an infant who is so congenitally deformed that it can never become self-conscious, or the doctor may abort an embryo for therapeutic or social reasons. In one case there is no potential for personhood; in the other no actual personality has developed. Those who do not have to deal with such dilemmas often tend to assume wrongly that it is easy to decide the question of humanness.

Americans generally agree that life is one of the rights with which they have been endowed by their Creator and that no person ought to be deprived of it without due process of law. There is considerable agreement now on criteria for ascertaining when human life ends, but there is no consensus on when it begins. A couple may refrain from birth control because they think the essence of human life is in the seminal fluid. An expectant mother who is convinced that human life begins at conception may abstain from voluntarily aborting her embryo. Likewise a pregnant woman who believes that aborting an embryo or a defective fetus is not murder may choose not to bring the organism in her uterus to a state of viability. Until a consensus develops, it would be tragic if one religious or political faction attained the power to impose its definition on all citizens and thereby remove our present freedom to act on the dictates of conscience.

Attempting to define death and life illustrates well that any study of death and dying necessitates a study of what constitutes life and living from womb to tomb. The next chapter will continue our discussion of the quantitative and qualitative aspects of life and death.

3

LIFE EXPECTANCY AND AGING

Longevity Data

Of all the revolutions in the modern era, the mortality or longevity revolution may be the most spectacular. The dimensions of the sudden change are revealed by the graphs in this chapter.

Life expectancy refers to the average duration of life in a population. The first graph shows that life expectancy has been extended radically in technologically developed nations. What has not significantly altered over recorded history has been the maximum length of life. Life span has remained fixed at about one hundred years, but in some areas of the globe more people are now living until they approach that limit. If death from disease, violence, and accidents were eliminated in some future century, then, as the dotted line indicates, most people would die in their tenth decade.[1] Due largely to progress in disease control, the Census Bureau forecasts that within the next century the current nine percent of the United States population over eighty-five will rise to twenty-five percent. However, less than one percent will live to become centenarians.[2]

Historians can only make educated guesses regarding the average

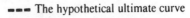

- - - The hypothetical ultimate curve

━━━ Technologically developed countries, 1980

● ● ● United States, 1900

. . . . Average of recorded history

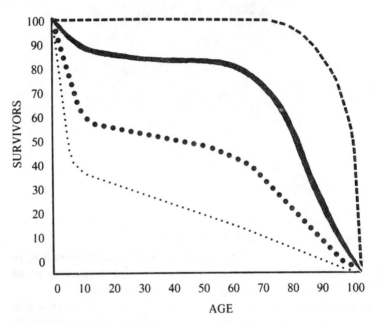

Modified from *Scientific American,* 242 (Jan. 1980): 60.

Fig. 1: Longevity Revolution

length of life before modern times. Death certificates and the statistical compilation of mortality data have been public policy only for the past century in the United States and other industrialized nations. The earliest date in our National Vital Statistics for obtaining information on which comparisons can be made is 1900. Those who have examined ancient Greco-Roman graveyards have found that the average life span was about twenty-five years. Since the improved living conditions of civilized life presumably increased life expectancy in that era, it was probably no more than twenty years among the uncivilized. In medieval Europe, life expectancy rose to thirty years, though it fluctuated erratically due to bubonic plagues called Black Death.[3]

Those who believe in the inerrancy of the Bible reject the general assumptions stated above regarding life expectancy or the maximum life span in primitive times. According to Genesis 5, the average life span was 847 years for the men who are listed as having lived between human creation and the flood which covered "all the high mountains under the whole heaven" (7:19) at the time of Noah. Methuselah, who lived 969 years, would probably have become the first and only millenarian had he not been drowned with the wicked in the flood. But Methuselah holds the longevity record only if an even more ancient record of preflood people is rejected. The Sumerians listed on a clay tablet the years when their kings ruled. The average rule was 30,150 years, and one named En-men-lu-Anna lasted 43,200 years![4]

How can these implausible early records be explained? Ancient people of Western Asia had little interest in precise recording of time, and consequently they had neither written family records nor a standardized calendar. Also in contrast to current Western values, the ancients assumed that the longer the life, the nobler the ancestor. Thus there was a tendency to exaggerate more and more the orally transmitted stories about heroic forebears. After technology arose for making contemporaneous recordings, distinction was no longer given to ancestors by lengthening their ages. Record keepers began to be utilized during the era of the Israelite monarchy after 1000 B.C., and consequently the range of the ages of citizens at death was within what would now be regarded as normal. We find nothing unusual about the length of life expected by a psalmist of the first millennium B.C.: "The years of our life are threescore and ten, or . . . fourscore" (Ps. 90:10).

In developed countries there are two related reasons for rapid progress during the past century toward the "ultimate curve." One is the improvement of sanitation and nutrition. The use of purified water has prevented transmission of many deadly germs. The availability of sufficient and wholesome food has also extended life. Developments in medical science are the second reason for life extension. Maternal and infant mortality has plummeted as obstetrics has advanced and vaccines have greatly contributed to humans surviving their childhood. Also, the discovery of sulfa drugs and penicillin during World War II has affected the subsequent increase in life span.

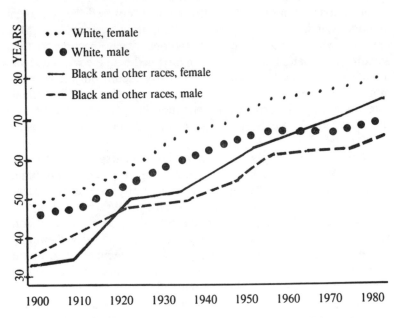

U.S. Department of Commerce, Bureau of the Census, *Social Indicators*, III, p. 715.

Fig. 2: Life Expectancy at Birth in the United States

A study of this graph discloses that there has been a constant rise in life expectancy among all major segments of the United States population during the twentieth century. The unprecedented rate of increase during the first half of the century has tapered off. A comparison of infants born in 1900 with those born in 1950 shows an increase in life expectancy from forty-seven to sixty-eight years. This twenty-one-year increase in fifty years equals the previous increase over the past two thousand years.

Whereas the life-expectancy increase ran at the rate of four years per decade (or about five months per year) during the first half of this century, it has slowed to two years per decade in the second half. The United States Census Bureau estimates that the rate of increase will continue during the remaining years of the century, so the overall life expectancy in the United States for infants born in the year 2000 will be around seventy-eight years. The three-decade rise in life expectancy in one century will be equivalent to the rise in the entire course of recorded history prior to the twentieth century.

Throughout most of recorded history, infancy has been the period for the sharpest drop in survivors. Only about half of all children born have lived to the age of procreation. When survival of the naturally fittest reigned among humans, as it still does among other species, early death was more the rule than the exception. Up until a century ago, the death rate among the young was higher than among the old. Even today stillborn infants are so common in some nations that no public record is kept.

At the turn of this century more than half of all deaths in the United States occurred among children under fifteen, and sixteen percent of all deaths took place during the first year. But now the diseases that were especially devastating to children—diphtheria, smallpox, whooping cough, and polio—have been virtually eliminated. Less than six percent of American deaths are among those under fifteen, and infants account for less than two percent of the total deaths. At the beginning of this century it could have been reasonably expected that teenage Americans would survive into their retirement years; now it can be expected that infants will survive that long. Between 1980 and 1984 there was a nineteen percent increase in Americans aged eighty-five and over, but because of the lower birthrate, the teenage population fell by nine percent. Infectious diseases, especially flu, pneumonia, and tuberculosis, were the principal causes of death in 1900. The toll of these diseases is now only four percent of the total deaths in America.[6]

While death by acute disease has greatly decreased among the young, chronic disease has correspondingly increased among the elderly in total amount and in rate. Approximately seventy percent of those who will die in the United States in the last quarter of the twentieth century will be at least sixty-five years old. There has been a rapid rise in degenerative diseases which generally bring about death more slowly. If heart disease, stroke (cerebrovascular disease), and arteriosclerosis (hardening of the arteries) are all considered as one circulatory disease, then nearly half of all American deaths are from a single cause. The rate of death from cardiovascular disease has tripled during this century, largely because people are living longer. Since the death rate in the United States is one per hundred, approximately one million die of this disease annually.

Cancer, which accounted for only four percent of the deaths in 1900, is now five times higher and is still rising. However, since cancer is the most dreaded of all diseases, only five percent of the American population think they will die of malignancies—in spite of constant warnings about "cancer-causing" food ingredients, environmental conditions, and tobacco smoke. The "second most common cause of death in the United States," cancer kills almost one a minute. It kills more children than any other disease, and it seems destined to kill about one in four of all persons now living in the United States.[7] About thirteen hundred per day now die of cancer, almost one per minute.

The gender gap in life expectancy has fluctuated dramatically in history. In ancient times, because of the large number of deaths in childbirth, male life expectancy exceeded female by several years.[8] In some technologically underdeveloped countries of the world, males still exceed females in life expectancy. By 1900 this traditional pattern was found in America only among Blacks. Now both Black and white females have a longer life expectancy than American males of either race, and the gap has widened from two years in 1900 to seven years in 1984.[9] Whereas in 1900 female life expectancy did not extend beyond the age of menopause, the years beyond the normal childbearing years now exceed the years before.

There are approximately 140 male fertilized ova to every 100 female. At birth the ratio has lessened to 105 males per 100 females because of the disproportionate natural wastage of male conceptions. Most neonatal mortality is among males, probably because the XY gene configuration of males is not as protective to health as the XX redundancy of females. Hormones that females secrete at puberty provide additional gender advantage, enabling them to outnumber males from the age of eighteen onward.[10]

Among adults cultural conditions overtake genetic conditions in causing a higher male mortality rate. Our culture encourages women more than men to develop wide social networks that enable them to survive crises. Also, while women are trained to be security conscious, men are generally expected to take life-threatening risks in war, mines, hunting, collision sports, racing, fire fighting, and the like. Consequently, males have a much higher accident rate than females. Car crashes are the leading cause of death among young men. Women outnumber men by forty-three percent after age sixty-five, sixty-nine percent after seventy-five, and a hundred and two percent after eighty-five. In 1984 there were in America ninety-five males per one hundred females.[11]

Muscular strength may actually accelerate male demise because of the macho roles which culture has imposed upon the brawny. Were Shakespeare's Hamlet alive today and informed of our gender mortality facts, he might exclaim, "Frailty, thy name is *man!*" As the percentage of women increases in high-pressure and high-risk roles previously reserved for men—such as police work, military careers, and business management—the gender gap may decrease.

It is intriguing to speculate on how the difference in gender longevity might change marriage patterns. In past centuries, when males usually lived longer than females, men generally married women who were several years younger. By this marital arrangement there was less likelihood of one spouse surviving the other for many years. Often the most severe emotional stress of elderly life is caused by a spouse's death—a trauma from which some never adequately recover. There are now three times as many widows as widowers, an imbalance due to men marrying younger women as well as to the gender life expectancy differential and to more widowers remarrying. Those who associate lifelong companionship with marriage should look at the way in which the difference in gender mortality might affect the relationship in the distant future. When our ancestors pledged themselves "till death do us part," it was no big deal as compared with contemporary vows. Before the nineteenth century the average marriage lasted only a dozen years before one spouse died. Now partners who do not opt for divorce have marriages that average four times that long. Since wives will generally live years longer than their husbands, it would tend to increase long-range happiness if husbands were younger than their wives.

If men wedded women about seven years older, they would more likely end their sexual functioning as well as their biological lives at about the same time. Studies show that women's interest in orgasms sometimes increases after menopause, and anxiety over intercourse lessens when pregnancy is not possible.[12] With men, however, impotence becomes an increasing problem in the latter half of life. There is some truth in the double pun: tri-weekly at twenty-five, try weekly at fifty, try weakly at seventy-five! Foresighted women who seek matrimony and who want to diminish years of widowhood and insure a vital sexual relationship in the latter years of life should focus on younger men. In our couple-oriented society, it is widows who are especially faced with both emotional and financial insecurity. The majority of nursing home patients are widows who cannot afford the thirty thousand dollars or more it costs annually for adequate care. Some of those homes are tombs where the elderly are buried alive.

The twentieth-century progress of American Blacks is even more remarkable than that of whites, for they have more than doubled their life expectancy. In 1900 nonwhites, of whom ninety-five percent were Blacks, lived in 1900 an average of thirty-three years—fifteen years less than whites lived. That overall racial longevity advantage has been reduced to five years. A Black female born in 1982 will probably live two years longer than a white male, but a white female will live fourteen years longer than a Black male. The physical qualities of race are not a factor in longevity. The higher overall mortality rate can be attributed largely to the fact that Blacks generally have not been able to afford the quality of health care that whites receive. This economic factor is reflected in the death rate of Black infants—

still nearly twice that of whites. Also, dietary differences may explain why a significantly larger number of Black men die of cardiovascular disease than white men.[13]

The red race, however, has seen little improvement in life expectancy. It is now only forty-five years for North American Indians. Interrelated factors that contribute to the forty-percent lower life expectancy than most Americans enjoy are poverty, despair, and inadequate health care. Native Americans suffer a high infant mortality, five times the alcoholism rate of other Americans, and a significant amount of tuberculosis.[14]

Internationally there is a forty-year gap between the countries with the highest and lowest life expectancy. The Japanese are the global leaders in longevity, for their females have a life expectancy of eighty years, their males seventy-four years. Other countries with a life expectancy significantly higher than the United States' overall average of seventy-five years (1982 figures) include the Scandinavian nations and Australia. At the opposite end of the spectrum are countries with primitive medicine and marginal living conditions. It is difficult for the United Nations to gather statistics on such countries because their census records are often not reliable. Even so, the life expectancy of thirty-two in the Sahara Desert country of Chad is one of the lowest in Africa, the continent with the lowest on the globe. In the Sahara area approximately twenty-five percent of the children die before the age of five because of undernourishment, unsafe water, and lack of immunization.

A decade ago the media widely accepted astonishing claims of long life in several remote places on earth. An article published in the January 1973 issue of the *National Geographic Magazine* described those areas in Russia, Ecuador, and Kashmir. In 1975 a segment of the television program "Sixty Minutes" was devoted to interviewing an allegedly 136-year-old person. These and other reports were largely based on the investigations of Alexander Leaf, a professor at Harvard Medical School. He claimed, for example, that 9 of the 819 residents of an Ecuadoran village were centenarians, an incredible rate when compared to the seven per hundred thousand United States rate. A search for qualities that made life there distinctive disclosed that the village lacked modern sanitation and medical care. Many villagers bathed only once every two years and smoked heavily. High altitude is a feature of the Ecuadoran village and the other two areas where extremely long life was reported, so Leaf suggested that low altitude is life-shortening. In fact, however, the thinner atmosphere increases ultraviolet radiation, and this may have caused premature leathery skin which investigators interpreted as extreme age.[15]

Leaf's reports on particular global areas stimulated other scientists to go there to study the lifestyles of the old timers, and attracted tourists in search of the legendary fountain of youth. A Japanese group announced plans to construct a health spa and a longevity center at the Ecuador enclave. It was then discovered that some poor inhabitants of these regions were hoodwinking researchers in order to keep the revenue from visitors flowing in. Leaf became suspicious on finding that a man who had given his age as 121 in 1970 vouched four years later that he was 132.[16] Researchers, eager to report striking finds, had failed to check carefully to see if the old people were lying about their ages. In fact, some had earlier falsified records to avoid a military draft; others had misleadingly identified themselves as different persons who had the same name in church birth registers. A critical investigation disclosed that there were no bona fide centenarians in the special areas.[17]

Accurate ascertaining of the age of death is, of course, dependent on well-documented data on the year of birth. State registration of birth certificates has been practiced only since the late nineteenth century. According to *The Guinness Book of World Records* a Japanese man who died in 1986 at the age of 120 and an American woman who died in 1981 at the age of 113 hold the records for the oldest humans with authenticated ages. There is no reliable evidence to substantiate claims that some humans have lived longer than twelve decades.

How do species compare with one another regarding life span? Most wild animals die of starvation, disease, and predators, so it is difficult to ascertain their natural limit. Even so, some claim that tortoises have a maximum life span of about 150 years, while vultures have lasted 120 years. *Homo sapiens* greatly outlives most other animal species. Among mammals, humans have by far the longest span, doubling that of our nearest primate relative, the chimpanzee. A human generally lives nine cat lives![18]

It has been suggested that our brain size may be a factor in explaining why we live, for example, about thirty times longer than mice. However, if brain makes a difference in the biology of aging, why have brainless giant sequoia trees lived thousands of years? Others suggest that there is a rough correspondence between bodily bulk and longevity, since mammals live longer than insects. Why then does a human weighing a couple of hundred pounds have several times the life span of a horse weighing a couple of thousand pounds? Perhaps longevity is related to the time it takes an animal to reach maturity, for horses and other mammals grow up much more rapidly than humans. There may be a correlation between metabolism rate and the duration of life. For example, a mouse with 650 heartbeats per minute and an elephant with 25 heartbeats per minute both have a life expectancy of about one billion heartbeats, even though the elephant's longevity is two dozen times that of the mouse. Research has yet to clarify why some species age so much more rapidly than others.

Life-extension Factors

(Before reading this section, use Appendix B.1 to calculate your "Individual Life Expectancy.") With longevity, as with everything else organic, heredity and environment are the two broad causative factors. Studies show a significantly higher percentage of long-living parents and grandparents having offspring who do likewise.[19] Similarly, offspring are several times more likely to have heart disease if one parent had it. Alzheimer's disease, formerly inaccurately called senility, and diabetes are also influenced by heredity. Unfortunately the heredity factor is one over which a person has no control. Especially determinative of life span are artery size and elasticity, qualities which are partly inherited. The smaller the vessel, the more the risk of blood blockage. As cardiac output diminishes so does agility, and life cannot continue when circulation is overly constricted. There is truth in the old adage, "We are as old as our arteries."

Heredity is the cause of much of the gradual debilitation that is apparent during the second half of the normal life span. Each species has a limited duration because cellular aging is intrinsic to all organisms. Genetic blueprints called DNA program the body's aging clock. The biological slowdown includes reduced circulation, stiff joints, and wrinkled skin. Although it is often imprecisely said that so-and-so died of "old age," the body actually dies a little each day through all stages of life. Normal cells eventually lose the ability to function or divide. Therefore, if all the leading causes of death were eliminated, life expectancy would only rise about a dozen years. Continually the hope is expressed that in the not too distant future the monumental cancer research now under way will find a miraculous cure to wipe out that hideous disease. But even if that dream of eliminating cancer, heart disease, and stroke becomes a reality, the average life would only be extended about fifteen years.[20]

Some gerontologists, specialists in aging, have questioned whether humans need to submit to nature's one-century longevity limit. Were they able to develop an anti-aging serum, then aging could be arrested or even reversed. However, more within the realm of probability is the discovery of a treatment that could slow down aging and raise by a few decades the outer limit of human life.

Collagen, the fibrous protein that surrounds cells, is the focus of some gerontological research. Binding the cells together is connective tissue called cross-linkers which lose flexibility as age increases. Resembling rods with hooks on either end, cross-linkers hamper the work of the protein molecules that are essential to life. This process is manifested when joints become arthritic and skin becomes wrinkled. If scientists could alter the aging instructions contained in the DNA, then there might be less collagen thickening. Such intervention might allow cells to function with perpetual elasticity. But an unlimited life span may not be attainable—and might not be desirable if it were.

Although there may be little humans can do to alter their inborn inheritance, at least in the near future, a great deal can be done by way of altering individual habits and social environment. In 1982 Surgeon General Everett Koop reported that smoking is annually responsible for some 340,000 deaths in the United States.[21] One way to comprehend the magnitude of this figure is to realize that it is six times as large as the total number of American fatalities in the Vietnam War. One-third of these deaths are caused by lung cancer, and the rest by a variety of heart diseases, respiratory diseases, and other forms of cancer. Smoking is a major cause of larynx and esophagus malignancy and is a contributing factor in bladder, kidney, and pancreas cancer. The deaths of Americans from lung cancer have risen fivefold since 1950 even though a lower percentage now smoke. The reason for this rise at a time when millions have quit smoking is that lung cancer often takes decades to develop. Only ten percent of lung cancer victims survive for five years or more after their cancer has been diagnosed. Lung cancer kills more American men than any other form of cancer.

The movement toward sexual equality has resulted in a lessening of the gender differential of previous generations in smoking-related deaths. Although the use of tobacco has traditionally been predominantly a male habit, teenage females are now outsmoking their male peers. In the nineteen-eighties lung cancer is surpassing breast cancer as a killer of women. Smoking during pregnancy is related to miscarriages, premature births, and birth defects.

The danger of death from smoking varies according to consumption. Whereas any regular use of tobacco significantly increases the risk of cancer, there is a two hundred percent increase among those who smoke more than one pack of cigarettes a day. The American Cancer Society also implicates cigar, pipe, snuff, and chewing tobacco in a variety of cancers. Some studies also suggest that nonsmokers increase the risk of lung cancer just by being continuously exposed to smoke-filled rooms. In 1982 the Surgeon General cautioned, " 'Prudence dictates that nonsmokers avoid exposure to secondhand tobacco smoke to the extent possible."[22] On the basis of an enormous amount of clinical data the Surgeon General concludes, "Cigarette smoking is clearly identified as the chief preventable cause of death in our society."[23] The Surgeon General's judgment can be extended internationally because the millions of adults killed annually by tobacco use exceeds even the number killed by famine and war throughout the world.

The ten million problem drinkers in America experience health problems almost as serious as the much larger number of problem smokers. Liver cirrhosis, heart damage, and malnutrition are the main results of alcohol abuse. Excessive use of alcohol is also associated with cancers of the mouth, larynx, esophagus, and liver. If both tobacco and alcohol are used, the interaction causes a much greater cancer risk. It has been estimated that chronic alcoholism decreases life expectancy by about one decade. The poisoning from this drug is a worldwide problem. It is the main reason why the overall life expectancy among Russian males declined from sixty-six to sixty-two years in the last twenty years while it was increasing in other industrialized nations. The typical Russian family spends one-third of its food budget on vodka.[24] In spite of the global problem of alcohol overconsumption, it should be acknowledged that there is no evidence that its moderate use shortens life.

It has been proven that a low-cholesterol diet is an important factor in the prolongation of life. Cholesterol is produced in the body by the intake of animal fats. Blood vessels begin to harden as fatty cholesterol deposits build up in them. Excessive cholesterol is especially found in people who are overweight. The average American consumes twice as much cholesterol as is needed. The Japanese have one-third our intake of cholesterol and one-fourth our rate of heart attacks. Each year one million Americans have heart attacks, one-half of them fatal. According to a 1984 report by the federal government, one hundred thousand lives would be saved by a ten-percent reduction in the national average of cholesterol consumption.[25] The role of food choice in mortality is conveyed by the saying, "You dig your grave with your teeth." Or, to compose a less gruesome one: Girth control reduces unwanted deaths.

Daily mile walks, jogging, bicycling, and sports add extra years to life. After an extensive study of the relationship between exercise and longevity among Harvard alumni, Ralph Paffenbarger concludes, "For each hour of physical activity, you can expect to live that hour over—and live one or two more hours to boot."[26] This means that young people who average an hour of exercise daily throughout life can expect to live several years longer than their inactive counterparts.

Avoiding unnecessary transportation risks is another factor in promoting longevity. The choice among different modes of air and surface transportation can often be a life-and-death matter. Highway speed has proven to be a significant factor in this regard. Since the speed limit in the United States was reduced to fifty-five miles per hour, an average of three thousand lives have been saved each year. The use of a bicycle, motorcycle, or automobile without utilizing the best safety devices available proves all too often to be a shortsighted attempt to defy death.

The use of vehicular seat belts is a good case in point. In Britain, where a heavy fine is imposed for noncompliance, over ninety percent buckle up on entering a car. The resulting lower accident rate has saved the British much in public health expenditure as well as citizens' lives. Many think a similar law throughout the United States is needed, for only fourteen percent of the population use belts voluntarily.[27] However, the oldest compulsory seat belt law in the world was enacted in Brooklyn, Ohio. Since the law took effect in 1966, no one wearing a seat belt has been killed in Brooklyn, but thirty-three persons not wearing belts have. Serious injuries as well as fatalities have been curbed, for there has been a sixty percent reduction in the number of accident victims needing hospital treatment since the law took effect.[28] The National Highway Traffic Safety Administration estimates that at least half of all automobile fatalities could have been prevented had adults and children worn seat belts at all times.[29] Recognizing that seat belts could save approximately thirteen thousand lives annually and that they greatly reduce the likelihood of severe injuries, lawmakers are moving to require their use. In 1985 New York became the first state to adopt a mandatory seat belt law for adults. In its first nine months of enforcement the state's monthly traffic fatality record dropped seventeen percent below the numbers for previous years.[30] Legislatures in other states are rapidly responding to statistics showing that 180 lives may be saved annually in America for every one percent increase in seat belt use. All states have now enacted legislation requiring restraints for young children; as a result their death rate has decreased by one-third during the last five years.[31] The *Journal of the American Medical Association* has evaluated such laws as "the most practical approach to 'immunizing' . . . children against their leading killer."[32]

It is instructive to examine American resistance to voluntary use of seat belts from the standpoint of death psychology. Massive campaigning urging their use has resulted in most citizens recognizing on a rational level that a simple buckle click might save their lives or protect their bodies from serious injury. Some also realize that if travelers had the seat belt habit, automobile insurance rates would be lowered. In view of the personal advantages at stake, why do the vast majority of Americans have to be coerced to protect themselves and their children? The bottom-line answer might be that humans have an unconscious aversion to admitting the real possibility of death for themselves. To commit themselves to seat belts would be an open admission that they are vulnerable to death. In a parallel manner, only about twenty percent of Americans compose a simple last will and testament, even though the overwhelming majority admit that it is something they ought to do. Humans shun actions that declare their mortality.

Satisfaction in employment or volunteer activities is another longevity predictor, as was confirmed by a lengthy study of older people by Erdman Palmore of Duke University. Keeping busy at work which they perform well was found to be more important than physical condition in extending the lives of those over sixty. Palmore also found that men with high scores on a hostility test had cardiovascular disease at five times the rate of those with low scores. "His blood was boiling" is apt because blood flows with greater pressure within hostile folks.[33]

Other research has revealed that gregarious people have a longevity advantage over introverts. After Lisa Berkman of Berkeley studied seven thousand people for a nine-year period she concluded that the outgoing are more resistant to debilitating disease.[34] The body is more likely to rust out from lack of activity than wear out from exercise. The slogan "Use it or lose it" applies to both mind and body. Brains that are kept stimulated have less loss of memory; muscles that are stretched have less arthritis; hearts and blood vessels that are given a regular workout have less arteriosclerosis.

What relationship is there between longevity and religious commitment? From the story of Abraham onward, the Old Testament assures that long life is a reward for right living (see Gen. 15:15; Job 42:16; Ps. 91:16; Prov. 3:2, 16). But the New Testament does not make such a glib connection, probably because the founder of Christianity died in his early thirties. The saying, "The good die young," describes martyrs such as Jesus, Stephen, Joan of Arc, and Martin Luther King, Jr. However, less courageous Christians seem to live longer on earth than the general population, perhaps because they are more socially outgoing and take more care of their physical health than ordinary sinners. In 1983 the Ministers Life Insurance Company advertised widely that "ministers go to heaven twenty-three percent slower."

Psychological versus Chronological Age

In his 1932 bestseller *Life Begins at Forty,* Walter Pitkin maintains that ninety percent of the world's greatest work has been done by people who have passed their physical prime. When his son revised the book in 1965 he changed the title to *Life Begins at Fifty,* because in this century life expectancy has increased about ten years with each ..ew generation. In the nineteen-nineties there should be a second revision entitled *Life Begins at Sixty!* The age of sixty will soon leave as many productive years as the age of forty did earlier in this century.

Even in centuries when life expectancy was much less than it is now, there were striking illustrations of outstanding achievements by older people. If Socrates had died before his seventh decade, he probably would not be famous. Plato, who wrote dialogues about him, did not get to know the one who would become his greatest inspiration until Socrates was over sixty years old. *The Laws,* one of Plato's finest dialogues, was written when he was about eighty years old. When Michelangelo was over seventy he was commissioned to design the magnificent St. Peter's Cathedral in Rome. At ninety-five Titian completed his masterpiece, "Christ Crowned with Thorns."

In the early years of our nation Benjamin Franklin was our leading diplomat while in his seventies. He was governor of Pennsylvania and helped to frame the United States Constitution during his eighties. Franklin invented bifocals at seventy-nine and made an appeal to Congress for the abolition of slavery when he was eighty-four. "His mind was ever young," commented Thomas Paine, "science, that never grows gray, was always his mistress."[35] Likewise, when he was seventy-five, Thomas Jefferson began creating the architecture and curriculum of the University of Virginia, an activity which his self-composed epitaph shows he regarded as more important than being president of the United States.

In this century Grandma Moses started painting at seventy-six when her arthritic hands could no longer hold an embroidery needle. Ranked as one of the top judges in American history, Oliver Wendell Holmes assisted Franklin Roosevelt in establishing the New Deal after his retirement at the age of ninety from the Supreme Court. Winston Churchill was sixty-six when he first became prime minister. After he brought Britain through World War II, he was again elected to that highest office at the age of seventy-seven. The noted philosopher Bertrand Russell was leading demonstrations to ban nuclear weapons at ninety-four and was writing about the problem of Jewish settlements in occupied areas of Palestine when he was ninety-eight. At ninety-three George Bernard Shaw wrote the play *Farfetched Fables*. Robert Frost's eighty-eighth birthday was the publication date of his book *In the Clearing*. Pope John XXIII, one of the most forward-looking pontiffs in the history of the papacy, did not assume office until he was seventy-seven. At eighty-nine Artur Rubinstein gave a recital at Carnegie Hall and performed concertos with the London Symphony. While in his eighties Bob Hope has entertained millions, and George Burns continues to do so in his nineties.

In the poem *Morituri Salutamus*, which he wrote to celebrate the fiftieth reunion of his college class, Henry Wadsworth Longfellow asserts, "Nothing is too late / Till the tired heart shall cease to palpitate." The examples given in that poem are worth repeating: "Sophocles wrote his grand Oedipus" after "more than fourscore years." And Goethe "completed Faust when eighty years were past" (lines 239–253). Longfellow declares that such persons demonstrate "how far the gulf stream of our youth may flow / Into the arctic regions of our lives." Thus, history records that many have done some of their best work at a time when, by ordinary standards, they would be considered "too old" to do any worthwhile thing.

Harvey Lehman discovered that fifty-five to fifty-nine was the median age for eminent Americans in government, business, and education. It is likely that the median age has risen since his research was published in 1942.[36] In spite of the many significant accomplishments of older adults, Americans tend to idolize those who are young. As a result, many who have lost their physical bloom regard their age as a source of embarrassment. Consequently there is a ready market for the hair dye industry and for face-lift surgery. As Franklin observed, "All would live long, but none would be old."

Depreciation of older adults in the United States is reflected in employment practices and in mandatory retirement policies. It is often difficult for talented and healthy persons in their late fifties to find new employment. How did Americans come to associate retirement with reaching the mid-sixties? The Social Security retirement policy was strongly influenced by Johns Hopkins professor William Osler. In 1905 that distinguished medical scientist delivered a retirement address which was widely publicized. In it he asserted that people over sixty were useless in every vocation and that it would be of immeasurable commercial, political, and professional benefit if employees were required to stop work at sixty. Ironically the entire second half of Harvey Cushing's *Life of Sir William Osler* deals with accomplishments after Osler went to England to live. He was a professor at Oxford from the age of fifty-six until he died at the age of seventy.[37]

Osler's outlook is now rejected among scientists because it is not in accord with research findings. The human brain's capacity often increases throughout the years that are customarily marked for retirement. Brain specialist Wilder Penfield knows that an old brain is quite capable of new tricks. He states: "At sixty the body has certainly passed beyond its greatest strength, and physical demands should be lessened and changed. But the brain quite often is ready for its best performance in certain fields."[38] Compulsory retirement rules occasionally deprive organizations of persons at the peak of their abilities. Research reveals that more than half of those past sixty-five believe that anyone who wishes to work and still can do a good job should not be required to retire.[39] There are millions of well-qualified citizens even over seventy who want to work and are unable to find paid or unpaid work that matches their skills.

The term *ageism* has been coined—to join *racism* and *sexism*—to name the false attempt to gauge individual capability by merely counting years. After the election successes of Ronald Reagan, *Time* essayist Frank Trippett commented on the continued aversion to age in the American culture:

> While mandatory retirement has recently been relaxed, with the age advanced to 70, popular thinking still falsely tends to take age as a sure index of vitality. The stereotype of an old person as a doddering, drooling, irrelevant nuisance is much circulated. . . . But the troublesome truth is that the higher the age the less it dependably reveals about the human being. . . . It is ignorance of that truth, among others, that sets the stage for ageism, that patchwork of prejudices and predispositions.[40]

In the ancient world the Strait of Gilbraltar at the mouth of the Mediterranean Sea was considered to be the last outpost of the earth. Ancient coins had stamped on them the Pillars of Hercules, the mythological designation for Gibraltar, and underneath were the words *Ne Plus Ultra*, meaning no more beyond. When Columbus proved there was, in fact, *plus ultra*, the negative had to be stricken. In venturing forth into uncharted seas, Columbus expressed what has come to be the distinctive spirit of great Americans. That spirit is well depicted by a certain statue in our nation's capital. Outside the Hall of Archives is a bronze statue of a young woman who is seated in a chair and leafing through a book. Beneath the figure is this graphic quotation from *The Tempest*: "What's past is prologue" (II. i. line 260). Shakespeare would have us think of human history as a colossal and continuous drama, the prologue just over and the play about to begin.

Individually and as a nation it is invigorating to live with such expectancy. As an unknown writer has put it, "Youth is not a time of life—it is a state of mind. . . . It is a temper of the will, a quality of the imagination, a vigor of the emotions; it is a freshness of the deep spring of life." There is a sense in which no persons or nations *grow* old; they become old by not growing. It is despair, cynicism, and apathy that turn the spirit back to dust. Youth is not basically a physical matter but an attitude of anticipation, an urge to press on to new goals. One may be mentally deteriorating at twenty, or one may be a vibrant "keenager" at ninety. One's psychological age often bears little relation to one's chronological age. It has been said that "A man is as old as he feels; a woman, as old as she looks." Actually, however, all persons are as old as they think. If they think they are good for nothing, that becomes a self-fulfilling prophecy. One may have bunions and bulges and still be buoyant and bullish. Those with whitened hair and wrinkled skin can discover new frontiers as the years roll. Both psychology and religion affirm that our spirits need not decay with our bodies. Indeed, our spirits can become rejuvenated and "mount up with wings like eagles" (Isa. 40:31) with the march of time.

4

THE DYING PATIENT

Mortals are by definition a dying lot, but some are under the shadow of medical prognoses—predictions of the probable course of a disease—which count *termini* in months. The considerations in this chapter are devoted to such terminal patients. An appropriate place to begin is with an examination of Dr. Elisabeth Kübler-Ross, who for the past two decades has done more than anyone else to focus awareness on the psychological outlook of patients with life-threatening illnesses. She has brought out of the closet matters previously presumed to be too ugly and miserable for full viewing. Her impact on health care professionals and on the general public has been enormous.

Critique of Kübler-Ross

Born and educated in Switzerland, Kübler-Ross came to the University of Chicago in 1965 to teach psychiatry, and she soon became involved with dying patients. She assisted theology students enrolled in her Crises of Human Life course who were in search of dying patients to interview. At first the students were unable to obtain permission to talk with anyone in the large hospital with which Kübler-Ross was associated. Some members of the staff expressed hostility toward her, and one even thought the psychiatrist needed a psychiatrist because she insisted on being permitted to talk with patients about dying. One medical worker protested: "About dying? There is no one dying here!" Desiring to protect the terminally ill, the physicians and nurses isolated them from those wanting to learn from them. Kübler-Ross perceived that health care professionals in the death-denying American culture tended to treat the terminally ill as though they were quarantined.

Eventually Kübler-Ross' persistence was rewarded, and the hospital staff realized that a number of patients were willing and often eager to share their outlooks with whoever would listen. A seminar was organized as a result of initial interviews. The dying patients, ranging in age from sixteen to ninety, were the main teachers; physicians, nurses, counselors, seminarians, priests, and rabbis were the learners. The patients agreed to let students sit behind a one-way glass partition where they could see and hear. Kübler-Ross interviewed individually patients who had days, weeks, or months to live.

After interviewing hundreds of patients, Kübler-Ross published *On Death and Dying* in 1969. *Time* magazine correctly states in its book review, "The Chicago seminar has vanquished the conspiracy of silence that once shrouded hospitals' terminal wards." The interest stirred by *On Death and Dying*—which has now sold more than one million copies—was so widespread that Kübler-Ross soon found herself in great international demand. Through workshops, films, and subsequent books, she has disseminated her ideas and raised public consciousness about persons who had previously been kept in a psychological isolation ward.

The core outline of Kübler-Ross' landmark book, a main ingredient of her subsequent popular lectures, is what she calls the five stages of dying. In order of occurrence, these stages are denial, anger, bargaining, depression, and acceptance. How does she distinguish these psychological responses, and what do other clinical psychologists think of her stages?

First is the denial or the not-me stage. Learning of one's terminal illness brings on shock and disbelief. Kübler-Ross illustrates this initial stage from a patient's response in her Chicago hospital:

> She was convinced that the X-rays were "mixed up"; she asked for reassurance that her pathology report could not possibly be back so soon and that another patient's report must have been marked with her name. When none of this could be confirmed, she quickly asked to leave the hospital, looking for another physician in the vain hope "to get a better explanation for my troubles."[1]

Second is the anger or the why-me stage. Someone must be blamed for the personal disaster that has been forecast. The patient may be resentful that fate did not single out a person more deserving to die or may be irritated over the presumed incompetence of members of the medical staff. Occasionally the anger is rational. Nurses apparently do prefer to focus attention on patients with optimistic prognoses. Kübler-Ross cites one study which reveals that terminally ill patients wait twice as long for response to a help signal as do those who are expected to get well.[2]

Third is the bargaining or the yes-me-but stage. Having found that venting fury against others is ineffective, the patient pursues a new strategy. The patient is like a child who, on finding that stomping in rage does not accomplish what he or she wants, attempts to get the same by promising to do a household chore with regularity. The dying patient desires the prolongation of life until something eagerly awaited occurs, such as the marriage of a daughter or the birth of a grandchild. In return, promises are made to do specific acts of goodness. The deals that are made are often the result of an internal theological dialogue. Kübler-Ross writes:

> Most bargains are made with God and are usually kept a secret or mentioned between the lines or in a chaplain's private office. . . . We have been impressed by the number of patients who promise "a life dedicated to God" or "a life in the service of the church" in exchange for some additional time. Many of our patients also promised to give parts of or their whole body "to science" (if the doctors use their knowledge of science to extend their life).[3]

Fourth is the depression or the yes-me stage. Rapid physical deterioration now displays that the bargaining to extend the "deadline" failed and that death will not be postponed. The patient thinks that it is not just a single friend that will be lost by the impending demise but everyone and everything he or she has ever loved. There is a feeling of impotence and utter despair.

Fifth is the acceptance or the I'm-ready stage. The patient has adjusted to the finiteness of life and the inevitability of death. This final stage is characterized by much sleep and little verbal communication. Here is Kübler-Ross' description:

> Acceptance should not be mistaken for a happy stage. It is almost void of feelings. It is as if the pain had gone, the struggle is over, and there comes a time for "the final rest before the long journey" as one patient phrased it. . . . the dying patient has found some peace and . . . wishes to be left alone or at least not stirred up by news and problems of the outside world.[4]

By way of critique, what merits and demerits exist in Kübler-Ross' interpretation of her findings? Many in the health service professions have found the logic of her "stages" compelling. It relieves the anxiety of some persons who care for dying patients to assume that there is a neat and normal sequence. For them death is like the countdown for a rocket lift-off: although there may be a temporary hold at one stage, there are certain definite steps until the departure is accomplished. Nurses who have memorized Kübler-Ross' five-stage checklist have been known to be disturbed by patients who have "regressed" from one phase to a previous one.

It should be pointed out that the stages of dying may be more in Kübler-Ross' mind than in the clinical data she presents. Other clinical psychologists who have worked with dying patients do not find evidence of a standard progressive pattern. Two noted thanatologists evaluate Kübler-Ross' stages in what follows.

Edwin Shneidman writes in *Deaths of Man:*

> While I have seen in dying persons isolation, envy, bargaining, depression, and acceptance, I do not believe that these are necessarily "stages" of the dying process, and I am not at all convinced that they are lived through in that order, or, for that matter, in any universal order. . . .
>
> One does not find a unidirectional movement through progressive stages so much as an alternation between acceptance and denial. Denial is a most interesting psychodynamic phenomenon. For a few consecutive days a dying person is capable of shocking a listener with the breathtaking candor of his profound acceptance of imminent death and

the next day shock that listener with unrealistic talk of leaving the hospital and going on a trip.[5]

Shneidman's criticism of Kübler-Ross' stages is even stronger in a more recent publication:

> My own experiences have led me to radically different conclusions, so that I reject the notion that human beings, as they die, are somehow marched in lock step through a series of stages of the dying process. On the contrary, in working with dying persons, I see a wide panoply of human feelings and emotions, of various human needs, and a broad selection of psychological defenses and maneuvers—a few of these in some people, dozens in others—experienced in an impressive variety of ways.[6]

Robert Kastenbaum offers this judgment about Kübler-Ross' theory of dying:

> The stage theory of dying assumes a single primary path of movement. . . . Variations are acknowledged, but are seen as deviations from a central mode of progression. . . . The theory implies that there is a valued destination to be reached, and that one should keep moving toward acceptance, if at his or her own pace. . . . There is . . . a disturbing tendency for description to be converted imperceptibly into prescription.[7]

Indeed, Kübler-Ross has done a disservice in going beyond describing how people die to recommending how they ought to die. Such prescribing tends to depersonalize individuals by placing them in a questionable schema. What she calls stages may more accurately be termed *moods* in dying patients, several of which may coexist at the same time. Anticipation, resignation, hope, and fright are other observable responses of dying patients. Moreover, Kübler-Ross presumes that all ages and both sexes respond to death in the same basic stages. Age and gender are factors needing investigation, as are the types of disease and the environments of the patients. For example, dying patients may have quite different patterns of response, depending on whether they are living at home or in a hospital. Anger may be less common among retired persons than among younger persons who expected to accomplish much more in life. Who is to say that anger is not an appropriate finale for some individuals? The outrage recommended for dying persons by Dylan Thomas may be as appropriate as Kübler-Ross' "acceptance" stage:

> Do not go gentle into that good night,
> Old age should burn and rave at close of day;
> Rage, rage against the dying of the light.
> ("Do Not Go Gentle" . . . , lines 1–3)

What Kübler-Ross calls "acceptance" may be due more to medication or physical exhaustion than to psychic tranquility.

Despite the preceding negative evaluation, Kübler-Ross' work has a number of positive aspects. She should be credited with much of the recent movement toward open communication with dying persons. With the help of her counseling, they were able to unload their feelings of fright, loneliness, inadequacy, and embarrassment. Kübler-Ross' approach has also been personally helpful to millions of nondying persons whom she has directly or indirectly instructed. In this regard Kübler-Ross writes, "Many of our young students who originally were petrified at the thought of facing dying patients were eventually able to express to us their own concerns, their own fears, and their own fantasies about dying."[8] She has enabled many to take off their masks when handling situations involving death. Previously there had been little willingness to deal honestly with the actual predicament. Dying patients had been approached with words such as these: "You will soon be getting better. . . . Your flowers are lovely." Kübler-Ross' message is that those who confront the terminally ill in this manner may have more problems with their own mortality than with the mortality of those they are attempting to comfort. They expose that they only want to talk about beautiful things and are unaccepting of unhealthy persons. Ultimately we are all terminal cases, with some arriving at the end of life earlier than others. Acknowledgment of this by all parties establishes a companionship among mortals. Then people can share the bad happenings as well as the good in a healing manner.

By opening up lines of communication among all who are involved in situations of imminent death, Kübler-Ross has had an impact that can be measured statistically. Studies made a few years before the publication of *On Death and Dying* showed that approximately eighty percent of American physicians did not favor telling terminal patients the truth.[9] Serving as the patients' advocate against medical doctors' conspiracy of silence, Kübler-Ross has written:

> Patients should not be told that their illness is terminal or that they are dying. A patient should be informed that he is seriously ill but that everything possible will be done to keep him comfortable and to help him. When the patient becomes "beyond medical help," he will ask the doctor if he has any chance. If the physician levels with the patient and gives him an appropriate idea of his expectations without leaving him without hope, the patient will then be able to come to grips with it much better than if he is told that he is going to get well.[10]

Some elements in death education parallel those in sex education. When children take the initiative to ask about reproduction, they deserve nonevasive responses from authoritative sources. It may be damaging to their growth either to inflict on them answers to unasked questions before they are able to assimilate them or to give the silent treatment to frank questions. Considerations of when and how are needed in communicating the facts of death as well as the facts of life. Kübler-Ross counsels that a sense of timing is needed and that attention should be given to the method by which the truth is conveyed. Truth without love is devastating, but love without truth is deceptive. The truth can be told in a cold and cruel manner, or it can be told in a warm and considerate way. When inquiring patients are informed early of the gravity of their situation, they have time to do what Kübler-Ross calls taking care of "unfinished business." They may want to do such things as straighten out their financial records, give away some of their treasured possessions to friends who will most appreciate them, write reconciliation letters to relatives, or reestablish a spiritual relationship. When given full information about their plight, dying patients retain more dignity and control over their lives. They are not distressed by a loss of trust in those whom they had considered sources of reliable information. They can plan ways of living the remaining days to the fullest.

As a result of the efforts of Kübler-Ross and others who have been inspired by her, physicians' attitudes have changed dramatically in one decade. A 1979 issue of the *Journal of the American Medical Association* reports that ninety-eight percent of physicians now prefer to inform terminal patients of their condition.[11] There is now a similar overwhelming proportion of physicians who want to inform on the one hand and patients who want to be informed on the other.

The Hospice Movement

Institutional and noninstitutional alternatives are being explored and adopted for dying patients. But first, what are the limitations of modern hospitals which have caused much dissatisfaction with their customary way of dealing with the terminally ill?

Hospitals are oriented toward cure rather than care. Their staffs are trained to keep patients alive as long as possible. Death is often viewed as evidence of failure. Thus, when death occurs the camouflaged corpse is quickly trundled off to the morgue or the mortician. Increasingly hospitals are centers for the treatment of short-term, acute illnesses. Get-well medicine is stuffed in around the clock. The average hospital stay is less than one week, and nearly all patients are discharged with improved health. The purpose of hospitals is diagnosis and rehabilitation. In making a diagnosis the physician is not interested in what makes a patient distinctive as an individual but in what makes her or him like all others who have similar symptoms. Impersonal computers are now being used effectively to match symptoms with diagnoses. Elaborate medical equipment is often needed for diagnosis and treatment. Patients may be confronted with massive brain scan machines or hooked up to devices that monitor pulmonary and cardiac functioning. X-rays, hypodermic injections, blood tests, gastric tubes, and bladder catheters are standard procedures. For more severe cases, implants, chemotherapy, and radiation treatment are also routine in the sophisticated medical world. Should a patient's heart stop, open-chest cardiac massage and electric shock are often used in an effort to resuscitate. The shock treatment is sometimes like jump starting a worn-out engine, enabling it to quiver and sputter on a little farther.

The cost of the massive equipment needed in hospitals has been one of the main reasons per capita hospital expenses have more than doubled in the past decade. A cure-at-any-cost outlook has pervaded decision making in some hospitals.

Beyond this intense focus on cure, the organizational pattern of hospitals is detrimental to the dying patient. Physicians generally rule without much input from nurses, technicians, and other staff members. Many of the stringent regulations are made to minimize inconveniences to the doctors. Unlike the family physician of past generations, who was as much interested in the patient as the disease, the specialist physician now may become so focused on the course of an illness that the full needs of the patient suffering from it may be overlooked.

Those who control hospitals in America may be more apprehensive about death than are the patients. Herman Feifel discovered from extensive interviews that physicians have an above average fear of death.[12] Doctors tend to have an aversion to a dying patient, who is a deviant from the normal recovery pattern. Consequently, the opinions of such a patient are often not sought or taken seriously. Moreover, the patient's family is usually informed but not consulted. In a time of crisis the common place for an exchange with the family is in the hospital hallway; conference rooms for private family consultation are usually lacking.

Nurses as a group do not treat patients as impersonally as physicians, but studies show that they generally put terminally ill patients off with evasion, denial, or falsification. Kastenbaum found these typical responses by hospital nurses: "You are not going to die," "Let's think of something more cheerful," "You'll be feeling like your old self again."[13]

The growing impersonality of the technological jungle confronting the terminally ill has evoked this comment from Robert Kavanaugh: "a dying human being deserves more than . . . a mouth full of pills, arms full of tubes . . . and a rump full of needles."[14] Consider the following illustration of what can happen in a hospital. A patient in an advanced stage of cancer had his stomach removed. It was then found that the malignancy had spread farther. The patient, a retired physician, fully understood his condition. His pain was constant despite the continual administration of drugs. While he was in the hospital, another operation was performed to remove a clot from his lung. The patient then asked members of the hospital staff that he be allowed to die peacefully should he have another crisis. To make sure everyone understood his feelings, he wrote a note to that effect and had it placed in his case file. However, two weeks later he had a heart attack and was resuscitated. The hospital team rushed to revive him four more times that same day. The patient lingered on for three more weeks, kept "alive" by intravenous feeding and blood transfusions. Violent vomiting and convulsions marked his intense suffering. His frequent heart stoppages damaged his mind. A whole battery of machines was used feverishly to sustain his life. At last the hospital technicians were unable to revive the old doctor despite an aggressive effort when his heart stopped again. Technology appears to have grown faster than humane methods for controlling it.

Over the past generation a hospice movement has emerged in response to the maltreatment of incurables in hospitals. The hospice is a return to the original purpose of hospitals (from the Latin term *hospitium*, meaning a hospitality place). Hospitals or hospices were established by Christians many centuries ago to carry out Jesus' expectation that his followers would welcome the stranger, feed the hungry, and help the sick (Matt. 25:35).[15] They were maintained by religious communities and were not primarily places for medical treatment. Medieval physicians practiced elsewhere.

The hospice movement in America was inspired by two institutions in London. St. Joseph's Hospice, established in 1905 by an order of nuns, is the oldest modern hospice. One-third of its beds are for patients with a prognosis of three months or fewer to live. Cicely Saunders trained there as a nurse before later becoming a medical doctor with an aim to incorporate the old hospice concept in contemporary society. In 1981 on receiving the prestigious Templeton Prize for Progress in Religion, Saunders described the hospice purpose in this way:

> For over 1,000 years hospice was a resting place for pilgrims, giving them a welcome that lasted till they were ready to go on. . . . Over the past decade the word has been filled up with new meaning. . . . I would define the modern hospice as a skilled community working to improve the quality of life remaining for patients and their families

struggling with mortal and long-term illness. . . . Hospice is about a special kind of living and in a sense is still concerned with traveling; patients, families, elderly residents and the staff and volunteers who meet them find they are drawn into a journey of the spirit.[16]

In 1967 Saunders opened St. Christopher's Hospice, named for the patron saint of travelers and almost entirely devoted to those whose journey is nearly over. This hospice has served as a model for dozens more that have been formed subsequently in Europe and in the United States. In comparison with nursing homes where most chronically ill patients survive for some years, the average stay at St. Christopher's is two months for those in an advanced stage of malignancy or neurological disease. Some stay much longer than the average because the hospice has, in Saunders' words, "beds without invisible parking meters beside them."[17] Since there is no expectation for recovery, the expensive technology for prolonging life is absent. Patients are not treated as things to be manipulated by respirators or intravenous feeding.

At St. Christopher's the rooms are homelike. Smoking and alcohol are permitted, and sherry or beer is served before meals as an appetite stimulator. Family visits are unrestricted throughout the day, and lounges are available to accommodate them. Children are encouraged to visit, and unsanitary pets may come too. For some hours after a death the family is permitted to be with the body in the bedroom or in the hospice chapel.

High priority is given to relieving pain, with phenomenal success. A study of English hospices showed that thirty-seven percent of those admitted were experiencing severe pain. All but one percent of them found relief after admission. Narcotic dosages are skillfully regulated to give comfort without destroying alertness. A mixture of cocaine, heroin, alcohol, and fruit syrup is given in anticipation of pain. Addiction to powerful drugs is not the concern it would be in a hospital. Saunders tells of the way painkillers fit into the philosophy of St. Christopher's: "There is a stage when the treatment of a hemorrhage is not another transfusion, but adequate sedation, or someone who will not go away but will stay and hold a hand."[18] Caressing the body, spoon-feeding a favorite soup, stroking the hair, and uttering reassuring words are also soothing pain relievers. Saunders relates a case illustrating this holistic approach:

> Mr. P came to us from a teaching hospital with an unsolved problem of pain, unhappy and breathless.
>
> He quickly settled to our regime of drugs, and pain was never a problem again. Mr. P used the ten weeks he was with us to sort out his thoughts on life and faith. . . . He enjoyed meeting students and visitors, and he made good friends in the ward.
>
> After Christmas I took him some copies of a photograph I had taken of him at one of our parties. I wanted to give it to him, he wanted to pay for it. We ended by each accepting something from the other. As we were discussing this I held my hand out. At this he held both his, palms upwards, next to mine and said, "That's what life is about, four hands held out together." [19]

There are two main experimental approaches to hospices in the United States. One of these is inpatient based and is quite similar to St. Christopher's. The hospice may be a separate hospital wing or an autonomous facility. It has been found that it is not as disturbing for dying patients to be with those sharing their plight as to be spread throughout a hospital where they can watch other patients leaving with improving health. The hospice rooms are colorful, in contrast to the starkness of hospital walls, and patients are encouraged to wear bright clothing. Knowing that change in environment can lift morale, attendants may move a patient's bed for a better window view. Those who are able may sit on the porch, play games, attend chapel, and walk or ride outside.

Special training is provided staff members to orient them toward adding quality rather than length to life. The sensitive hospice worker may play music, hang pictures, arrange privacy, and select foods that reflect individual differences. Flexible scheduling that accommodates personal needs is another way to minister to individual well-being. Attempts are made to establish in-depth discussions with patients so that mental anguish and irrational guilt can be relieved. Staff self-esteem is raised as personnel come to view death not as a sign of their personal neglect but as an appropriate and holy remedy.

The other current approach in this country is the home-care-based hospice, a program rather than a place. The hundreds of hospices of this kind established in the past few years are popular because of their financial and emotional benefits. Maintaining a patient at home costs much less than at a hospital and significantly less than at an inpatient hospice. Medicare has recognized this savings to the government and has begun to fund home-based hospices. Also most patients have a sentimental attachment to the place where they have long lived, and they want to spend their declining days there. They would much rather be surrounded by their relatives and their furniture than by strange people and humming machines in a hospital. A recent study found that eighty percent of the population would prefer to die at home, but in practice the vast majority do not.[20]

The effectiveness of the program type of hospice depends on a skillfully administered interdisciplinary team. A key component of the team is trained unpaid volunteers. The ideal ratio is one dozen part-time volunteers per patient, because unpaid aids cannot individually be expected to donate large amounts of time each week. Their jobs are limited only by their imaginations. They could construct a bird feeding station outside a window, contribute a weekly morning of shopping for the patient's family, or sit in the home for an evening to give the family a time to get out. Volunteers could read books to or write letters for the terminally ill. Those with special skills could assist with unfinished business, such as writing down memoirs or revising a will.

Involvement of the dying person and the family in team decisions is of prime importance. Family members need to give as well as receive support. Some of the family's satisfaction comes from the opportunity to serve tasty food or to provide entertainment that would not be possible in a hospital or nursing home. Returning kindnesses prior to death assists in healing the grief to follow, because family members will recall that they did all they could to provide enjoyment while life was present. In a home hospice, children and grandchildren both give joy to the dying and receive an understanding of dying that is unobtainable elsewhere. The primary experience of beholding someone actually die in a loving home is healthier than the impersonal experiences of looking at pictures of death in the media.

Home hospice teams are also composed of nurses, physicians,

social workers, and ministers, as well as the patients themselves, as long as they are able. Professional people come into homes as needed. Donald McCarthy has informed his fellow clergy regarding their opportunities:

> Theology teaches that spiritual growth continues to occur even as the body decays and dies. Spiritual growth seems to occur most readily in the intimacy of family relationships and through the love and support with which family members watch and wait with a dying member for the inevitable moment of final separation. Often the final stages of terminal illness occasion various forms of family reconciliation and a healing of wounds that have festered for years. The hospice environment fosters this grace-filled process more effectively than the typical hospital environment.[21]

Inpatient and home-based hospices need not be viewed as complete alternatives. The two can be coordinated so that a dying person could be shifted temporarily from home to institutional hospice in order to prevent family burnout or to provide a backup when members of the home hospice team neglect their responsibilities.

The hospice is an idea whose time has come. Although only a small percentage of dying patients now receive hospice care, the movement is rapidly gaining favor. Dr. Saunders is most deserving of the international recognition she has received in spearheading an innovative means of maximizing life with dignity. The hospice helps fill the gap left when the general practitioner stopped making house calls and was partly replaced by specialized personnel in hospitals. The burgeoning growth of health care necessitates a division of labor, with the primary goal of hospitals being cure and of hospices being care. More hospices are needed like the one in Cincinnati which has set forth this aim in its charter: "To express reverence for human life, not by prolonging the terminal illness of patients but by assisting them to live fully, to preserve mental alertness, and to experience the support of family and a caring community."[22]

Options in Terminal Situations

The hospice movement is one expression of euthanasia, if that term is defined literally. Meaning good dying, *euthanasia* compounds the Greek word *eu,* good, with *thanatos,* death. In recent years euthanasia has been primarily associated, especially by its opponents, with killing the incapacitated. In this sense, euthanasia among humans is not unlike shooting a crippled horse or aged dog to put it out of its misery. Humans do not like to be treated like animals who have no freedom to decide when or how they die. Hence, there is general abhorrence of euthanasia when it describes situations in which patients capable of expressing themselves are given no choice regarding when and how they will die. The pejoratively defined term *euthanasia,* only one of several possible ways for dealing with terminal situations, will be avoided in the following considerations since the use of a word that now commonly has such a narrow and emotionally charged meaning hampers discussion.

In terminal situations both physicians and patients have two possible roles. The physician may be active or passive, and the patient may be involuntary or voluntary. Combining the two parties results in four options: active-involuntary, active-voluntary, passive-involuntary, and passive-voluntary. These will be dealt with sequentially from the most difficult to the least difficult to justify morally.

Cases in which a physician exercises the active option and kills an unwilling patient are rare in America because they are regarded as murder. Doctors have been convicted of intentionally prescribing lethal dosages which resulted in the death of patients who had not requested to die. At the beginning of World War II Hitler ordered the extermination of all physically incurable and mentally defective persons, under the guise of vacating hospital beds and conserving food. Thousands of Germans perished when his cruel orders were executed. In modern nations where there is prejudice against the elderly, it would not be difficult to rationalize killing the incapacitated and the obsolete for the convenience of the younger citizens.

The active-voluntary option of physicians and patients with respect to terminal illness is gaining favor. For forty years the National Opinion Research Center has asked Americans this question: "When a person has a disease that cannot be cured, do you think doctors should be allowed by law to end the patient's life by some painless means if the patient and his family request it?" In 1947 thirty-seven percent answered yes; by 1973 a bare majority were in favor; and in 1983 sixty-three percent answered yes.[23]

The biography of Sigmund Freud illustrates the active-voluntary option. He had throat cancer for many years and was unable to speak in spite of numerous operations. Biographer Ernest Jones, who was with Freud during his last days, when the cancer had eaten through his cheek, observes, "The exhaustion was extreme and the misery indescribable." Freud arranged for his physician to give him an infusion of morphine adequate to cause death when the pain became unbearable. The physician responded after Freud, at the age of eighty-three, said, "It is only torture now and it has no longer any sense."[24]

Withholding treatment and letting nature take its course exercises the passive-involuntary option that is widely but quietly practiced by physicians. Many members of the health care professions see little point in prolonging the suffering of irreversibly comatose patients and of such patients' families. In 1986 the American Medical Association decided that it would be ethical for physicians to discontinue "all means of life prolonging medical treatment"—including artificial feeding and respiration—in hopeless cases even when death is not imminent. The economic as well as emotional stress on the family cannot be overlooked. Terminal illness now consumes half of the lifetime medical expenses of the average American.[25] Intensive care, costing many hundreds of dollars daily, can quickly bankrupt a family of moderate means who lack insurance coverage. For those families who can afford it only with government assistance, there is the question of allocating scarce public health care funds for this purpose.

Americans now generally support physicians who take a passive or "benign neglect" approach to treatment even if the dying patient has not requested to die. A poll in 1983 showed that sixty-five percent believe that "doctors should be allowed to stop treating an incurably ill patient at the request of the patient's family."[26]

In *The Making of a Surgeon* William Nolen describes a young man who was ventilated and tube-fed for several weeks after a motorcycle accident which had caused serious brain damage and internal injuries. When the patient caught pneumonia, Nolen decided not to administer antibiotics, and the patient was declared dead three days later. Nolen was relieved when the complication hastened total death.[27]

It should, of course, be recognized that the judgments of physicians are fallible and that in some instances they make wrong prognoses. A patient may regain a fairly normal life after being comatose for many weeks. For example, a boy who was president of the student body of his high school broke his neck while playing football. His breathing stopped for almost ten minutes before he was placed on a respirator. Doctors presumed the oxygen deprivation had caused severe brain damage and advised the parents that their son could die with some dignity if the life-sustaining machine were disconnected. The parents refused to give up hope, and after some months the boy slowly came out of the coma. After rigorous physical therapy he overcame tremendous odds and began to walk and speak again.

Physicians are occasionally confronted with life-and-death decisions with respect to the very old and the very young. Consider the Alzheimer's patients who have dropped irretrievably into dementia. Intelligence and willpower have withered away and the patients do not know who they are or who any of their loved ones are. When infection arises, the physician decides not to administer medication, recognizing that it will prolong dying rather than prolong living. Consequently, the dehumanized body soon expires. As slower, debilitating dying becomes more likely due to medical developments, the preposition *from* in an Elizabethan prayer might better read: "*To* sudden death, good Lord, deliver us."

At the other end of the age spectrum, one out of every six hundred babies is born with mongolism, now professionally called Down's syndrome. Though many of these infants are trainable, most are severely retarded and/or physically handicapped. When a Down's syndrome infant is born with another congenital defect—such as an intestinal obstruction—requiring corrective surgery for survival, the physician may elect not to operate, especially if those who will be burdened with the infant's care agree.[28]

The least difficult terminal decisions are those involving the fourth option—a willing patient and a passive physician. In a 1985 nationwide Gallup poll, eighty-five percent agreed with the statement that "a patient with a terminal disease ought to be able to tell his doctor to let him die rather than to extend his life when no cure is in sight."[29] The percentage is not significantly affected by differences in religious persuasion. Although allied with the "pro-lifers," Pope John Paul II stated in 1980, "It is permitted in conscience to take the decision to refuse forms of treatment that would only secure a precarious and burdensome prolongation of life."[30]

Cases of massive burns are among those in which an earlier death can be chosen. During a two-year period, the Los Angeles burn unit diagnosed twenty-four patients as "having injury without precedent of survival." Those victims were lucid and without pain for the first several hours after being burned, because the injury anesthetized nerve endings. They were able to make a rational choice on the treatment they preferred. All but three chose ordinary medical care, consisting of painkillers and death in a few hours, rather than the maximum treatment which involved the use of life-prolonging machines. The other three died within a week. Relatives of the victims were relieved that the burden of decision making was never on their shoulders.[31]

Occasionally patients have enough intellect and willpower to assert their right to refuse even ordinary care. After suffering a stroke in 1983, an eighty-five-year-old former college president decided the quality of his life was so unsatisfactory that he did not wish to live on. A judge ruled that it was legal for the medical professionals to withhold treatment and for the patient to refuse food and therapy. In six weeks he starved himself to death by refusing solid food.

Terminal patients are sometimes not in a healthy enough mental condition to make an informed decision on whether life continues to be worth living. Even if they are conscious and are able to think clearly, they lack the energy to take the initiative to see that their wishes are respected. In anticipation of such situations a *Living Will* has been developed to enable healthy persons to express in writing what should be done regarding artificial life-prolonging equipment if they become ill and the physician foresees no hope of recovery. Approximately half of the states have approved right-to-die legislation, and a dozen others have bills under consideration. The statutes offer individuals the opportunity to express legally their wishes regarding extraordinary medical treatment in case of subsequent incompetence caused by terminal illness. Should there be a change of mind when a person is faced with the imminent prospect of dying, the declaration can be revoked orally or by destruction of the written statement. Physicians generally support the Living Will, which millions have now signed, because it enables them to know more fully a terminal patient's wishes as to extent of treatment. Also it relieves them of malpractice fears when they turn off the life-prolonging machines after judging the chances of recovery to be nil. (The Living Will distributed by Concern for Dying can be found in Appendix B.2.)

An illustration of the way the Living Will has been used is found in John Sherrill's description of his eighty-two-year-old mother's situation. Severely afflicted with pneumonia, she was moved to the skilled-care unit of her retirement home. She was unable to respond verbally to anyone by the time her son arrived, but her body language showed she regarded her bed as a torture chamber. Sherrill eloquently tells of the final hours of her life:

> Plastic tubes, which ran from the upside-down bottles over Mother's head, were connected to two I.V.'s. The needles, hidden beneath adhesive, were imbedded in each of Mother's arms. . . . Her restless, constantly moving wrists were tied to the bars. . . . A nurse came in. She looked at Mother and shook her head. "I think I'll turn her," she said. She untied Mother's left hand. Instantly, before the nurse could stop her, Mother's free hand swept across her body to her right arm. With awkward fingers she began to grope and claw and pull at the adhesive which held the needle in her vein. . . . The nurse snatched at Mother's left arm. "Here now," she said, "we can't do that." She forced Mother's hand back to the bars on the near side and struggled to tie the gauze again. . . .
>
> Mother had little fear of death, but she did fear a bad dying. Like most of us, she dreaded the idea of being incapacitated, and then being hooked up to machines, put on chemicals, fed intravenously and kept alive artificially. Nine years ago, when she was in excellent health, Mother had written out a Living Will which she distributed to a dozen family members. It was a statement which instructed all concerned that, in the event of irreversible deterioration, we were not to take extraordinary measures to prolong her life. . . . I asked Dr. Haller if he knew of Mother's standing request not to resort to life-prolonging measures. "No, we didn't get those instructions, and I'm afraid that's not unusual

when you change institutions. Failures of communication . . . do happen." There was a long pause. And then I asked the question I'd been avoiding. . . . "What would happen if we asked for those I.V.'s to come out?" Dr. Haller's voice was neutral as he said, "The body does surprise us at times. But in my opinion, your mother would probably go ahead with her death. . . . The pneumonia would get worse. . . . There's a saying among doctors that pneumonia is the old man's friend. . . . Nobody dies of 'old age.' We die of something specific. Pneumonia is a kind way to go. Relatively quick and painless. A friend when we need one most. . . ."

The needles out, the nurse untied the first strip of gauze. I expected Mother's left arm to start flailing. So did the nurse apparently; she held Mother's free hand in her own, then released it. But this time Mother's hand did not move. . . . Mother's whole being, starting with her hands and arms, virtually melted into total relaxation. . . . Was it possible that she was this very moment making a transition to a new depth of being? Was she resting completely in the arms of her Lord? . . . Mother's eyes opened. . . . Her eyes were brilliant blue. . . . The stare was steady. Unblinking. . . . There was agelessness in Mother's look, just as in a newborn's. The baby is coming from God; Mother was going to God. And both conveyed to me the same whisper of eternity.[32]

The death education movement, initiated in large part by the unfatiguing efforts of Dr. Kübler-Ross, is now coming of age. Over the past generation there has been a remarkable shift in the attitudes of both the health care professionals and the general public toward the rights of the dying. Much is now being done to provide a humanizing context for the burgeoning growth of medical technology. The previously undreamed of replacement of vital organs and treatment by sophisticated machines have their place as long as the patient's needs are kept central. With a diminished uncritical faith in scientific progress, fewer Americans are awaiting a *deus ex machina* spectacle that will rescue those playing out the last act of their mortal dramas. An acceptance of the wisdom of W.N. Hubbard, dean of the University of Michigan Medical School, is abroad in the land. He said, " 'To sacrifice human dignity at the time of death . . . or to make the process of dying a burden upon the living, is not in the highest tradition of medicine, nor is it justified in the humanistic traditions.' "[33]

5

SUICIDE

Defining suicide, which literally means self-killing, is not as simple as it might at first glance seem. The lethal hemlock that Socrates drank was self-administered, but his court-ordered death was not a suicide. Neither should a woman who dies of anorexia be so classified, even though she has slowly starved herself to death. A man who dies in a hurricane because he did not heed a radio warning is not a suicide victim, nor is someone who carelessly consumes an overdose of barbiturates and dies. A woman who kills herself by jumping from a burning building has not committed suicide, nor has a child who is killed by a train while exploring a railway tunnel. A motorcyclist who dies from head injuries because he or she did not wear a helmet would not be reported as a suicide. None of these examples involves voluntary extinction of life. Suicide is a fatal act of self-destruction undertaken with conscious intent.

Statistical Data

In the United States a person is more likely to commit suicide than to be killed by someone else. Each year the number of reported suicides exceeds by thousands the number of reported homicides. This is not commonly recognized because newspapers make headlines of homicides but make little mention of suicides. Edwin Shneidman, America's leading suicidologist, estimates that the actual annual number of suicides is about fifty thousand, or one every ten minutes, since as many as half of the suicides may be officially reported by coroners as accidents.[1] If this is the case, then there are nearly as many suicides annually as there are names listed on our national memorial for the twelve years of the Vietnam War.

It is often difficult to determine absolutely if a death was intentionally self-inflicted. And because suicide is taboo in our culture, the official record reflects that the benefit of a doubt has often been given in order to avoid stigmatizing the family name or voiding a life insurance policy. "Autocides" illustrate the difficulty in establishing accurate suicide figures. If a single-driver car crash is a suicide in disguise, it is often impossible to arrive at this firm conclusion because of the state of the wreckage. An alcoholic who runs head-on into a concrete barrier at 140 miles per hour may, at least semi-intentionally, have had termination of life in mind. The official record, however, would probably show this to be an accidental death. It is also unlikely that a drowning victim who had strong self-destructive habits would be certified as a suicide.

The chart on page 70 shows the striking (and unprecedented) statistical shift over the past generation in the ages at which American suicides are committed, even though the rate for the total population has not increased significantly. Teen suicide has more than doubled since 1950, with the rate for college students doubling that. Nationwide one member of the younger generation takes his or her life every hour. Sometimes one teen suicide seems to motivate other teenagers living in the community to do the same. A Texas town had seven in 1983, and during one month in 1984 there were five in Westchester, New York, four of these using the same method of strangulation. At an Omaha high school in February 1986, seven students tried to kill themselves and three succeeded.[3]

Even though the most tragic suicides may be among the young, the greatest number of suicides continues now, as in the past, to be among those of the older generation. While the overall suicide rate is declining for those who are sixty-five and older, for men it in-

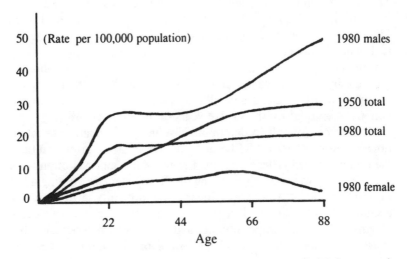

Modified from *Vital Statistics of the United States, 1980* vol. 2 (Hyattsville: U.S. Department of Health and Human Services, 1985), pp. 32-33[2].

Fig. 3: Suicide in the United States

creases with each year of old age, peaking at forty-five per hundred thousand at age eighty-five or older. Nearly three-fourths of the suicides among Americans over fifty are by white men.[4]

It is estimated that there are about ten attempts for every suicide accomplished. This ratio is much lower for the older generation and much higher for the younger generation. Pregnant teenagers are seven times more likely than other women to attempt suicide. Females try three times more often than males, but males actually commit suicide three times more often than females.[5] There has been little change in the suicide rate for women over the past thirty years.

The disagreeable means used in bungled suicides sometimes remove the determination to try again. In her poem *Résumé* Dorothy Parker observes that unappealing methods cause minds to change:

since razors, rivers, acids, drugs, guns, nooses, and gas can't be trusted to do the job satisfactorily, "You might as well live" (line 8).

With regard to the methods used by those who succeed at suicide, guns account for fifty-eight percent; solid, liquid, or gas poisoning for twenty percent; hanging, strangulation, and suffocation for fourteen percent; jumping and drowning for five percent; and cutting and piercing for two percent.[6] Gas poisoning is usually by carbon monoxide exhaust fumes from a car, and solid poisoning is usually by pills intended for medication. A suicide landmark is the Golden Gate Bridge of San Francisco from which more than seven hundred have dropped two hundred feet to death.[7] However, home is the most likely place for suicides. As for gender differentiation, more than twice as many women as men prefer poisoning. The latter prefer guns, which are more macho and have more lethal certainty. The aggressiveness of feminism has brought more use by women of the formerly male-dominated firearms.

Suicide statistics also show a significant racial difference. For both males and females, the white rate is about double that for Blacks. Among Blacks there are almost five times as many males who commit suicide as females. As with white males, there is an increasing proportion of Black male suicides among youth. The lowest suicide rate in the United States is among older Black women, even though they are among the most disadvantaged citizens. Among those over the age of sixty-five, white men commit suicide fourteen times as often as Black women; white women, twice as often as Black women.[8]

Lifestyles also affect suicide rates. Married people have a lower rate than singles, and heterosexuals have a much lower rate than homosexuals. Rural dwellers are less suicide prone than urban dwellers. Alcoholics have a rate about ten times higher than nonalcoholics.[9] The more affluent take their lives more frequently than those who are less affluent. Chicago's suburban North Shore, one of the wealthiest areas of the nation, is known as "the suicide belt." In a seventeen-month period in 1979 and 1980 eighteen teenagers there took their own lives by means of guns, eight more hung themselves, and two lay down in front of trains.[10]

Among the professions, lawyers have a higher suicide rate than teachers and the clergy. The rate among military officers is higher than among enlisted soldiers. Physicians, who are among the top-paid Americans, have a much higher suicide rate than the average. Psychiatrist Matthew Ross reported in 1973 that suicide accounts for twenty-eight percent of physician deaths in the under-forty age group, compared with nine percent for other white males of the same age. Female physicians have the highest reported rate for any group of women, nearly four times that of the general female population. Ironically, psychiatrists, who are especially trained to counsel with the suicide-prone, are in one of the medical specialties most suscep-tible to suicide. Highly stressful careers and the abuse of easily ac-cessible drugs are the main reasons doctors are a relatively high-risk suicide group.[11]

Religion is a statistically significant factor in suicides. For ex-ample, the suicide rate in Egypt is one-sixtieth that of the United States. The Egyptian outlook on life has been heavily impacted by the Muslim condemnation of suicide. The *Quran* does not prohibit suicide, but from early times onward Muslim tradition has asserted, "Whosoever shall kill himself shall suffer in the fire of hell, and shall be excluded from heaven forever."[12]

Countries with a predominantly Roman Catholic population— such as Ireland—generally have a lower suicide rate than Protestant countries.[13] This differential may be due in part to Catholic teaching, which has condemned suicide for many centuries. Fourth-century Bishop Augustine calls it "a detestable and damnable wickedness" unless a person is, like the biblical Samson, specially commanded by God to take his own life. The command "You shall not kill" (Exod. 20:13) implies, Augustine argues, that one's own life as well as the lives of others should be preserved.[14] Extending Augustine's position, Thomas Aquinas declared that the self-killer has committed a triple sin: against God who alone has the right to give and take life; against the human community of which he or she is a part; and against oneself who has the natural inclination of self-preservation. ". . . to bring death upon oneself in order to escape the other afflic-tions of this life, is to adopt a greater evil in order to avoid a lesser," Aquinas reasons. He concludes that suicide "is most dangerous since no time is left . . . to expiate it by repentance."[15] The poet Dante, following Aquinas' theology, placed those who take their own lives on the seventh level of hell, below the greedy and the murderous (*Inferno*, Canto 13). For centuries the bodies of those who committed the unconfessed and therefore unforgivable sin of suicide were not buried in cemeteries that Catholic priests had consecrated. The somewhat more tolerant attitude toward suicide among Protestants and Jews may be due to the fact that it is not a specifically forbidden sin in the Jewish Scriptures or the Christian Bible.[16]

On the basis of actuarial data, what would be the appearance of a likely suicidal person? The composite portrait would show an elderly male WASP in the medical profession. He would be a gay alcoholic who had made previous suicide attempts. He also would live in Denmark, for that European country may have the world's highest suicide rate—twice that of the United States.

Psychological and Social Causes

Since suicide is usually a secretive and private act, it is difficult to discover reasons why people take their own lives. The few who leave notes do not usually reveal much about the underlying causes of their self-killing. The causes are elusive also because of the frequent and emotional reactions to the very idea of suicide among those who comment on it. The first scientific treatment of the subject was by the French sociologist Emile Durkheim. *Le Suicide,* written in 1897, is still the most influential study of the subject. His thesis is that suicide risk increases when an individual is too little or too much integrated into the group in which he or she lives.[17] In modified form, Durkheim's outlook is presented in the following discussion of several social causes.

One main cause of suicide is the shattering loss of someone or something highly valued. The death of love drives some to a love of death. The loneliness that results from the death of a lover and the abandonment anxiety that can follow a divorce make persons vulnerable to suicide. The Romeos of real life, devastated without their Juliets, commit suicide. Those who are unhappily married often look forward to becoming unfettered again. However, most divorced persons find the single life miserable and soon remarry; those who remain unattached have a higher rate of suicide. Divorced men commit suicide four times more often than married men, and divorced women commit suicide three times more often than married women.[18]

Some who are separated by death imagine that suicide affords a means for quick reunion. Socrates observes that "there are many who have chosen of their own free will to follow dead lovers and wives and sons to the next world, in the hope of seeing and meeting there the persons whom they loved."[19] Psychologist Robert Kastenbaum tells what agonies recently bereaved persons can have:

> Loss of a loved one can be experienced as so unbearable that the survivor is tempted to "join" the deceased. . . . desperate longing may impel a person to follow the dead all the way "to the other side" if the relationship has been marked by extreme dependency. . . .
>
> Some components in our cultural tradition encourage suicidal fantasies and actions of this kind. Heaven is such a delightful place—and it is so miserable here. Death is not real; it is only a portal to eternal life. There is an insurance advertisement that depicts a dead husband gazing down with approval from the clouds. Messages of this type encourage a blurring of the distinction between the living and the dead. . . .
>
> Children are particularly vulnerable to reunion fantasies. They do not yet have a firm cognitive grasp of life and death. . . . The child is still in the process of attempting to establish identity as an individual. The parent or older sibling who has "gone off to heaven" has left the survivor with painful feelings of incompleteness and yearning.[20]

For individuals who have high aspirations, the loss of status often triggers thoughts of suicide. White men, who tend to identify their sense of self-worth with occupational success, are likely to be severely disturbed when they are fired, demoted, or passed over for promotion. By contrast, Blacks, who generally have been barred from high status, are not as often overwhelmed by hard times because they have learned to cope with disappointment for much of their lives. In 1985 it was reported that for every fifteen-percent increase in unemployment in the United States there are 318 men who commit suicide.[21] The self-inflicted termination of lives clusters around the age of sixty-five, the time when most careers are terminated. Those who identify themselves with their jobs share Ernest Hemingway's view: "Retirement is the filthiest word in the language. Whether by choice or by fate, to retire from what you do—and what you do makes you what you are—is to back up into the grave."[22] That novelist shot himself to death at the age of sixty-two.

For youth, low grades may be the final overwhelming blow that provokes self-killing. In American culture, self-esteem is closely tied to victory in competition. Youth are sometimes placed under unbearable pressure by adults to win in all their activities. For many, school achievement is the principal arena for proving to their parents that they are responsible. Youth may be assigned few household chores and have no paying job outside the home, especially if they belong to well-to-do families. Those who do not earn high grades or other school distinctions fail to attain the presumed parental standard for acceptability and goodness. Students whose school records cease to show progress may be crushed with shame. Losing out to others in the upward mobility race—whether real or imagined—is one of the multiple factors that intensify the risk of suicide.

Parents who impose too few standards may unwittingly cause as much self-destructive behavior as those who impose an intensely competitive orientation on their children. Many youth grow up with little sense of emotional or moral bonds with their families or their larger community. They have been left to "do their own thing" at day-care centers or with teenage peers. Although adequately provided for in material things, they have not been given the affection and the time with role models needed for inculcating normative values. The underparented youth feels unwanted and isolated from traditional goals of life. Research also shows that in a number of adolescent suicide cases, parents were seen as adversaries and physical violence in the home was a common pattern. Psychiatrist Herbert Hendin, the author of several books on suicide, maintains that many children perceive themselves as a source of their parents' unhappiness. Those parents communicate that they could have a more pleasurable life and successful career if they were not burdened with the time and money demands of child care. Hendin attributes the mushrooming rise in youth suicide in the present generation primarily to the frequent absence of shared concerns, intimacy, and love in family relations.[23]

Offering yet another motive for suicide, Sigmund Freud held that it is a way of expressing revenge over being rejected. Thus suicide carries out the urge to kill that all have some time during life. People fantasize that by murdering themselves they can devastate everyone who is tormenting their conscious or subconscious minds and at the same time can remove the guilt over their death wishes.[24] Two English poets have expressed well the psychodynamics of this inverted aggression. G. K. Chesterton muses:

> The man who kills a man kills a man.
> The man who kills himself kills all men.
> As far as he is concerned, he wipes out the world.

In a lyric about a knife, A. E. Housman conveys similar self-assassination sentiments:

> Here is a knife like other knives,
> That cost me eighteen pence.
>
> I need but stick it in my heart
> And down will come the sky,
> And earth's foundations will depart
> And all you folk will die.

Fear of the future is also a component of some attempted and completed suicides. Personal and national happenings can be so destructive of any hope of achieving goals that deadly psychological numbness settles upon individuals of all ages. For one person it could be an unwanted pregnancy that threatens educational and career plans; for another it could be a malignancy which precipitates paralyzing thoughts of infirmities ahead. Events of national scope can also be traumatic. The suicide rate in the United States peaked in 1932 when economic depression caused personal depression for those who had been ruined financially. The happy days when there were cars in their garages and meat in their pots were over, and there was no hope for the recovery of lost fortunes.[25]

War and the prospects of war can have either a positive or negative effect on suicide rates. World War II strengthened social bonds in the United States and gave a new meaning to life. It ended the Great Depression and fueled patriotic hopes of liquidating evil total-itarianism. As sacrificial death for one's country soared, the suicide rate sank. By contrast, the legacy of the Vietnam War and the grow-ing awareness of the potentiality for total destruction by nuclear war have resulted in some being scared literally to death. A survey con-ducted between 1975 and 1978 showed that twenty-eight percent of high school seniors believed that "nuclear or biological annihilation will probably be the fate of all mankind in my lifetime."[26] In a 1984 referendum at Brown, one of America's most prestigious universi-ties, students voted to have suicide pills stocked on campus in case of nuclear war.[27] The unpopular Vietnam War crushed the idealism of some young Americans, resulting in some using drugs or guns to kill themselves partially or totally. International politics, which fre-quently appears to be on a suicidal course between the superpowers, has had a spin-off onto individuals contemplating doom for them-selves. In an *Encyclopaedia Britannica* article, Shneidman states that "suicide always involves an individual's tortured and tunneled logic in a state of inner-felt, intolerable emotion."[28] Rips within the fabric of a society can contribute to that state of mind.

Durkheim labeled another type of suicide as "altruistic," meaning other-directed. Far from being alienated from family or country, these individuals are so totally absorbed by their groups that they die enthusiastically for it in a show of loyalty.[29] Due to the impact of individualism in Western culture, altruistic suicide is a rarity. In war-time, however, there are occasionally reports of such, as when sol-diers throw themselves on grenades and absorb in their bowels the deadly explosion in order to save nearby buddies.

In traditional Asian cultures altruistic suicide is more frequently practiced and has been deemed a meritorious way of fulfilling social expectations. For many centuries a custom called *suttee* has been practiced in India. It involves a widow's voluntarily throwing herself on her husband's funeral pyre. (Widowers in that patriarchal culture were not reciprocally obligated!) The British outlawed this practice in the nineteenth century, but a few women still express total devo-tion to their dead spouses in this way.[30]

The sacrificial self-incineration ideal of Indian culture has influenced Buddhism. Zen Buddhism in Japan approved of serene self-destruction as a way of showing inner strength. Hence, it became a part of the samurai warrior's code of conduct. Ritual self-disembowelment, called *seppuku* in Japan or *hara-kiri* (literally, belly cutting) in the West, was expected, and even demanded in certain situations. It was a laudable way of protesting an injustice, of atoning for disgrace in battle, and of avoiding capture by an enemy.[31]

The long Oriental tradition of honorable suicide has been illustrated in twentieth-century wars. Thousands of kamikaze pilots became martyrs for Japan during World War II by diving their planes filled with explosives into enemy ships. One kamikaze, who was a Christian convert, wrote his parents: "We live in the spirit of Jesus Christ and we die in that spirit. This thought stays with me. It is gratifying to live in this world but living has a spirit of futility about it now. It is time to die. I do not seek reasons for dying. My only search is for an enemy target against which to dive."[32] Another example of martyrdom comes from the Vietnam War. Some Buddhist monks set themselves afire as a political protest while sitting in a passionless lotus position. On the opposite side of Asia in the nineteen-eighties, suicidal attackers of Shiite Islam have killed hundreds by driving trucks of explosives into buildings housing those whom their religion has designated as enemies.

Durkheim also refers to fatalistic suicides. They occur when schemes for a better life have been blocked and all prospects for a brighter future have disappeared. He points out that such suicides can be "very contagious." Durkheim tells of fifteen hospital patients who hanged themselves in swift succession and of frequent suicide imitation among soldiers.[33]

In 1978 one of the largest mass suicides in history occurred in a Guyana jungle when contagious fatalism struck nine hundred cultists from California. They drank cyanide-spiked punch at the urging of their disillusioned leader. The last hypnotic words of the Reverend Jim Jones were recorded on tape. Here is what he said amid much applause and some protest:

> . . . death is not a fearful thing. It's living that's cursed. It's not worth living like this. . . . everybody dies. . . . I like to choose my

own kind of death for a change. I'm tired of being tormented to hell.
. . .
    The best testimony we can make is to leave this goddamn world.
. . .
    it's the will of sovereign Being that we lay down our lives in pro-
test. . . .
    Lay down your life with dignity. . . . Stop this hysterics. . . . This
is not the way for people who are socialistic Communists to die. . . .
    Lay down your life with your child. Free at last. . . . death is a
million times preferable to spending more days in this life. If you knew
what was ahead of you, you'd be glad to be stepping over tonight. . . .
    Hurry, my children. . . . No more pain. . . . take a drink to go to
sleep. That's what death is, sleep. . . . This world was not our home.[34]

What Can Be Done?

    ("Suicide Issues" in Appendix A.4 should be considered in con-
nection with this section.) There is more stigma against suicidal conduct than any other behavior in our culture. Consequently many
dangerous prejudices are circulated about people who have contem-
plated, attempted, or completed suicide. To substitute correct information for half-truths is the first step toward preventing a potential
suicide. It is frequently asserted that suicide is the product of a diseased mind. The fact is that psychotics are higher suicide risks than
the rest of the population, but most of those who commit suicide have
no history of severe mental illness. Another half-truth is that suicide
runs in families. The fact is that there is no evidence that genetic
inheritance predisposes some to self-destruction. However, a child
who grows up in an environment where one family member has committed suicide is more likely to copy that way of solving problems.
Ernest Hemingway, for example, killed himself in the same way as
his father had done. It is also misleading to say that it is only depressed people who commit suicide. Not all suicidal persons have
been depressed, and those who are in a despondent mood may lack
the energy to complete their resolve. Many suicides occur after individuals come out of depression and are presumed by their friends
to have regained mental health. It is also unsupported folk wisdom
that suicide tends to be seasonal, with more occurrences during bad
weather or at Christmas time when some people are most lonely.

Actually there is a statistical but insignificant increase of suicide in the spring, when the revival of life is celebrated.

Some people distance themselves from those who talk about suicide, believing that there is no stopping those who have decided on that course of action. Actually, most who seem intent on suicide are ambivalent and never carry out their decision. Shneidman has observed that "an individual is at a peak of self-destructiveness for a brief time and is either helped, cools off, or is dead."[35] Many who attempt suicide hope that they will not succeed, and they appreciate rescuers who arrive on the scene unexpectedly. Persons may slash their wrists and immediately call for help. A related half-truth holds that the suicide-prone are so deeply disturbed that only a professional psychotherapist should deal with them. This assertion is little more than a rationalization made by those unwilling to be of help. Distributed among American cities are hundreds of "Contact" centers which are largely operated by lay volunteers. From these round-the-clock hotlines a suicide attempter can learn nonspecialized techniques for stress reduction and life preservation.[36]

Sensitive listening is much needed in all areas of our social life, but it is crucial in counseling with persons who say they feel like killing themselves. That warning signal should not be taken lightly because, contrary to folklore, those who talk about it also may do it. For example, in 1985 a Boston youth laughingly told friends that he was going to shoot himself. No one took him seriously until he stood up in math class, pointed a pistol at his head, and destroyed himself.

Effective communicators do not convey to suicide-prone persons how much stronger counselors are in coping with adversity, because this may prompt feelings of even greater weakness in those they are attempting to help. If persons who are contemplating self-destruction are encouraged to talk about qualities of value in themselves and in things they like, they may soon find matters of worth from which they do not wish to be separated. By contrast, if such persons are humiliated further by challenges to their resolve, the very thing not desired may be done. To say I don't think you have the guts to pull the trigger or jump off the ledge may strengthen the will to do just that. It is also counterproductive to add to the guilt feelings of such persons by informing them that suicidal thoughts never cross the mind of a normal person.

Some things can be done to control the external means for accomplishing suicides. Three-fourths of all suicides in America are inflicted by guns or drugs. To work for more effective laws and police action to control lethal weapons and substances is a sure way to reduce suicides. Many would never get beyond the stage of contemplating suicide if tempting pistols and deadly pills were not so easily accessible in homes or in stores. If they do attempt suicide by means of a knife or gas rather than a gun, there is often time for intervention by a rescuer, and, in many cases, a fatal outcome is not as likely.

Birth control is a long-range means of suicide prevention. As we have seen, children who feel unwanted and are deprived of tender, loving nurture are prime suicide candidates. If children were brought into the world only by parents who genuinely make child guidance a primary commitment, the youth suicide "epidemic" probably would be removed.

The family of a suicide also needs counseling. It is appalling to a family when one of them decides to die rather than continue to share their company. Since there is no illness or accident to blame for the killing, the family are consumed with guilt. A father whose son committed suicide said: "Everyone has a skeleton in their closet. But the person who kills themselves leaves their skeleton in another's closet."[37] Family members tend to think that if only they had avoided those quarrels, the suicide would not have happened. Sometimes they are so ashamed that they dread facing their acquaintances in the community. Not only do they feel socially isolated, but they may also feel spiritual alienation, expressed in resentment toward God for allowing this injustice to happen to them. Or there may be self-hatred for contributing to the nurture of those who would arrogantly take their own lives, a prerogative of God alone. A survivor's grief may be so severe that it can become a cause of self-execution by the bereaved.

In view of the tragedy of suicide and its horrendous impact on survivors, are there any situations when it is morally right? The proscription of suicide was one of the traditional Judeo-Christian values rejected by German philosopher Friedrich Nietzsche. Tormented by various illnesses, he testified, "The thought of suicide is a powerful comfort: it helps one through many a dreadful night."[38] He penned these words a few months before he lost his mind and vegetated for the last decade of life:

> In a certain state it is indecent to live longer. To go on vegetating in cowardly dependence on physicians and machinations, after the meaning of life, the right to life, has been lost, that ought to prompt a profound contempt in society. . . . To die proudly when it is no longer possible to live proudly. Death freely chosen, death at the right time, brightly and cheerfully accomplished amid children and witnesses: then a real farewell is still possible, as the one who is taking leave is still there.[39]

Nietzsche's advocacy of suicide a century ago does not seem to be so rash now. Consider the cancer case of artist Jo Roman, which was featured in the 1980 television program entitled "Choosing Suicide." Roman decided that ending her life by means of a lethal dose was a better option than gambling that the malignancy could be placed in remission. Becoming a helpless invalid was for her a fate worse than death. Roman declared: "I want to die on a day when I feel well and in command of myself. It's my life canvas and I am going to end it my way." Although her husband and daughter tried to dissuade her, they supported her personal autonomy.[40]

Is Roman's act of self-termination an example of what psychiatrist Alfred Hocke called "balance-sheet suicide"? He used that expression for instances in which rational individuals size up their current life situations and decide to end their lives after finding the bad things outweigh the good things.[41] However, Roman may have made an irrational assessment of the effect of her illness. She had been diagnosed at the age of sixty-one as having a breast tumor which could have been surgically removed. Judging by the recovery of many other women who have been treated for breast cancer, Roman probably cheated herself out of many productive years of life and deprived others of the pleasure of her companionship. Mastectomy trauma may have impaired her judgment about possibilities for her personal future. English novelist Barbara Pym, for one, survived breast cancer surgery at age fifty-eight and wrote two more novels and other material before her death at age sixty-six. By her choice she also gained the privilege of seeing a dramatic rise in her reputation as a writer.

The distinguished biologist Max Delbrück has recommended a new kind of education:

> I would suggest that our society provide "suicide education" as it now provides birth control information. A person should be given instruction in the techniques of control over his or her own death. . . . Society must have free access to information about forms of suicide that are not too repulsive. . . .
>
> There is an interesting modern example where suicide instruction was denied to a seriously ill patient. In 1961, seriously ill with cancer at the age of 80, Percy W. Bridgman, the 1946 Nobel laureate in physics, took his life. He left a note that said: "It isn't decent for society to make a man do this thing himself. Probably this is the last day I will be able to do it myself." He then shot himself.
>
> Both his family and his physician should have given him the opportunity of taking his life in a dignified way. But because of society's emphasis on the prolongation of life at all costs, he had to end his own life in a lonely and agonizing way.[42]

In 1980 a group of psychiatrists, philosophers, and theologians prepared a statement on suicide for the terminally ill that has been published by an organization known as Concern for Dying. The statement asserts that suicide should not be advocated but that there may be exceptions to the general prohibition. Excerpts from that statement follow:

> Historically, suicide has been judged as "sinful" by organized religion. . . . We do not dispute the contention that the majority of suicides represent a rejection of the "gift of life" and, as such, are evidence of severe emotional distress. We believe, however, that a person with a progressive terminal disease faces a unique situation—one which calls for a new look at traditional assumptions about the motivation for choosing suicide. In our view, this choice might be found to be reasoned, appropriate, altruistic, sacrificial, and loving. We can imagine that an individual faced with debilitating, irreversible illness, who would have to endure intractable pain, mutilating surgery, or demeaning treatments—with added concern for the burden being placed on family and friends—might conclude that suicide was a reasonable, even

generous, resolution to a process already moving inexorably toward death. . . . Under no circumstances do we wish our efforts to encourage a more accepting attitude to be construed as support for the institutionalization of suicide assistance. We oppose organizations which offer practical help or disseminate printed material describing methods of committing suicide. Not only is such material subject to misuse, its advice is standardized and cannot make allowance for individual differences. . . . Wrong dosage can produce paralysis or massive brain damage without killing, a fact which is not known to many laymen. A decision to choose suicide, we believe, should be an independent and private one, made in consultation with family, friends, and trusted health care professionals. If assistance is required to carry out such a decision, we believe it should be provided by those who have an intimate knowledge of the patient and would be acting out of compassion, knowing that the choice had been made voluntarily.[43]

This Concern for Dying position paper makes allusion to the Hemlock Society, an American organization formed in 1980. Derek Humphry was its founder and also the publisher of *Let Me Die Before I Wake*. Dozens have committed suicide by taking the lethal dose of drugs which Humphry's manual recommends.[44]

In *Suicide: The Philosophical Issues* Margaret Battin raises the question of whether it was moral to prohibit suicide in a cancer case involving an eighty-year-old blind widow who had lived for years in a nursing home. The widow endured uninterrupted pain for a week to save up enough morphine tablets to swallow all at once and, hopefully, die. She sank into a coma but regained consciousness after she was rushed to a hospital emergency room and injected with an antimorphine drug. She was returned to the nursing home to suffer much longer.[45]

Battin predicts that the day may come when there will again be a general change of viewpoint among Christians on suicide. According to A. Alvarez, before the time of Augustine, the church did not regard it as contrary to divine law.[46] There are a number of suicide accounts in the Bible, but no moral judgment about them is made by the narrators (see Judg. 16:30; 1 Sam. 31:4–5; 2 Sam. 17:23; 1 Kings 16:18; Matt. 27:3–5). In early Christianity women who protected themselves from rape by killing themselves were considered virtuous.[47] Battin thinks that the church may find suicide morally acceptable for the terminally ill. Indeed, she speculates that it might become a kind of sacrament, involving serious decision making.[48]

John Donne, prior to becoming a famous Anglican preacher, defended suicide as fitting in certain situations. He wrote a treatise entitled *Biathanatos* in which he defends this thesis: "Selfe-homicide is not so naturally sinne, that it may never be otherwise."[49] He was the first Englishman and one of the few Christians ever to argue that suicide could be a response to a "summons from God." Donne believed that the voice of God is transmitted to humans through conscientious reasoning, especially on matters on which the Bible gives no definite judgment. Would Donne have approved the decision of the kamikaze Christian who felt summoned by God to kill himself, as the biblical Samson had done, in a scheme aimed at the destruction of enemies whom God was thought to despise? Clear reasoning on personal moral matters is generally difficult and may be impossible when suicide is at stake.

Lutheran theologian Dietrich Bonhoeffer did not share Donne's outlook on suicide. While this leader of German resistance to Hitler was being persecuted, but before his imprisonment and execution by the Nazis, he affirmed: "God has reserved to Himself the right to determine the end of life, because He alone knows the goal to which it is His will to lead it. . . . Even if a person's earthly life has become a torment for him, he must commit it intact into God's hand, from which it came."[50]

Congregational pastor Charles Luckey agreed with Bonhoeffer. A month before his death in 1974 he dictated this letter to his friends:

> What . . . does the Christian do when he stands over the abyss of his own death and the doctors have told him that disease is ravaging his brain and that his whole personality may be warped, twisted, changed? *Then* does the Christian have any right to self-destruction, especially when he knows that the changed personality may bring out some horrible beast in himself? Well, after 48 hours of self-searching and study, it comes to me that ultimately and finally the Christian has to always view life as a gift from God, and every precious drop of life was not earned but was a grace, lovingly bestowed upon him by his Creator, and it is not his to pick up and smash.
>
> And so I find the position of suicide untenable, not because I lack

the courage to blow out my brains, but rather because of my deep, abiding faith in the Creator who put the brains there in the first place. And now the result is that I lie here blind on my bed and trust in the sustaining, loving power of that great Creator who knew and loved me before I was fashioned in my mother's womb. But I do not think it is wrong to pray for an early release from this diseased, ravaged carcass.[51]

Our last case is the much-publicized one of Elizabeth and Pitney Van Dusen. Pitney, age seventy-seven was the former president of New York's Union Theological Seminary and a distinguished Presbyterian minister. Before taking an overdose of sleeping pills, he and his wife, Elizabeth, age eighty, wrote:

We have both had very full and satisfying lives. . . .

But since Pitney had his stroke five years ago, we have not been able to do any of the things we want to do . . . and my arthritis is much worse.

There are too many helpless old people who without modern medicinal care would have died, and we feel God would have allowed them to die when their time had come.

Nowadays it is difficult to die. We feel that this way we are taking will become more usual and acceptable as the years pass. . . . We are both increasingly weak and unwell, and who would want to die in a Nursing Home. . . .

"O Lamb of God, that takest away the sins of the world,
Grant us thy peace."[52]

Battin's hopes for a new sacrament may be unrealistic, but most Christians and non-Christians will probably agree that the traditional Christian condemnation of all suicides is too harsh. In spite of the usual debilitating impact of suicide on survivors, we must ask: are there any situations in which it is morally right? Donne's position is a helpful guide for facing the broad range of circumstances confronting the religiously oriented person. There may well be situations in which suicide can be a conscientious act resulting from a careful weighing of alternatives. The Van Dusens' suicide note, for example, displays serious and rational decision making by Christians. After the couple died, a committee of the Presbytery of New York City wisely concluded that "for some Christians, as a last resort in the gravest of situations, suicide may be an act of their Christian conscience."[53]

6

VIOLENCE AND DEATH

Violence is an especially prominent social disease in American culture. United Nations' statistics show that the United States has a higher homicide rate than most other countries. In North America, Mexico has a higher rate, but Canada's rate is one-fifth as high. The further south on the continent, or the further south in the United States, the higher the homicide rate, a geographic pattern due more to poverty than to heat. The homicide rate in this nation has doubled in the past generation, so that there are now several killings every hour. One-third are killed by relatives, one-third by acquaintances, and one-third by strangers. To curb this growing social problem the federal Centers for Disease Control has established a Violence Epidemiology Branch. "Violence in American public and private life has indeed assumed the proportions of an epidemic," claims Surgeon General Everett Koop.[1]

Why is violence endemic in American society? Some clues can be found in our history. The cynical outlook that "the only good Indian is a dead Indian" resulted in wanton decimation of Native Americans. The contempt and brutality of some Anglo-Saxon Protestants who had immigrated to America is also displayed in their relations with other ethnics. Africans were kidnapped and brought as slaves to this nation. The treatment of captured Blacks was so harsh that fewer than half survived the Atlantic passage to work and die on plantations. Torture and lynching of Blacks were tolerated after as well as before emancipation. The violence "virus" seems to have been transmitted to the victims, resulting in a current homicide rate seven times higher for Blacks than for whites in America.[2]

As the nation's frontier expanded westward, getting away with murder was more the rule than the exception. During the first six years of the California gold rush, forty-two hundred murders were committed with the result of only one court conviction. Retaliation against some murderers was arbitrarily administered by private citizens at the end of a rope or gun. Self-appointed vigilantes became a law unto themselves to mete out severe and sudden punishment to the "bad guys."[3] Those "Wild West" days set a pattern for acceptable behavior and partly account for the inordinate attractiveness of violence in the American mass media.

In order to probe the disease of violence as it relates to death, a brief description of various types of homicide is needed. The word homicide refers to killing other *homo sapiens,* and this includes both noncriminal and criminal acts. As regards noncriminal homicide, except during wartime, only a small percentage can be classified as justifiable. Examples of this type would be a police officer who kills a fleeing murderer, a woman who shoots an intruder who intends to attack her, or a soldier who destroys enemy invaders. Another noncriminal type of homicide, distinct from this, is called unavoidable, as for instance, when an engineer is unable to stop a train to avoid running over someone who has fallen on the tracks immediately ahead.

The two main types of criminal homicide are avoidable manslaughter and murder. Industrial deaths are often cases of manslaughter. Companies who neglect to provide adequate safety procedures and devices are likely to have disasters in mines and factories. In 1984 Union Carbide was involved in the largest industrial accident in history. Many hundreds were killed and many thousands were injured from a toxic chemical leak at one of their plants in India. Because of design flaws, management mistakes, and operating errors, Union Carbide has been charged with manslaughter.

Murder refers to intentional killing as the result of malice. Murders without advance deliberation are the more numerous. Some seventy percent of murders have been blamed on anger and jealousy. Quarrels often become violent when drunkenness is involved. Humans have occasional death wishes or urges to kill, and if the means are easily accessible at moments when they are overcome with rage, a murder may result.

Currently there is a move to reclassify as murderers those who cause death while driving drunk. An organization called Mothers Against Drunk Driving (MADD) was formed in 1980 to protest the light penalties commonly given convicted drunk drivers. MADD, recognizing that about half of the fifty thousand vehicular deaths annually in the United States are caused by drivers who are legally drunk, advocates a more severe classification of such killers.[4] One case MADD cites is that of a hit-and-run driver in California who killed a pedestrian two days after he had been arrested for another drunk driving hit-and-run crime. After the second arrest he was convicted of manslaughter, which carries with it a brief prison term.[5] Drivers know road performance is directly related to the amount of alcohol imbibed, because newspapers are constantly reporting the hundreds of alcohol-related accidents that happen each week in America. Even though they have little control over their vehicles while intoxicated, they could have chosen to stay sober if they planned to drive. Hence, it could well be argued that they consciously and maliciously decided to use their vehicles as deadly weapons against anyone who got in their way. In fact, in 1984 the California jury determined that a drunk who plowed into a car at high speeds up to one hundred miles per hour and killed the occupant exhibited enough malice to justify a murder conviction.[6]

Throughout human civilizations the heaviest penalties have gone to those convicted of first-degree murder. It is called premeditated because prior meditation is devoted to plotting what is intended to be coolly executed. For those apprehended and convicted of this capital crime, sentences of life imprisonment or death may be given. Since much press coverage is given to court trials of this type of homicide, the public presumes that premeditated murder is the most common kind of slaying, though this is actually not the case. The moral and legal issues pertaining to punishment in capital crime cases are complex and should be examined carefully.

Reasoning About the Death Penalty

Americans regard the death penalty as one of the most important of current moral issues. An indication of its importance can be found in the letters the editor of *Time* received about a January 24 cover story on the topic. It drew the news magazine's largest 1983 response: 1,697 letters, 1,009 of which favored capital punishment.[7]

A week seldom passes without the media presenting something about someone being executed or sentenced to die. Whereas executions averaged less than one per year in the nineteen-seventies, during the first half of the nineteen-eighties there was about one per month. Considering the more than seventeen hundred inmates now on death row and the rate of new arrivals, at least one execution per day will be needed to keep up with the sentencing. Since the murder rate in the United States is more than one per hour, executions may become so common that they will no longer be regarded as nationally newsworthy. Like most murder coverage, they will be only a matter of the regional press.

Throughout American history the death penalty has been approved for the most serious crimes. Only in the nineteen-sixties did public opinion polls show less than majority support. At that time a number of states outlawed the practice, but most have reinstated it. Polls show that about three-fourths of Americans currently favor the death penalty, and correspondingly about three-fourths of the states permit it.[8]

The various reasons for and against the death penalty will now be weighed. The arguments can be classified as sociological, psychological, economic, theological, and judicial. Although these areas overlap, they are helpful categories for purposes of analysis.

The sociological argument relates to the impact of an action on society, claiming that the death penalty deters others. Many consider it the most persuasive argument for the death penalty. It assumes that facing one's own untimely but scheduled death is the greatest horror. Thus, knowing that a death sentence could also be in one's future is the most effective way of decreasing the grossest of crimes. The appeal of this argument comes from realizing that the certainty of heavy punishment often keeps both younger and older people in line. After a child is severely punished for crossing a busy street or for breaking a valued object, other siblings in the family will probably avoid similar conduct. Now that citizens are losing licenses and going to jail for driving when drunk, more adults arc separating alcohol from driving as they reflect on the grim consequences. Penalties do much to decrease bad behavior in the private as well as in the public arena. Hence, many find compelling data which suggest that fear of the death penalty deters crime. For example, it has been reported that in China in 1983 five thousand executions resulted in a forty-two-percent drop in crime.[9] Also, New Hampshire has a death penalty and one of the lowest murder rates in the nation. Many terrible crimes might have been committed had individuals not paused to think about being executed. Self-preservation is a basic instinct, so the threat of death is a powerful way of discouraging people from acting on urges to kill.

Death penalty abolitionists, however, point out that statistics have to be used quite selectively, and therefore unscientifically, to provide evidence that a higher execution rate lowers the murder rate. Here are some facts that do not fit the claim that the death penalty is a deterrent. Georgia leads the nation in capital punishment, but it has one of the highest murder rates. The ten states with the most murders all have the death penalty. On the other hand Wisconsin, which abolished the death penalty over a century ago, has one of the lowest murder rates in the nation, one-fifth that of Georgia. In 1984 the thirty-seven states where capital punishment is permitted had a murder rate fifty-one percent higher than the other thirteen states. Criminologist William Bowers argues that executions have a brutalizing effect on society and thereby encourage more murders. He found that during the month following each of the six hundred executions in New York state from 1907 to the last in 1963, an average of two more homicides occurred than in the months not following executions. In the nineteen-eighties Florida and Alabama had a murder rate increase in the year following the reinstating of executions.[10] If social problems can be solved acceptably by executing offenders, then potential murderers may feel justified in killing to solve their individual problems.

The deterrent argument also presumes that a person who is on the verge of killing generally reflects on the severe sentence society will give the action. However, as we have seen, murders are much more likely to be hot-blooded than cold-blooded. Most murders are done without premeditation by people reacting to a surge of angry passion. Their blind rage obstructs visions of the electric chair, gas chamber, or lethal injection that may lie ahead.

Second, there is the psychological argument, which is simply that a few people are incorrigible and are too dangerous even to be imprisoned. For instance, two Marion federal penitentiary life-timers, at different times on the same day in 1983, killed the guards who were escorting the handcuffed inmates from their separate cells. Proponents argue that due to environmental conditioning or genetic disorder some become pathological killers by the time they become adults, and they should be executed as a safety precaution. If they are not apprehended for subsequent murders in or out of prison, it is because they have become more clever. The threat of killers behind bars is increasing, and in 1985 the homicide rate in prisons was three times higher than in the general population.

On the other side of the psychological argument is the fact that reformation of presumed hardened criminals does occasionally happen. The National Council of Crime reports that 11,404 murderers were released from prison from 1965 to 1975. Only thirty-four (three-tenths of one percent) of them were convicted of murder subsequent to their release.[11] Many teenage killers are rehabilitated in prison—often just by growing older. Adults over the age of twenty-five do not engage in nearly as much antisocial destructiveness as young people do.

Third, consider the economic argument for the death penalty. Some individuals will never be safe enough to be released from prison, but across the United States the cost of maintaining each prisoner now averages close to twenty thousand dollars per year—more than it would cost to enroll a student at one of our most expensive universities. Capital crimes inmates require more surveillance than the average, so they cost more than the average. Allowing for inflation and an average term of forty years for those imprisoned for life without parole, it will cost taxpayers about one million dollars to provide one caged person a marginal life. Moreover, our current prison population is at an all-time high, having increased forty percent since 1980. Most facilities are overcrowded, and little is being done positively to prepare inmates for life outside. Some argue that the limited funds now used to coop up permanently the most hardened of criminals would better be diverted to rehabilitate those who are scheduled for parole. The situation here is similar to what hospitals face: should exorbitant sums be expended on one patient who has little potential for a quality life when the same money could provide less expensive therapy for many who have promising futures?

Those who oppose the economic argument for the death penalty point out that prison costs could be lowered, and even eliminated, if inmates were given pay-your-own-way work to do, learning skills and making saleable products. Prisoners could perform adequately in a number of jobs for which the state now pays salaries. Also, even if it might cost one million dollars per life imprisonment, this cost is not out of line for a nation which pays that much for a single piece of military hardware.

Theological reasons both for and against the death penalty are rooted in the Judeo-Christian heritage. Both start with the biblical assumption that all are created "in the image of God" (Gen. 1:27). Those for the death penalty reason that since life is sacred, anyone removing that life should be executed. This is the most ancient of all arguments: "Whoever sheds the blood of man, by man shall his blood be shed; for God made man in his own image" (Gen. 9:6). Commandments associated with Moses reinforced this principle by imposing the death penalty for premeditated murder. Thus the commandment "You shall not kill" (Exod. 20:13) was not intended to outlaw the death penalty.

Theologically motivated people who oppose the death penalty draw their position mainly from the New Testament. Given the sanctity of life, taking a life to avenge a murder doubles the wrong. In his Sermon on the Mount, Jesus replaced Moses' "life for life" (Exod. 21:23) law with a principle of nonretaliation (Matt. 5:38–39).

The last and most difficult category is the judicial. The judicial argument for the death penalty asserts that justice is upheld by equal retaliation. Our Bill of Rights permits the government to deprive persons of life after "due process." Judicial review by our court system adequately protects the innocent from execution. While it is true that certain groups have been unfairly discriminated against in the past, equity can now be achieved by extending executions to include more from groups who have previously received preferential treatment.

Those who cite judicial reasons for their opposition to the death penalty focus on two matters. First, judges and juries are fallible. Socrates and Jesus are ancient examples of the execution of the innocent. Recent history offers occasional illustrations of the same. In 1984 Howard Metzenbaum presented to the United States Senate details of dozens of American mistakes in administering the death penalty. In Nebraska, in one of several such cases, years after one person was executed for a murder, the true killer confessed to the crime.[12] When courts err, reparations are possible in many cases, but compensation cannot be given if the unjustly condemned person has been executed.

The second and most significant judicial reason for abolition of the death penalty is its unequal application. The injustice in administering it in the United States is related to four factors: one's state, gender, race, and wealth. Only six states were responsible for the twenty-three convicted killers executed in the United States in 1985. In a dozen states no murder or series of murders can be atrocious enough to warrant the death penalty, yet in some states a person does not even need to murder to warrant it. Three-fourths of those now on death row in the United States are in four states of one region: Florida, Texas, Georgia, and Alabama.[13]

Or look at gender and racial discrimination. Men commit murders four times as often as women, but they are one hundred times more likely to be executed for such behavior. Of the thirty-nine hundred executions in the United States since 1930, only thirty-four have been of women. As for racial discrimination, a Black who kills a white is forty times more likely to be sentenced to die than a white who kills a Black. Eighty-nine percent of all executions for rape have been Black.[14] While in graduate school I worked at the penitentiary in Richmond where seven Blacks were on death row for raping one white woman. They were electrocuted in 1952 even though Virginia has never executed a white for rape.

Lastly, there is economic discrimination. Virtually no convicted murderers who are affluent have been given the death sentence in America. Most capital offenders have been unable to hire a lawyer and have been defended by one who was appointed by the court. Such an attorney is usually not as persistent an advocate for a client as is one who is highly paid.

Due to various types of unfair discrimination, the United States Supreme Court declared in 1972 that the death penalty as practiced in our nation was "cruel and unusual punishment" and therefore unconstitutional. Even though most states have rewritten laws in order to eliminate discrimination, little has been altered in the past dozen years in the proportion of nonsoutherner to southerner, female to male, white to Black, and rich to poor on death row.

A nationwide Associated Press sampling in 1984 disclosed that the majority of Americans believe that the death penalty is not imposed fairly from case to case. In spite of this only twelve percent wanted to see the penalty abolished. According to this poll, the main justification for the death penalty is neither to punish the criminal nor to deter others from committing serious crimes but "to protect society from future crimes that person might commit."[15] This sampling shows that Americans lack confidence in prison reformation and tend now to believe that only drastic action will protect citizens' lives from the cold-blooded murderers in the land. They are sure, however, that the death penalty deters the person who is executed from future killings regardless of whether it deters others. Occasionally there are guards and inmates who are killed by "life-timers." Since torture and dungeon confinement are forbidden "cruel and unusual punishments," what else can be done to stop these serial murderers?

The time may come when our nation will develop prisons in which life is not threatened. The Japanese criminal justice system provides a model in this regard. In Japan inmates killed no prison guards and only one inmate in the past decade. Guards there are well trained as counselors, and the prison system is given priority in social planning.[16] By contrast, in most American states penal institutions are deteriorating and guards are poorly educated. In view of the inhumane condition of some overcrowded prisons, perhaps certain persons convicted of premeditated murder should be allowed a choice of death rather than life imprisonment.

To curb the chronic disease of violence in America, the spotlight should also be aimed at conditions outside prison walls. Preventive medicine is needed. Children and adults should learn to avoid verbal as well as physical violence. Derogatory labels tend to dehumanize victims, making them the target of fanatics who would rid society of "vermin." For example, by calling physicians who perform abortions "Nazi baby butchers," some religious leaders have incited their followers to engage in terrorist acts against abortion clinics.

Economic conditions do have some bearing on violence and should also be addressed. Sociologist Colin Loftin observes, "The majority of the more than 20,000 people in this country who are victims of homicide are dirt poor people who have been killed by dirt poor people."[17] However, in some nations poverty is much more extreme than in the United States, but the homicide rate is not high. Even if unemployment could be eliminated and wealth redistributed, it is likely that much violence would remain.

Franklin E. Zimring, who directs the Center for Studies in Criminal Justice at the University of Chicago, has examined homicide extensively for the past generation and has come up with a practical measure for reducing murder and its consequences in capital punishment. He believes we can do something to remove the primary means by which violence is perpetrated even though it may be impossible to root out the psychological and social causes of such behavior. Zimring thinks that much can be done by way of public laws and education to make people aware of the handgun hazard. He says, "I think it is scandalous that when people purchase a gun to protect themselves from a robbery, they are not informed of their statistical chance of being killed or having someone in their family killed with that gun."[18] The complex gun issue deserves further treatment.

Reasoning About Gun Control

There are few social issues now facing Americans on which there is more emotional heat and less rational light than handgun control. Selective pathetic or heroic stories of individuals whose lives were lost or saved by handguns too often replace careful consideration of the important legal and ethical facets of the problem. Many obfuscate the crucial issues by focusing on the most extreme position of their opponents and then easily burning down that straw man. Thus it wrongly appears that the issue is between those who believe the state should confiscate all guns and those who think that anyone should be free to brandish submachine guns in public. The views of most Americans should not be confused with such fanaticism.

A person should consider at least a dozen significant factors before taking a position on handgun legislation. Assuming that in a free country the burden of proof should be on the side of those who advocate government restrictions, more attention will be given to the arguments for handgun regulation. After the summary position of those who are against handgun control is stated in italics, the opposing arguments will be presented.

1. *If guns were outlawed, only outlaws would have guns.*

The issue is not the outlawing of all guns or even the outlawing of handguns. It is presumed that the police, the military, security guards, and other licensed persons would be permitted to use firearms. Handgun laws would probably not stop most outlaws from obtaining handguns. However, most killings are not the result of cold-blooded intent by criminals. Strong handgun laws would at least reduce the number of nonpremeditated shootings and killings.

2. *Guns don't kill—people do. Thus a person who uses a gun in a crime should be punished by imprisonment or execution. Guns, like knives, can be used for good or bad purposes. Those pieces of steel are not in themselves evil, for they are devoid of a will of their own.*

In most handgun deaths the gun did kill even though the one pulling the trigger did not deliberately plan to kill. In acts of passion a relative or a friend may use a lethal weapon that is handy. Humans, especially under the influence of drugs, may have momentary urges to kill. When rage is being vented, fists, feet, clubs, or even knives are not nearly as deadly as guns. The death rate for gun victims is five times that of those assaulted with a knife—the second most common weapon used in homicides. To kill with gunless hands takes a special skill and determination which many lack. Also, guns make killing more impersonal, enabling many who do not have a killer's temperament to accomplish far more than they intended. It is often the bullet from an easily accessible and operated handgun which tears apart human flesh. If handguns were less available, accidental deaths would decline.

Agreed, stiff penalties should be exacted against the criminal who uses a gun in a crime. Also, unlicensed persons who carry unregistered, loaded guns in public should be punished, as is already the case in Massachusetts and in New York.

3. *Gun registration laws are ineffective. For example, the Gun Control Act of 1968 prohibits convicted felons and persons with mental disorders from owning firearms. In spite of that federal law those people continue to acquire firearms.*

If failure to catch most offenders is a reason for removing a law, then there should be no laws against reckless driving or against drug pushers. Handgun control could be effective if the 1968 law were modified and fully enforced. Presently a handgun dealer merely takes a customer's word that he or she has not been a felon or had a history of mental illness. The Handgun Crime Control Bill now before Congress would establish a twenty-one-day waiting period before a handgun could be purchased. This would allow time for dealers to check on the identification of the would-be purchaser and to obtain police verification of the applicant's claim of no previous criminal activity, drug addiction, or mental illness. Also, those weeks of delay might serve as a cooling-off period during which murderous or suicidal impulses might pass away. Suicides declined in Canada after that nation began to require a wait between gun application and purchase. The attorney general's office in California reports that some twelve hundred handgun applications were rejected in 1981 alone as a result of the state's background check on those who declared their eligibility. Such a check on John Hinckley, President Reagan's attempted assassin, would have exposed Hinckley's psychiatric history and previous arrest for carrying handguns at an airport where President Carter was scheduled to visit.

4. *Even if handgun registration could be made effective, personal change would not follow. Registration does not change the motivations of individuals obtaining guns, so it would assist little in crime reduction.*

A uniform federal law that effectively controlled the registration of all handguns at the time of purchase or transfer of ownership would provide a means for tracing stolen handguns. This would aid in finding criminals just as the registration of motor vehicles in all states has aided in finding vehicles and those who stole them.

It may be a part of human nature to have the urge to kill occasionally. Even if that motivation cannot be changed, enforced laws do affect outward behavior.

5. *Licensing of handguns runs counter to the individual freedom Americans value most highly.*

The handgun is like a motor vehicle in that both can be lethal instruments in the hands of those who define freedom as doing as they please rather than as they ought. Requiring licenses of vehicle operators and handgun owners protects everyone's freedom. A license, complete with photograph and physical description, should be issued only after the applicant has successfully completed testing designed to ascertain whether applicants are competent to use the instrument. Such testing should be repeated periodically, for continual vigilance is needed to screen out convicted felons, persons under indictment, mentally deranged people, and those addicted to narcotics.

6. *Our rate of violent crime is rapidly rising, so honest citizens increasingly need handguns to protect themselves against muggers and robbers.*

Americans already own more handguns per capita than any other people, yet our gun homicide rate is fifty times that of Japan, England, or Germany. Presently there are approximately fifty million handguns in private ownership in the United States, and this number

is increasing by more than two million each year.[19] Handgun prolif-
eration in this nation has resulted from a search for greater personal
security.

New York Police Commissioner Robert McGuire stated that his
department found that innocent bystanders and the victims of hold-
ups and burglaries are far more likely than criminals to suffer wound-
ing or death in shoot-outs. A study showed that resistance occurred
in only eight percent of Chicago robberies but produced fifty-one
percent of the fatalities. Another study made in Cleveland showed
that those who kept and used guns as protection in their homes accidentally shot and killed six times more friends, neighbors, and family members than robbers and intruders. Moreover, weapons used by
murderers are often those that have been stolen in home burglaries.[20]

7. *Handgun control deprives Americans of what is guaranteed
by the Second Amendment of the United States Constitution, which
states, "The right of the people to keep and bear arms shall not be
infringed."*

The first part of the single sentence which makes up the Second
Amendment reads, "A well-regulated militia being necessary to the
security of a free state. . . ." That amendment is not concerned with
individual rights but with the collective right to have what is now
called the National Guard in the fifty states. Repeatedly the Supreme
Court has ruled that the purpose of the amendment is to protect state
militia from being disarmed by the federal government.[21] In 1939 the
Court ruled that firearms control laws for the protection of citizens'
lives are constitutional.

8. *The law-abiding hunter has a right to own and use firearms
without government harassment.*

The prohibition of handguns in the possession of unlicensed persons would not restrict hunters from having rifles and shotguns.
Since they are hard to conceal, long guns are seldom used in crimes.
Nor are they often used in accidental deaths or in suicides. Only one-
quarter of the firearms in the United States are handguns, but they
account for over fifty percent of all homicides and for more than
sixty percent of the accidental gun deaths (about two thousand per
year, including many children).[22]

9. *Since Americans don't want handgun control, imposing it on*

them would never be successful. It would be as unenforceable as Prohibition was in the 1920s when the majority wanted freedom to drink alcoholic beverages. From our pioneer days onward we have prized guns, and we now publish a number of gun magazines.

Opinion surveys of Americans do show that a substantial majority disfavor *banning* handguns, but polls have repeatedly indicated that Americans, by a landslide, favor *controlling* handguns. A 1982 Harris poll shows that two-thirds of Americans favor "a federal law requiring that all handguns people own be registered by federal authorities." Gallup reported in 1981 that eighty-one percent of the public favor requiring a license for anyone wanting to carry a handgun on the streets. Another survey taken by NBC News in 1981 shows that seventy-one percent favor a law requiring persons to obtain police permits before handgun purchase.[23] The will of the minority prevails because of the influence of the powerful National Rifle Association, which spends about fifty million dollars annually to defeat gun control legislation. The money is spent for campaign contributions, computerized mailings to mobilize letters to members of Congress, and other lobbying efforts. Politicians often do not realize that only a small fraction of gun owners in America belong to the NRA and that its own membership is not united behind the legislative position of its present leaders.[24] The billion-dollar United States industry that manufactures millions of handguns annually also puts pressure on politicians.

Unlike any other nation in the world, America has a gun culture that is kept alive by movies, novels, and magazines. Some who have a nostalgia for the romanticized frontier days believe that carrying side arms is the macho thing to do, and that shoot-outs are the traditional American way of settling disputes. In *The Interpretation of Dreams* Sigmund Freud describes the gun as among the powerful phallic symbols in the unconscious mind.[25] Some males have been conditioned from childhood to play with toy and real guns; thus they feel an absence of full masculinity as adults if they have no gun to oil, fondle, and shoot off. But proper education can result in youths' learning to have fun apart from deadly weapons and realizing that they can be red-blooded Americans without loving handguns.

10. *Effective gun control would cost millions of dollars. The bur-*

densome bureaucracy that would result cannot be justified by the alleged benefits it might give.

In a society that professes to believe in the supreme worth of the individual, how many lives do we need to save in order to make gun control cost-effective? In this century the American mortality by handguns has exceeded those killed in our four wars. In 1982 there were 8,474 handgun murders (one every hour) and about 250,000 handgun-related woundings, rapes, robberies, and threats.[26] Many who are not killed are permanently injured. A robbery occurs every minute in this country, nearly half of them involving handguns. Behind these statistics lies tragedy after senseless tragedy. There is the mentally ill woman who went on a killing rampage with the gun her husband bought to protect the family. Or the intoxicated husband who killed his wife and children after an argument. Or the six-year-old child who accidentally shot his younger brother in the head with the gun his father had left in the dresser drawer. Or the depressed person who inserted into her mouth the pistol she had at hand and pulled the trigger. The money saved by the reduced number of intentional and unintentional killers prosecuted would probably more than pay for the cost of effective control. Also, the incalculable expense of the loss of many productive citizens would be saved.

11. *If any gun controls are needed, they should be handled by state rather than by federal government.*

The effectiveness of gun control laws is reduced if a person can go to a neighboring state, where laws are looser or absent, and easily purchase handguns. For example, since 1976 the District of Columbia has had tough gun control laws, but nearly forty percent of the handguns used in crime there come from Virginia and Maryland dealers.[27] The handgun used to shoot President Reagan in Washington was acquired in a Texas pawnshop. In New York City ninety-six percent of the handguns used in crimes come from out of state. The handgun used there to kill John Lennon was acquired in Hawaii. State handgun statutes are more effective if there is a comprehensive national law to provide a uniform standard. What is needed is a combination of city, state, and federal laws to bring about consistent regulation.

12. *There is no evidence that stringent handgun laws result in a corresponding decrease in homicides.*

The United States is the only major country in the world without effective national handgun control laws. We also have a higher firearm death rate per capita than any other country. Great Britain has some of the strongest gun laws in the world, and we have some of the weakest. Our murder rate is many times that of Britain, even though that country also has complex economic and ethnic problems. In 1974 Massachusetts passed a law requiring a mandatory one-year jail sentence for carrying a handgun without a license. As a result, handgun homicide dropped forty-three percent in the first two years the law was in effect.[28] In 1976 handgun murder in South Carolina declined from 264 to 147 after a handgun control law went into effect in 1975.[29]

Perhaps the above exchange of arguments against and for handgun control will stimulate the serious consideration that the social problem merits. Informed citizens who make their voices heard can have more influence over politicians than the pro-gun lobbies. Like war, handgun control is too important a matter to leave to the exclusive consideration of government employees. Facing the reality and acting on the control options available can diminish the present one in five chance that a member of your family will be assaulted by a handgun.

Reasoning About War

Americans have traditionally separated microviolence—individual against individual—from macroviolence—nation against nation. *War* is the term used to designate the latter type of violence, and it is defined as the socially organized and approved killing of those who are deemed enemies. War is generally accepted as legitimate whenever it is sanctioned by one's government, while the killing of citizens is treated as generally unjustifiable.

Much can be learned about different moral outlooks by understanding when and why wars have arisen. The eminent historian Arnold Toynbee studied the role of warfare in the course of many civilizations. From his examination of more than a thousand years of human history, he concludes that the institution of war is not intrinsic to human culture: "War is not a spontaneous vent for human nature's innate pugnacity. . . . War is a recent institution if measured by the time scale of the age of the human race." Primitives do not have the leisure to devote themselves to the complex planning required to organize a war. Toynbee traces its beginning to occasions of spare time after survival needs were met. Not until five thousand years ago did humans living in certain agriculturally productive valleys have the surplus time and large resources needed for invading other territories.[30]

War is also dependent on the development of national ideology. Social forces must transpose killing, a crime of great magnitude on the in-group level, so that it is viewed as a glorious expression of patriotism when committed on a battlefield under public orders. Consider, for example, two killers of the past generation. One American youth killed fourteen strangers from a tower on a Texas campus, and another one killed fourteen strangers in a Vietnam village. One is slain and is considered crazy by people who react as humans have reacted from earliest times onward. The other one is decorated and acclaimed a hero by people who react as humans have generally reacted ever since they moved from the "savage" to the "civilized" age. It is difficult for people to handle opposite judgments on carnage as they compare domestic and international conduct. This may explain why a philosophical analysis of war is rarely made by people conditioned to detest microviolence and to accept macroviolence.

The holy war has been the most recurring type of warfare in history. An example of such is described in Numbers 31, a chapter usually overlooked now by those who believe every Bible verse is the Word of God. Moses, who delivered in God's name the unconditional command, "You shall not kill," assumed that some other ethnic groups were not included in the prohibition. One such outside group was a shepherd people called Midianites, into whose terrItory Moses had led his fellow Israelites after escaping from Egyptian bondage. Believing that the wiles of Midianite women had corrupted Israelite men, Moses ordered, as the Lord's spokesman, vengeance against the Midianites. Twelve thousand warriors attacked the enemy when signaled by a priest's trumpet. After the battle Moses was furious because only the Midianite men had been annihilated. He commanded that all women and children be slain, with this exception: "all the young girls who have not known man by lying with him, keep alive for yourselves" (vs. 18). The share of the booty received by the priests was 675 sheep, 72 cattle, 61 asses, and 32 virgins. In a holy war the certified representatives of the divine power play a central role. In the scriptural story they are called Levites, a tribe to which Moses and other priests belonged.

The Aztecs also felt driven by their priests to wage war continually. The purpose of fighting was to capture victims for ritual sacrifice. The Aztecs were convinced that their god of war liked to consume enemy hearts, freshly carved out on the altar while still thumping. Thus the normal sanctions against killing become strangely reversed in the context of holy war.

In Muslim countries holy war, called *jihad*, is still the reason given by the *ayatollahs*, Allah's agents, for fighting outsiders. The *Quran* instructs Muslims to retaliate on behalf of Allah, "fighting those that fight you." In the Iran-Iraq war, in which a million or more may be killed, each adversary is certain Allah has commanded the destruction of the "infidel" army of the neighboring country. In European history there have been similar wars between peoples who worshiped the same God. Catholics and Protestants have been motivated by pious belligerence to turn the cross, the symbol of their shared religion, into a sword for slaughtering one another.

The founder of Christianity was inspired by an Israelite who declared that neither macroviolence nor microviolence was sanctioned by God. As Jesus read the scroll of Isaiah he found the criticism of murder within the Jewish nation followed by this vision of peace among the nations:

> and they shall beat their swords into plowshares,
>   and their spears into pruning hooks;
> nation shall not lift up sword against nation,
>   neither shall they learn war any more. (Isa. 2:4)

Jesus assumed the "Prince of Peace" messianic role forecast by Isaiah (9:6). Rather than advocating hatred and destruction of so-called enemies, Jesus radically commanded his disciples to love and assist all types of people.

Following Jesus' lead, Christians rejected warfare for hundreds of years. Church historian Roland Bainton states that until the time of Constantine the church was pacifist "to the degree that during this period no Christian author to our knowledge approved of Christian participation in battle." Moreover, "from the end of the New Testament period to the decade A.D. 170–180 there is no evidence whatever of Christians in the army."[31]

One dramatic testimony from the third century pertains to a twenty-one-year-old Roman named Maximilian who conscientiously objected to joining Caesar's army. Here is an excerpt from his confrontation with Dion, the governor of a North African province:

> Dion: Take his measurements. . . .
> Maximilian: I will not be a soldier. Cut off my head, if you will. I cannot be a soldier on behalf of the world. I am a soldier for my God.
> D: Who filled your head with these ideas?
> M: My conscience, and God who called me. . . .
> D: Among the guards . . . there are soldiers who are Christians, and they are in the service.
> M: They know what is good for themselves. . . .
> D: Be willing to serve, or I shall punish with death your contempt of military service.
> M: I shall not die; and if I leave this world, my soul will live with Christ my Lord. . . .
> D: You shall be punished as a salutary example to others. . . . It has pleased the court that Maximilian be beheaded, because out of disloyalty he has refused to take the military oath.
> M: Thanks be to God! (Then with a joyous countenance he turned to his father and said:) Give this executioner the new clothes which you prepared for my military service.[32]

It can be seen that Maximilian's conscientious objection to military service did not represent the sentiments of all the Christians then, for Dion states that some Christians had become soldiers—perhaps out of fear of the dire consequences of refusing to bear arms. The church bestowed on Maximilian the title of saint for his sacrificial loyalty as a soldier of Christ.

During Emperor Constantine's era, Christianity received approval as a tolerated religion and soon the formerly persecuted fringe sect was established as the official religion of the Roman Empire. Living shortly after this establishment, Augustine wrestled with a dilemma. That most influential of Christian intellectuals perceived that the gospel and the example of Jesus were incompatible with the use of violence. On the other hand, he realistically recognized that it was unlikely that violence could be averted if the Christian rulers of Rome opened their gates submissively to the pagan invaders. If the Christian community and the Greco-Roman civilization were to be preserved, armed resistance was needed against the barbarians who would kill, rape, and plunder.

In light of this situation, Augustine took the position that he would personally rather suffer death than inflict death if attacked when by himself. He would not use evil force against evil force on a one-to-one basis. However, if women and children were with him, it would be unloving if he did not come to their defense and even give his life to protect them against unjust attack. Augustine likewise thought that Christians should defend their larger state community against a more evil invader, keeping in mind the goal of establishing a peaceful and just society for all. He held that Christians could be obedient to a relatively righteous state when it commanded them to engage in a war of self-defense.[33]

The just war position which Augustine developed became the dominant position of Roman Catholicism and Protestantism. Eventually the church taught that war is justified if these conditions are met: (1) the enemy is not hated; (2) it is a defense against aggression; (3) civilians are not attacked; (4) the harm done is less than the benefits hoped for; (5) its purposes are to restore peace and promote justice; (6) it is waged by a legitimate authority; (7) it avoids wanton violence and looting; and (8) it is the last resort.

When the wars of history are measured by these exacting just war criteria, some meet the conditions better than others. Abraham Lincoln and Margaret Thatcher, for example, may have fulfilled all the conditions for the Civil War and the Falklands War. However, it was more difficult for Americans during the time of the Vietnamese conflict to rationalize that they were engaged in a just war. The North Vietnamese did not initiate threats against American territory or lives; rather, the opposite was true. The United States engaged in saturation bombing in which far more civilians than soldiers were killed. The harm done by chemical agents on the land and people, the siring of unwanted GI children, the wrecking of the economy, and so forth, did not make war the lesser of two evils. Wanton massacres occurred at My Lai and at other places. Moreover, it was a war that was never declared by Congress, the legitimate constitutional authority. Also the war was not the last resort. Had elections been held in the nineteen-fifties, there is little doubt that Ho Chi Minh would have been selected by citizens in the South and North to unify and head a government that had been divided by civil war. In short, the unjust Vietnam War may have been the greatest moral blunder in American history.

Most defenders of the just war concept do not see how a nuclear war between the two superpowers could possibly comply with the third and fourth guidelines. Many non-Christians as well as Christians agree with Pope John XXIII's assertion in his 1963 encyclical "Pacem in Terris": "It is hardly possible to imagine that in the atomic era war could be used as an instrument of justice."[34] We are currently faced with the realistic possibility of the complete destruction of organic life on earth. There are now over fifty thousand nuclear weapons in the worldwide stockpile, with a destructive power about one million times that of the bomb that devastated Hiroshima. Regarding the United States' deterrence doctrine, President Reagan admitted in 1985, "The only weapon we have is MAD—Mutual Assured Destruction."[35] Even if "Red or dead" were the only national option, it would be impossible for a sane person to hold that a radioactive ash heap is to be preferred to living under a political and economic system different from our own. The harm resulting from global incineration would be infinitely greater than any benefit hoped for.

Early in this century William James, America's most outstanding psychologist, wrote "The Moral Equivalent of War," an essay in which he observes the human craving to break out of the tedious routines of life and suggests that boredom will continue to be replaced by the momentary thrill of war unless a psychological sublimation is effected. Hence James believed that peace would never be satisfying if it was defined as the absence of struggle. Humans must have the joy of campaigning for attractive goals. James found certain positive qualities in the military life that should be devoted to more constructive ends, including a surrender of private interest for the public good and a contempt for softness.[36]

Some American presidents have valiantly attempted to place James' ideas into public programs. Franklin Roosevelt formed the Civilian Conservation Corps during the Great Depression to enable idealistic youth to join together in a military type of camaraderie and attack the problems of conserving national parks while developing them for fuller utilization. John Kennedy introduced the Peace Corps as an alternative to war corps. He successfully channeled the patriotism into programs for assisting technologically underdeveloped nations. Jimmy Carter also spoke of a moral equivalent of war at the time of an energy crisis. He hoped that citizens would become excited by the goal of discovering renewable sources of energy to replace vanishing fossil fuels.

What passion, if any, can ignite citizens of all nations in the next century to replace the wars of this century that have killed more than one hundred million people? World federalism? Ecological preservation? The kingdom of God? If a constructive goal is accepted, James says, "It is only a question of blowing on the spark till the whole population gets incandescent, and on the ruins of the old morals of military honor, a stable system of morals of civic honor builds itself up." James favors a citizens' conscription for a certain number of years. By means of this

> the military ideals of hardihood and discipline would be wrought into the growing fibre of the people; no one would remain blind as the luxurious classes now are blind, to man's relations to the globe he lives on. . . .
> We should get toughness without callousness, authority with as little criminal cruelty as possible, and painful work done cheerily because the duty is temporary, and threatens not, as now, to degrade the whole remainder of one's life.[37]

Is James' outlook realistic or naive?

It is ironic that the century in which individual life has been extended by technology beyond all previous limits is the very century when death from technology has killed more than in all the previous centuries combined. By honestly confronting our noble potentialities for life and ignoble potentialities for death, we may be able to avoid a much more horrendous megadeath in the next century and make the famine areas of this planet "blossom as the rose" (Isa. 35:1 KJV). In *Reason in Common Sense* Santayana has rightly observed that "Those who cannot remember the past are condemned to repeat it."[38] However, if we forget now the lessons of warfare history, there may be no opportunity for repeating the course in world civilization that we have failed.

7

BODY DISPOSAL

Burial Methods in History

Humans are the only animals who bury their dead. The custom has been found in the earliest cultures uncovered by archaeologists. Cro-Magnon people, who lived in European caves some twenty-five thousand years ago, dug shallow graves and covered them with stones. Some bones found there contain the red ochre which was rubbed on the body. By means of that cosmetic, ancient morticians simulated the ruddy glow of life.[1]

On display in the British Museum is a body that lived in Egypt more than five thousand years ago. It was preserved exclusively by the hot, dry sand of a land with very little rainfall. After the loss of water, which makes up eighty percent of body weight, hardened skin is left stretched over the skeleton.

Egyptian embalmers, encouraged by the desert in which they lived, developed a skill which assisted the natural dehydrating process. The embalming business, coupled with vast necropolises and pyramid tombs, makes Egypt historically unique in the amount of national resources expended on the dead. Greek historian Herodotus reported some twenty-five centuries ago on mortuary activity that had already been under way in Egypt for many centuries. Because of the impact of Egyptian morticians on subsequent practices, Herodotus deserves to be quoted at length:

> Embalming is a distinct profession. The embalmers, when a body is brought to them, produce specimen models in wood, painted to resemble nature, and graded in quality; the best and most expensive kind is said to represent a being whose name I shrink from mentioning . . . ; the next best is somewhat inferior and cheaper, while the third sort is cheapest of all. After pointing out these differences in quality, they ask which of the three is required, and the kinsmen of the dead man, having agreed upon a price, go away and leave the embalmers to their work. The most perfect process is as follows: as much as possible of the brain is extracted through the nostrils with an iron hook, and what the hook cannot reach is rinsed out with drugs; next the flank is laid open with a flint knife and the whole contents of the abdomen removed; the cavity is then thoroughly cleansed and washed out, first with palm wine and again with an infusion of pounded spices. After that it is filled with pure bruised myrrh, cassia, and every other aromatic substance with the exception of frankincense, and sewn up again, after which the body is placed in natrum, covered entirely over, for seventy days—never longer. When this period, which must not be exceeded, is over, the body is washed and then wrapped from head to foot in linen cut into strips and smeared on the under side with gum, which is commonly used by the Egyptians instead of glue. In this condition the body is given back to the family, who have a wooden case made, shaped like the human figure, into which it is put. The case is then sealed up and stored in a sepulchral chamber, upright against the wall. When, for reasons of expense, the second quality is called for, the treatment is different: no incision is made and the intestines are not removed, but oil of cedar is injected with a syringe into the body through the anus which is afterwards stopped up to prevent the liquid from escaping. The body is then pickled in natrum for the prescribed number of days, on the last of which the oil is drained off. The effect of it is so powerful that as it leaves the body it brings with it the stomach and intestines in a liquid state, and as the flesh too is dissolved by the natrum nothing of the body is left but the bones and skin. After this treatment it is returned to the family without further fuss.
>
> The third method, used for embalming the bodies of the poor, is simply to clear out the intestines with a purge and keep the body seventy days in natrum. It is then given back to the family to be taken away.
>
> When the wife of a distinguished man dies, or any woman who

happens to be beautiful or well known, her body is not given to the embalmers immediately, but only after the lapse of three or four days. This is a precautionary measure to prevent the embalmers from violating the corpse, a thing which is said actually to have happened in the case of a woman who had just died.[2]

Some explanation of Herodotus' description is needed. Necrophiliacs (literally, corpse lovers) were occasionally found in ancient times—as they are now—so attractive female bodies were allowed to decay before morticians were permitted to handle them. Embalmers recognized that putrefaction began in the internal organs; therefore, they were removed for first-class customers and preserved separately. The brain, however, was discarded as worthless. Natrum, the drying agent, is a mixture of sodium salts which are found in areas where ponds of Nile water have evaporated. After the moisture was removed from the corpse, it was wrapped tightly with bandages. Then it was soaked in hot resin, which had a glasslike surface on hardening. Sometimes asphalt was used to seal the embalmed body from dampness. The Arabs called asphalt *mumiya*, and from this comes the English word *mummy*. One of the earliest uses of Arabian oil was for corpse waterproofing.[3]

The mummification industry was integrated with Egyptian mythology. It was believed that the god Osiris was murdered and dismembered. Magically his fragmented parts were reassembled in a mummy, and his winged soul returned to give it vitality. Osiris then became the sovereign who presided over the final human judgment and the afterlife. Pious Egyptians hoped for a psychosomatic renewal like that of the resurrected god-king whom they worshiped. Priests chanted assurances from the *Book of the Dead* over embalmed bodies: "You live again, you live again forever, here you are young once more for ever."[4] On the coffin containing the mummy of an Egyptian, the hieroglyphs read, "Besenmut is alive and strong again, resurrected without blemish or fault."[5]

Burials among the Semites were generally quite different from those in the neighboring Egyptian culture. Included among the Semitic nomads of Western Asia were the Hebrews, and subsequently the Jews and Muslims. Abraham, the first to be called a Hebrew, is also the first in the biblical record to arrange for corpse disposal.

After the death of his wife Sarah, he purchased the cave of Machpelah so he could bury her body (Gen. 23). Acknowledging that humans are but "dust and ashes" (Gen. 18:27), Abraham accepted
realistically the return of humans to their originating elements.

Simple burial places continued to be popular in the Christian era.
Jesus' body, for example, was placed in a tomb, probably hewn out
of the soft limestone that was plentiful in Palestine. His body was not
embalmed by the Egyptian method of salt dehydration and spices
within the abdominal cavity. Rather, balms extracted from sweet-
smelling plants were placed around his linen-wrapped body to coun-
teract any anticipated unpleasant odors of decay (John 19:40).

The simplicity and promptness of Semitic corpse disposal is today best displayed in Arabia. Shortly after death the body is washed
and enshrouded; usually it is not encoffined. Family members carry
out the body on a bier and place it in an unpretentious grave. For
example, after the death in 1975 of Saudi King Faisal, the richest
man on earth, his corpse was wrapped in a sheet and buried facing
Mecca in an unmarked desert grave.

Among the Semites there was one striking exception to the customary burial method. The Genesis saga ends with an account of
what was done to the bodies of Jacob and his son Joseph after they
died in Egypt. Morticians took forty days to embalm Jacob's body.
The purpose of the corpse preservation was to fulfill the patriarch's
dying charge that his remains be transported the long distance back
to the land of his birth and buried in the Machpelah cave purchased
by his grandfather Abraham. Joseph likewise had his family swear
to carry his remains back to Canaan when they departed from Egypt
permanently. In preparation for that distant future occasion, a coffin
was used for storage. This single biblical account of an embalmed
body in a burial box was not intended to be an endorsement of the
Egyptian cult of the dead. It rather displays that the Israelites decided
against the tomb-centered religion of the land in which they were
aliens. The Jewish Scriptures also disapprove of giving offerings to
the dead, as the Egyptians did, or consulting the spirits of the dead
at tombs (see Deut. 18:11, 26:14; Isa. 65:4).

In ancient Greece there were two burial innovations, one to has-
ten and one to halt decomposition. From limestone the Greeks made

a burial container which they called a sarcophagus, meaning flesh-eater. Ancient historian Pliny tells of the rapid deterioration caused by the limestone: "Corpses buried in it are consumed within a period of forty days, except for the teeth."[6] On the other hand, honey was used as a preservative. When Alexander the Great died in Asia, rot was retarded by submerging the corpse in the sweet substance.

During the early centuries of Christianity the mode of Jesus' burial was the standard for church members. Their corpses were washed, wrapped in cloth, and placed in a tomb—usually within a day after death. Due in part to the impact of Christianity, mummification was abandoned in Egypt. Antony, the much admired fourth-century Egyptian monk, reminded Christians that the embalming custom of his country was "not right nor reverent at all." He asked that his remains be given a humble burial in the biblical manner.[7]

Throughout most of church history Christians have had no interest in the elaborate corpse preservation methods characteristic of the pagan Egyptian culture. In 1705 Englishman Thomas Greenhill described the "superstition" known as "the art of embalming" in this way: "It is by most despis'd and look'd on merely as an unnecessary expensive trouble."[8]

In Christianity the custom arose of using the churchyard adjacent to the sanctuary for burials, although prominent Christians could be buried under the floor of the sanctuary. After a few years little remained from a burial in the damp European soil, especially since coffins were seldom used. Space in the holy burial grounds was limited, so the reuse of plots of previous interment was a common practice. The church sexton opened the grave after a generation, and any remaining bones were deposited in the graveyard charnel house.

The term *coffin* came to be associated with death mainly as the result of the King James translation of the Bible in 1611. There *coffin* is used only in reference to a burial container for Joseph's corpse. The Greek word *kophinos* (originally designating a large wicker basket) was anglicized to refer to a formfitting wooden box that was wider at the shoulders and tapered toward the feet and head. Coffins were not commonly used in the West until the seventeenth century.

The unpretentious European methods for body disposal were adopted in North America from colonial times until the latter part of the nineteenth century, when changes in the treatment of corpses and places of interment made American burial practices unique. The word *embalm* acquired a meaning distinctively different from the Egyptian mummification process or the biblical use of aromatic balms to mask putrid odors. Embalming was developed by American physicians as a method of arresting decay in cadavers under study, even as Leonardo da Vinci had done for his study of anatomy. In the middle of the last century patents were issued in America for embalming fluids that were to be injected into arteries as a blood replacement. Alcohol, ether, and tannic acid were the main ingredients.

The initial public response to the use of embalming fluids by morticians was quite negative.[9] For example, in 1856 Henry Tuckerman saw "something revolting in the artificial conservation of what, by the law of nature, should undergo chemical dissolution."[10] The popularization of corpse embalming began with Thomas Holmes, who learned his technique while operating on cadavers in a medical school. During the Civil War he obtained government permission to embalm bodies of slain Union soldiers for shipment back to families who were rich enough to pay his fees. By the war's end the "father of modern embalming" had become wealthy from his 4,028 contracts and had publicized arterial embalming widely.[11]

The display of Abraham Lincoln's corpse for three weeks before burial did more than anything else to Americanize embalming. A funeral train carrying his body in an opened coffin toured a number of cities. Millions filed by to look at the remains of their assassinated hero and to examine the lead-lined mahogany box with silver handles. For those unable to make a firsthand examination, there were engravings and photographs—a recently invented art—depicting the body of Lincoln looking as though he were taking a nap. "Death had not changed the kindly countenance," sentimentalized one viewer. "It was as if the spirit had come back to the poor clay, reshaped the wonderfully sweet face, and given it an expression of gladness."[12]

In the eighteen-eighties another transformation occurred: undertakers renamed themselves funeral directors. Having appeared on the urban scene around 1800, undertakers had been appropriately named because they *undertook* to do things the bereaved family requested, such as arrange with a sexton to dig the grave or with a carpenter to construct the coffin or with a livery stable owner to provide the hearse and carriages. The undertaker's subordinate role was changed by the marketing strategy of the Stein Casket Manufacturing Company of Rochester, New York. In 1882 the company founded the National Funeral Directors' Association (NFDA). Bearing a new label, those who had been lowly undertakers now thought of themselves as directors. By self-appointment they moved into the decision-making role that had previously been the responsibility of family and clergy.

The Stein manufacturers decided that it would be easier to sell their product if it were called a casket rather than a coffin. Up until then the word *casket* generally had referred to a jewel box. A big design change in the burial box was introduced at this time. Realizing that a body-shaped coffin was a gruesome reminder of the decaying remains within, the burial container was disguised as an enormous, gleaming treasure chest. Stein funded a journal entitled *The Casket* to publicize the new creation.[13]

The aggressive funeral industry moved beyond providing merchandise and equipment. At places of local business, *parlors* or *chapels* were added in an effort to attract services away from home parlors and community churches. In 1885 the NFDA journal, *Proceedings*, informed its members that Harry Samson had built a chapel in connection with his funeral business in Pittsburgh. Today Samson's chapel has been copied all over the nation so that virtually all mortuaries now have auditoriums. They are blandly constructed in the hope that they will be inoffensive to customers of all faiths or of no faith. Historian James Farrell, in *Inventing the American Way of Death, 1830–1920,* has shown how "funeral directors created the demand for funeral homes because they would profit from their complete control of the corpse and ceremony."[14]

During the eighteen-eighties the arterial pump was introduced for replacing blood with embalming fluids more efficiently. When connected with the main blood vessels, the machine functions like an artificial heart. As fluid is pumped into the arteries, blood is forced out of the veins into a sewage pipe. After formaldehyde came on the market, it became a main ingredient in embalming mixes.

In 1885 a new journal called *Sunnyside* offered a thousand dollars to the mortician who could exhibit the "best appearing corpse" after it had been embalmed for two months. To win at this competition it was necessary to use creams to replace the color that had disappeared from the bloodless corpse. One mortician advertised that "the appearance of Christian hope and contentment" could be given for a certain price, while "a look of quiet resignation" could be provided for a lower price.[15] A Washington mortuary distributed pinup calendars proclaiming "Beautiful Bodies by Chambers." Morticians became skillful in the use of wax to restore youthful contours or to conceal disfigurement caused by accidental death. This art originated with Madame Tussaud, who made wax models from the death masks of some who were guillotined during the French Revolution. Although there was little profit in body "restoration," it caused customers to believe that the corpse was something valuable. They were then willing to pay for enshrining it in an expensive high-profit casket, complete with silver handles.

The nineteenth century also brought with it a shift in outlook on graveyards. The euphemistic word *cemetery,* literally meaning sleeping place, replaced what more candid earlier Americans called burial grounds. Mount Auburn Cemetery, opened in 1831 several miles from Boston, became the prototype of the back-to-nature romanticism that would be found a century later in every city graveyard. The rolling slopes of a former meadow were beautifully landscaped to become a garden paradise, and the grave markers were commonly inscribed with weeping willows, rather than with the dreadful skulls and crossbones of earlier centuries. The "perpetual care" provision in the contract of those purchasing lots insured that the sod would be kept ever verdant and the pathways ever fringed with fragrant flowers. It was said that a proper Bostonian earned a degree from Harvard University, rented a pew at Trinity Episcopal Church, and owned a lot in Mount Auburn Cemetery. ("Cemetery Visitation" questions are provided in Appendix B.5 to assist those interested in obtaining firsthand knowledge of the types of burial grounds described here.)

Places of burial preserve, in a symbolic way, the social structure of the living. When the church functioned as the community center in early America, the graveyard was usually adjacent to the sanctuary. Accordingly, garden cemeteries, which continue to be the most common type of graveyard, project on the dead the desire of modern Americans for a quiet home separated from the strife of the inner city. Mount Auburn, for example, was developed when affluent Bostonians were moving their residences away from the polluted industrial areas to be closer to Mother Nature. The suburban street names of Glen Brook and Meadowlark were mirrored in Mount Auburn's Swan Avenue and Primrose Path. Providing a carriage ride through the cemetery's curved and shady lanes was a fashionable way of showing hospitality. Visitors were uplifted, for example, by the sight of the conspicuous Greek temple memorial over the grave of Mary Baker Eddy. Her fame had come from founding in downtown Boston the Christian Science Church, which proclaims as a central doctrine the unreality of death.

In the twentieth century the phenomenally successful Forest Lawn Memorial Park in Los Angeles has been the model for thousands of imitators elsewhere in the United States. Essentially it is Mount Auburn without any personalizing tombstones, unappreciated reminders of death in a place devoted to forgetting its reality. Were it not for the chapels and the art works there, Forest Lawn could easily be mistaken for a well-manicured golf course. Sight-seeing buses in Los Angeles often include the park in tours of the city's distinctive institutions.

Hubert Eaton, the founder of Forest Lawn, is one of the most successful of American death entrepreneurs. While in college he learned from experience that expensiveness has snob appeal. When he was trying to promote college entertainment events, he found that attendance increased after he doubled the price of admission. He concluded that the well-to-do enjoy participating in what others cannot afford. Eaton then established in the public mind an association between ownership of a costly plot in one of his cemeteries and admission to an appealing celestial community. *First Step Up Toward Heaven* is the title of a book describing Forest Lawn; the book is sold in Forest Lawn's gift shop. Eaton used religious language in his promotional schemes and freely associated "his activities with God's will."[16] In spite of the stress he placed on Christian commitment, he followed the NFDA policy of serving only Caucasians until forced by a desegregation law to cater to all races.[17]

Many people must find it satisfying to know they are wealthy enough to be buried in the acreage where the bodies of prominent paradise-bound members of one's community are interred. At Forest Lawn this usually means being near the remains of movie stars.[18] Some people imagine that they will share the spectacle of immortality with those important persons who are in the same cemetery. The fantasy often includes being exclusively with those of the same race and religion as their cemetery companions.

A new huge expense has been added this century to cemetery use. A metal or concrete vault is now usually required, making the reuse of burial land, earlier complicated by the introduction of durable coffins, nearly impossible. The vault encases the casket to protect it from collapse and make it waterproof. Death-industry hucksters have found that they can double profits by selling customers on maximum "protection" from natural dissolution, rust, and even earthquakes. Few customers realize that the bacteria of putrefaction are already in the hydrated corpse and are working their ravages in the sealed container. Morticians would like their customers to think that embalming and double encasements will preserve everyone like King Tut, but modern embalming lasts days, not centuries, and caskets are usually "guaranteed" for only a few decades.

In recent years some Americans have expressed interest in converting old burial grounds into recreational land for the living. Americans are recalling a comment by Thomas Jefferson that "the soil is the gift of God to the living," not to the dead.[19] Some cities with inadequate playground areas for children have many acres for the dead. David Hendin comments on urban cemeteries: "The vast majority of them . . . are cold, gray wastelands which are spatially dead and all but irrelevant to the living. Entire communities lack real parks, but they have cemeteries."[20] He tells of St. Mark's Church-in-the-Bowery, which solved this dilemma by remodeling the oldest church graveyard in New York City into a stone park paved by gravestones. Now that the area is reclaimed it is no longer desecrated by litter, and many think it honors the dead more than the former eyesore did.[21] By contrast, the Boston graveyard where the body of the founder of America's oldest university lies looks like St. Mark's graveyard used to look. John Harvard would probably have preferred to be buried in an unmarked and now unknown place, as were some forebears of his Calvinist faith, rather than have his memorial marker defaced by vandals and his plot trashed by derelicts. The more fitting and properly honored memorial is his statue in the center of Harvard Yard.

One partial solution to the land scarcity problem is being introduced to American cities from abroad. In some Brazilian cities there are skyscrapers for the dead in which bodies are elevated to a crypt after final rites are conducted below. The idea of a vertical cemetery has also been introduced in Nashville, Tennessee. The twenty-story mausoleum provides seventy-five thousand burial spaces and uses one-seventh the land space of a conventional cemetery.

Underground grave stacking is another way of conserving space. Already in our national cemeteries, spouses of military personnel are commonly buried in an intimate double-depth arrangement. In New York City, where crowded cemeteries add thousands of new burials each year, triple-decker interments are being used. About eighty thousand acres of Long Island are already in cemeteries, and new developments are unlikely.[22]

It is possible to economize on land and retain customary burial plots by restoring biodegradable practices which have been used in centuries past. Even now New York authorizes the reuse every twenty-five years of interment places in its potter's field on Hart Island. Consequently some seven hundred thousand bodies of those who have died poor have been buried there during the past century. If those with means could overcome the arrogance of assuming that their dead bodies are worth more than the dead bodies of the indigent, cemetery land problems might be resolved.

During the past century the mortuary trade has vigorously continued promotional schemes. The campaign for arterial embalming has been so successful that embalming is routine procedure for about ninety percent of the corpses that mortuaries handle. Embalming is done as soon as possible after the body is received, and it was usually done without the expressed permission of the next of kin until that practice was outlawed in 1984. Contrary to what some morticians have long claimed, public laws do not require embalming. In spite of propaganda to the contrary, the main purpose of embalming is not sanitation but to slow the rate of decay so that the body can remain viewable for a few days. Having a body in a condition that is not offensive to eyes and nostrils enables morticians to sell a variety of merchandise that the bereaved might not otherwise purchase. Morticians have discovered that customers are more likely to purchase new burial garments, posh casket interiors with innerspring mattresses, and finer casket exteriors in solid hardwood or bronze if they can be persuaded that their loved ones are lifelike and impressible by the quality of materials that surround them.

"Restoration" is the name morticians give to their masking of reality. Abrasive plastic caps are inserted under the eyelids to close the staring eyes, and wire may be used to staple the jaws shut. Most of the attention is given to molding the face into the desired appearance. "Tissue builders" are injected to enlarge shriveled parts, cotton is used to puff cheeks, and a "healthy" tan is provided by cosmetics. On the presumption that age lacks dignity, the restorers remove ugly wrinkles, subtracting visible years from the corpse being prepared for viewing.

After the corpse is well dressed and the effects of death are glossed over, colored lights are strategically placed to give the flesh a vital look. Viewers are then welcomed to the mortuary exhibit hall to gawk at the skill of the restorer, to examine the quality of the casket, and to pay their respects to the bereaved. Those who fantasize that life is only skin-deep comment on how beautiful the person looks while sleeping.

Some distinguished writers have commented on attempts by Americans to escape from the tragic facts of existence. In *The Invisible Writing* Arthur Koestler observes, "Morticians endeavor to transform the dead, with lipstick and rouge, into horizontal members of a perennial cocktail party" (p. 158). Evelyn Waugh satirizes,

> Here pickled in formaldehyde and painted like a whore;
> Shrimp-pink incorruptible, not lost nor gone before.
> *(The Loved One)*

American economist Thorstein Veblen's *Theory of the Leisure Class* is a help for understanding why many Americans make useless expenditures. He perceptively points out that "conspicuous consumption" is a way of advertising one's wealth. Those who are affluent, or who pretend to be, assume that the more they spend wastefully, the more others will presume them to be wealthy.[23] Over the past century the American funeral industry has most willingly accommodated itself to the craving for tangible displays. Caskets can cost thousands of dollars. Funeral vehicles are also ways of consuming conspicuously. The "coach," an elegant renaming of the hearse, and a luxurious family limousine carry to the graveyard the notion which some accept throughout life, namely, that persons can be judged by the vehicles in which they ride.

Americans pay, and pay extravagantly, their last respects in the ways described, not only because of the cravings Veblen diagnosed but also because of the vast oversupply of morticians. In this country there is now an average of one funeral weekly per mortician.[24] The industry could function more efficiently and with much lower costs if there were half as many in the trade. In order to stay in business and make a profit, morticians are usually obliged to mark up the cost of their merchandise several times. They must subtly convey to their emotionally vulnerable customers that the worth of the loved one is closely associated with funeral costs. Due to guilt over not fully appreciating the value of the deceased during life, the next of kin may attempt to gain relief by enriching the mortician. Even though an inexpensive body bag in an economical vehicle can fill the actual need for corpse removal and disposal, the mortuary establishment strives to get its clients to regard as cheapskates persons who act in such a modest manner. As sociologist Vanderlyn Pine puts it, "Families who are seen as having considerable buying power and who purchase a well-below-average casket are seen as being 'strange' and possibly even 'disrespectful' of the deceased."[25]

Cremation in History

The four methods of body disposal happen to be the same as the four elements of ancient chemistry: earth, fire, water, and air. Disposal by fire ranks second to earth burial in historical frequency. The funeral pyre has been used by a number of cultures throughout history, but it has been principally associated with the people of India. There a shrouded corpse is smeared with butter from the holy cow and placed on top of a pile of wood, and then the pyre is ignited by a relative. Praise to the sacred fire is chanted as the body is rapidly consumed. Ashes are then gathered up in a sack and scattered—preferably in the holy Ganges River. The Indian cremation tradition continues in the Buddhist as well as in the Hindu religion. Japan, for example, one of the largest Buddhist nations, uses incineration for nearly all of its body disposals.

In the West cremation was widely practiced in the early Roman civilization and reached its height during the era of the Republic. Some corpse ashes were taken from the funeral pyre and placed in an urn. Urns were sometimes deposited in a building resembling a pigeon or dove shelter, filled with small compartments. *Columbarium*, the Latin designation of such a bird housing, was the name given then and is the name still used to refer to a place filled with niches for the deposit of urns.

Although the ancient Israelites did not have a prescribed mode of corpse disposal, the customary method was simple entombment or inhumation. However, the bodies of their first royalty, Saul and his sons, were honored by cremation after death in battle, and the practice of cremation is mentioned elsewhere in Scripture (1 Sam. 31:12–13; Amos 6:10). In biblical times fire had hallowed associations, so it was appropriate to incorporate flames in sacred ceremonies. At Mount Sinai "the appearance of the glory of the LORD was like a devouring fire" (Exod. 24:17).

Cremation was rejected, first by Jews and then by Christians, because they could not integrate the practice with a life-after-death doctrine that began to develop around 100 B.C. Some Jews believed that God would restore parts of an individual's body in a future resurrection (2 Maccabees 7:9–23). Cremation is prohibited in the *Mishnah*, an authoritative collection of acceptable viewpoints in ancient Judaism (Abodah Zarah, 1:2). As belief in physical resurrection became established in Judaism and Christianity, it was assumed that God would have less trouble reconstructing a body for paradise if the flesh had not been burned.

When Jews migrated to Rome around the beginning of the Christian era, they dug the first catacombs there. Eventually more than one hundred thousand Jews were buried in those underground chambers outside the city.[26] Tacitus wrote that one trait by which Jews could be distinguished from Romans was their custom "to bury the body rather than to burn [their dead]."[27] Christians, also generally endorsing postmortem revivification, borrowed the Jewish practice of catacomb construction to provide a dormitory (Latin, *coemeteria*) for those who were thought to be temporarily slumbering. By the fourth century, when Christianity became the official religion of the Roman Empire, it became firm doctrine that corpses rested in tombs until the Judgment Day. At that end-time the bones would join together, and the righteous would "walk all over God's heaven."

During the fifteen centuries of medieval and early modern European civilization, Christians joined Jews in viewing cremation as an abhorrent pagan practice. Even though cremation was not prohibited by biblical law, Roman Catholic canon law as late as 1917 stated, "The bodies of the faithful must be buried; their cremation is forbidden."[28] Due in part to religious attitudes, crematoriums have only been found in Europe and in America since the nineteenth century.

In recent years Christian spokespersons have shifted from banning cremation to accepting it and even encouraging it. As a part of church modernization, Pope Paul VI in 1963 ended the heavy penalties imposed on Catholics who choose cremation.[29] Catholic official doctrine still maintains that the physical remains eventually rise up, but the church believes that God reconstructed heavenly bodies for saints burned at the stake and that the Omnipotent can raise the bodies of other Christians from scattered ashes as easily as from tomb dust. In the nineteen-eighties, only a small percentage of Catholic or Protestant clergy oppose cremation.

Cremation is rapidly gaining approval around the world among religious and nonreligious persons. It now accounts for the vast majority of body disposals in Europe and for about fifteen percent of the disposals in the United States. In America the ratio of cremations to burials is rising about one percent a year, with a more rapid increase in metropolitan areas and in retirement areas of the South and West. A recent poll of elderly urban people showed that more than forty percent prefer cremation.[30] A California-based Neptune Society is now the largest funeral establishment in the United States. In 1983, a decade after being founded, it handled fourteen thousand cremations at as little as $370 each—about one-tenth the conventional funeral cost.[31] Thousands of funeral homes have closed in recent years because of the trend toward less expensive body disposals. Except for some ultraconservative Jews and Christians, cremation will probably become the most acceptable method for corpse disposal in the next century in America, as it is now for more densely populated areas of the globe. The relative plentifulness of land is the main reason the United States has been slower to endorse cremation than European countries have, for cremations and land values rise together.

The shortage of land with the accompanying higher cost of burial plots is only one of the reasons for the increasing acceptance of cremation. Some people who can easily afford a fancy casket and a cemetery lot or a mausoleum crypt prefer cremation for ecological reasons. They realize that millions of acres of choice land are already given over to perpetual care necropolises, and they are convinced that better use should be made of the limited soil. Assuming a three-by-six-foot area is needed per burial plot, 160 square miles—more than twice the area of the District of Columbia—would be needed for the burial of the current United States population. The ecologically oriented also believe that the hardwoods and metals used in casket manufacture should be used for more beautiful and beneficial purposes. Federal law prohibits requiring caskets for bodies that will be cremated. A sturdy wood-pulp container, costing a few dollars, leaves no nails, hinges, or other metal pieces in the ashes. The few pounds of remains, pulverized to a sandlike consistency, can then be distributed in a garden or forest as a symbolic aid to the growth of new life.

Family mobility in America is another reason for the trend away from interments and entombments. Many people have left the area where their ancestors lived and died. About twenty percent of United States citizens move annually, giving this nation the highest mobility in the world. Although they may not feel rooted in their new places of work or retirement, few long to have their bodies returned to former localities. Even fewer are interested in disturbing the dust of deceased family members and reinterring their remains near where the surviving family have moved. The search for family roots in

America has not diminished, but the focus is now less on where forebears were buried and more on what they did in life. Tombstone information sometimes provides valuable links with the past, but genealogy investigation in court and church records as well as historical preservation of letters and pictures of ancestors are other ways of keeping family traditions alive.

Disgust with the so-called "American way of death" underlies much of the shift toward cremations. The realistic person discerns that the only choice for mortals is between rapid or slow return to dust after death. An intense flame of natural gas effects in minutes what it takes a cool grave years to accomplish. Finding no value in slow decomposition, some see no point in having morticians temporarily arrest this inevitable process by replacing the blood with embalming fluid. Nor do they find comfort in being deceived by cosmetics into thinking that the body is just sleeping. On the contrary, a clean incineration which quickly reduces the body of the deceased to its component elements can be therapeutic to mourners by expressing the final severance of the physical bond.

Unless those who opt for cremation arrange for "direct disposition" at a crematorium or for a medical school to receive the body, they may find that few of the exploitative morticians' practices have been eliminated. Ordinarily morticians do not now discourage customers who request cremation because they know the bereaved can usually be persuaded to purchase lavish funeral paraphernalia anyhow. The presumption is made that an open casket for viewing will be desired prior to a funeral service, making embalming necessary. Subtle pressure is placed on customers to buy a high-profit hardwood casket that will be burned with the corpse. How could the conspicuous consumption of American culture better be expressed? In addition, the mortician tries to add on the expense of perpetual "inurnment" of the "cremains" in a columbarium or burial of the urn in a cemetery.

Religious considerations are also responsible for some of the shift away from the dominant burial practice in America. Many perceive corpse "restoration" as not only esthetically repulsive but also a brazen and phony attempt to counter basic biblical affirmations. The allegedly preserved body is a Promethean rejection of Isaiah's judgment that "all flesh is grass" that "withers . . . when the breath of the Lord blows upon it" (40:7), and of Paul's claim that "flesh and blood cannot inherit the kingdom of God" (1 Cor. 15:50). (Appendix C.3 is an exposition of the spiritual resurrection views of the Apostle Paul.)

Other Methods

Burials at sea originated out of necessity at a time when voyages were long and refrigeration was not available. In tropical waters especially, where corpse decay is rapid, it became customary to wrap a body in sailcloth, attach a weight, and slide it overboard after the ship's captain conducted final rites. Now that corpses can usually be quickly removed from ships by aircraft, water burial of those who die while sailing is seldom practiced.

Some have rejected water, fire, and earth as a means of body disposal. The followers of the ancient prophet Zoroaster believe that those elements should not be defiled by corpses. To maintain their stringent code of purification, they lay naked corpses in a place where birds of prey can strip clean the bones. In Bombay, a Zoroastrian center, vultures consume the flesh of loved ones at "Towers of Silence."[32] Although this method of honoring the dead is repulsive to many Westerners, organisms of various sorts consume corpses whether they are disposed above ground, below ground, or under the ocean. There is little point in trying to keep out of circulation the elements of human bodies, for the carbon compounds will be utilized again in new life.

Indians of the North American plains had another form of air burial. They placed their dead in trees and protected them against scavengers by wrapping them in animal skins. If trees were not available, they built a scaffolding for a platform on which the dead bodies decomposed. The Indians believed that bodies—dead or alive— should be presented to the sacred sun and wind.[33]

Cannibalism has been practiced among some tribes on several continents as a way of honoring the dead. Cannibals believe that by consuming the flesh of a deceased friend they are enabling the spirit to live on in the community. The Kallatians of India practiced cannibalism and regarded as barbaric the prevailing cremation custom of their country. The Chiribichi of South America roasted their dead in order to collect fat, which was drunk as a kind of holy communion to assimilate the personality of the departed.[34]

Those from other cultures might find equally bizarre some modern American ways of body disposal. In the nineteen-sixties a supercool method of body disposal called cryonics was introduced as an alternative to dust or ashes. In *The Prospect of Immortality* physicist Robert Ettinger advocates deep-freezing humans who died of currently incurable diseases and defrosting them decades or centuries later as cures are discovered. They would then obtain treatment and possibly resume their vitality forevermore. In *Man into Superman* Ettinger reports on cryonic groups organized to take care of those who have been able to establish enormous trust funds (seventy-five thousand dollars in 1982). The funds provide for replacing the blood with glycerol and inserting the aluminum-foil-wrapped "patient" into a thermos-shaped "forever flask" where liquid nitrogen cools it to $-320°F$. The accumulated interest on the trust is to be used for replacing the nitrogen that is constantly lost.[35]

What gives this "freeze-wait-reanimate" method plausibility? It is commonly recognized that frozen meat does not deteriorate for a long time. Cryonic suspension has proven to be an effective preservative for semen, corneas, and vaccines. In 1985 a Wisconsin child, accidentally quick-frozen in subzero weather, had no heart or brain damage after being thawed.[36] However, there have been no experimental revivals of any who were placed in cryonic suspension.

In the nineteen-eighties some cryonics companies have gone bankrupt, and a consumer fraud suit in California resulted in a nearly one-million-dollar award. Abandoned bodies have decomposed,[37] but certainly those who have already died after investing will never find out that they have been swindled.

The latest endeavor of the multi-billion-dollar United States funeral industry has been a high-tech form of air burial. A Celestis consortium of Florida undertakers is planning to launch heavenly hearses by 1987. For only $3,900, Celestis will compact cremains into a tiny titanium capsule, place it in the three-hundred-pound nose cone of a rocket, and blast it to kingdom come, along with 10,329 other capsules. Somewhat like the eternal orbiting of the medieval angels, this celestial cemetery will circle at nineteen hundred miles above the earth for sixty-three million years. The highly reflective surface of the spacecraft will enable relatives to watch their deceased pass overhead on clear nights. This is only the first giant leap for the ashes of humanity. In the more distant future, rockets with escape velocities will send payloads of cremains winging beyond our solar system on a trajectory into outer space.[38] For those with faith in the god of technology, this final devotional tribute is appropriate!

A more sensible means of body disposal has been made possible by medical technology. Americans are beginning to leave for recycling usable parts of their bodies, and "The Living Bank" has been established for matching donated organs with needs across the nation.[39] For purposes of transplantation, organs are removed within an hour after death. The donation procedure consists of filling out and carrying a card which conforms with the Uniform Anatomical Gift Act. Potential donors should attempt to persuade their loved ones of the wisdom of organ donation, because few surgeons will remove organs if the next of kin does not agree with the decision of the deceased.

There is an urgent need not only for certain vital organs but also for a variety of bones and bodily tissues which can be stored for long periods. Each year more people are overcoming their neurosis over the "pain" of postmortem organ extraction and are giving to recipients what may be worth more than the largest monetary legacy. Some conscientious moderns feel the need to repay their social debt to medical science. Due in part to its advancements, life expectancy has been extended by twenty-five years. Many respond to appeals such as this from the Kidney Foundation of West Virginia:

> There is a tremendous shortage of kidneys for transplantation in the United States. Consequently, thousands of men, women, and children are forced to spend eighteen hours or more every week attached to kidney machines. If your kidneys are usable at your death, they could bring the gift of a more normal life to one of these sufferers, or even two of them.

Organ reuse is dependent on the success of matching blood types and on whether the donated organ is free of disease.

Ophthalmologists are now using cornea gifts to assist some of the hundreds who go blind every day. For about ten percent of them, or thirty-five thousand of the total number of blind Americans, sight restoration is possible by means of a cornea transplant. These transplants have a high rate of success, and thousands of additional corneas could be used annually just within the United States. Some donors have been attracted to this means for modern miracle working by being reminded that purity of heart, not eyeballs, is needed to "see God." According to Jesus, "the pure in heart" are those who are generous without expecting something in return (Matt. 5:8; Luke 6:35).

A teenage recipient of two transplants expressed her appreciation by means of a "Dear Abby" letter. She marveled over her transformed life:

> I want to address my unknown donors: "I never knew you, yet your generosity changed my life. You died, yet a part of you still lives. You gave of yourself. It was the last thing you gave, and you gave it to someone you didn't even know. My life is so different because of you. Every day I am reminded of the gift you gave me. . . . With the help of God you created a miracle—the miracle of sight."[40]

Even though nearly two million people die in our nation annually, most medical schools find it difficult to obtain the few thousand cadavers needed each year to train future doctors and to develop new surgical procedures. These can only be obtained by donation, since medical institutions are not permitted to buy cadavers. Formerly bodies of unclaimed indigents were routinely sent to medical schools. Now that welfare policies in most states pay morticians to bury such bodies, there are usually some morticians who will solicit such business. But the current difficulty in obtaining bodies is in part due to morticians who discourage potential customers from considering this need. Morticians realize there is little opportunity to sell merchandise and services if they heed the medical school request that un-embalmed bodies be sent promptly after death to its anatomy department. Morticians have been known to convey to their potential customers that medical researchers are ghoulish and could cause bodies to rest eternally in pieces.

Actually bodies are treated with as much respect by the personnel of medical schools as they are by morticians. Although practices may vary from state to state, schools will usually cremate the remains after using cadavers in their anatomy laboratories or, at the request of the donor's family, return the body for burial. In West Virginia unclaimed cremains are deposited in a vault at the Medical Center garden. On that vault this inscription is engraved: " 'Greater love hath no man than this'—John 15:13. In memory of those who have donated their bodies for the advancement of mankind and the health sciences." Annually relatives of the deceased are invited to a memorial service there.

Mortuary history brings to mind a parable. Once when a leading citizen of Hong Kong was boating, he discovered an oyster which contained a pearl of exceptional value. Its shape, size, and color caused many to admire it. However, the possessor lost his priceless find and grieved over being deprived of its loveliness. A businesswoman in the city suggested that the man console himself by purchasing from her a golden chest with a silk lining and use it for exhibiting in her store window the polished and perfumed shell of the oyster that had produced the exquisite pearl. Moved by her suggestion, he bought the most expensive treasure chest available. The people in Hong Kong were at first surprised by the unusual window display, but out of respect for its prominent owner they commented to one another on its beauty. Some of the spectators even became convinced that such an exhibit was a fitting way of commemorating lost pearls. Showing off shells in caskets soon became an established custom, causing the value of pearls in Hong Kong to decline while the value of pearl oyster shells increased.

This story, implausible though it is, bears some similarity to the history of the funeral industry over the past several millennia. The opening chapter of *The History of American Funeral Directing* is appropriately entitled "Pagan Roots of Modern Funeral Practice." Described in that 1962 NFDA publication are Egyptian corpse embalming, funerary temples, and costly tombs which were first supplied for royalty, and eventually for all who could afford it.[41] The text does not point out that the Judeo-Christian culture during most of its long history has protested the theology and the economics of the Egyptian custom which it discarded. Synagogue and church leaders have affirmed that ultimate reality cannot be closely associated with the lifeless material body, because God is a living spirit. Hence the modern mortuary chapel, by placing a glorious "casket" and its contents in its holy of holies, misrepresents the dominant theology of Western civilization. To pay thousands of dollars to honor the shell in which a valuable pearl developed is both ludicrous and wasteful. Having had a century of Egyptian captivity it is time to become liberated from this neopaganism and find imaginative alternative ways of honoring the deceased.

8

GRIEF AND BEREAVEMENT

The Grief Experience

Grief is the normal response to the death of someone dear. Theologian Edgar Jackson, one of the best-known writers in the area of bereavement, puts it this way: "Grief is the other side of the coin of love. . . . Only the person who is incapable of loving another is entirely free of the possibility of grief. . . . When you love you become vulnerable, because the one you love may suffer and die and part of you suffers and dies along with him."[1]

Factors which determine the degree of grief are the emotional closeness of the deceased, the age at death, and the method of dying. An elderly grandmother who dies in her sleep after suffering from a degenerative heart condition would be recognized by her relatives as having a timely death, and consequently the survivors would be in a relatively low grief situation. The family of a young girl who drowned in a pool would probably feel that she was cheated out of the chance to make her full contribution to humanity, and thus a high grief situation would ensue. A woman would likely have higher grief over her husband's death in an airplane crash than over the death of her stillborn child with whom she had not had the opportunity to establish a long-term relationship. Although the deaths of the grand-parent, the girl, the husband, and the infant in these illustrations would likely prompt feelings of sadness and irreplaceable loss, the acuteness of grief would vary significantly. The quick accidental deaths of the young girl and the husband impose only brief ordeals on the dying but severe shock on the survivors.

Psychiatrist Erich Lindemann, a pioneer in clinical studies of grief, found among a variety of people a remarkable similarity of acute grief symptoms: "A feeling of tightness in the throat, choking with shortness of breath, need for sighing, an empty feeling in the abdomen, lack of muscular power, and an intensive subjective distress described as tension or pain."[2] Also commonly involved in the grief syndrome are these psychosomatic disorders: insomnia, night-mares, absentmindedness, trembling, high blood pressure, vomiting, overeating, diarrhea, constipation, colitis, and arthritis. In short, nei-ther mind nor body works properly in acute grief. The neurological, circulatory, glandular, digestive, and muscular systems are all af-fected. After the wrenching death of President Kennedy a number of surveys were conducted among American citizens to ascertain assas-sination reactions. Ninety percent reported experiencing one of these symptoms: headache, dizziness, fatigue, upset stomach, or loss of appetite.[3] In *A Grief Observed* C.S. Lewis describes the agony of the weeks after his wife's death:

> No one ever told me that grief felt so like fear. . . . The same fluttering in the stomach. . . . I keep on swallowing.
> At other times it feels like being mildly drunk, or concussed. . . .
> Then comes a sudden jab of red-hot memory. . . .
> Meanwhile, where is God? . . . go to him when your need is des-perate, when all other help is vain, and what do you find? A door slammed in your face. . . .
> . . . the same thing seems to have happened to Christ: 'Why hast thou forsaken me?'
> . . . Perhaps the bereaved ought to be isolated in special settlements like lepers.
> . . . Cancer, and cancer, and cancer. My mother, my father, my wife. I wonder who is next in the queue.[4]

Lewis articulates a rage that is often a part of the grief response. The target of the hostility varies according to the situation. Some direct it toward God or the clergy—the certified representatives of the divine. The most common expressions of theological anger are these: since this happened to me, God does not exist, God is not good, and the good God is powerless. Sometimes intense antagonism is directed toward the mortician, in part because the bereaved feel taken advantage of and in part because he represents the enemy death. Sometimes grieving persons pour out their bitterness on attending physicians, feeling that they bungled or were not personally interested in their loved one. A child's resentment toward the deceased is typically expressed: "Why did Daddy leave me? It's not fair!"

Guilt frequently accompanies grief. A parent may say, "I should never have let him drive when he was so young." A widower may say, "I should have taken her in for an examination when she first complained." A widow may say, "If I had persuaded him to stop smoking, he would be alive today." A youth may say, "If I had not asked my father to pick me up, he would not have been in the fatal accident." Lily Pincus says, "Perhaps the most painful and confusing guilt is about the moments—however fleeting—of triumph that the other one is dead, and I am alive!"[5]

Research has shown that the highest grief stress in American culture is over the death of a spouse.[6] By means of a social readjustment test, it was found that the impact of conjugal bereavement was twice that of being fired from a job. An accountant without a job, for example, still thinks of herself as a professional, but a wife without a husband is immediately transformed into a widow. Spouse loss hits harder than a term in prison or than the death of a sibling, parent, or child. Those who are happily married function as two halves coupled together; losing part of the larger self is then felt to be a dismemberment.

According to Colin Murray Parkes the word *brokenhearted* from biblical poetry (Isa. 61:1) aptly describes spouses who are crushed by grief. He cites *Medical Inquiries* (1835), a text by Benjamin Rush, the physician who signed the Declaration of Independence: "Dissections of persons who have died of grief, show congestion in, and inflammation of the heart." Research findings in recent decades prove that grief is indeed associated with heart-related death. A generation ago a British study revealed a forty percent higher death rate among several thousand widowers during their first six months of bereavement than among married men of the same age. Three-fourths of these deaths were attributed to heart and circulation disorders.[7] Grief can place an excessive stress on the heart, aggravating trouble already present in the cardiovascular system. The broken heart syndrome includes frightening loneliness from the loss of a daily companion, sexual frustration, economic confusion, improper nutrition, and inattention to driving hazards.

Emily Dickinson, the nineteenth-century American poet, poignantly describes brokenheartedness:

> The Bustle in a House
> The Morning after Death
> Is solemnest of industries
> Enacted upon Earth—
>
> The Sweeping up the Heart
> And putting Love away
> We shall not want to use again
> Until Eternity.
> (Number 1078)

A study published in the *British Medical Journal* showed that the death rate of widowers during the first year after their wives' deaths was about twenty percent and of widows during the first year after their husbands' death was about nine percent.[8] This was much higher than the one-percent death rate of spouses with living partners. A widower is twice as likely to die as a widow partially because men in Western culture are expected to keep a stiff upper lip while emotional expression among women is approved. In 1977 D. N. McNeill reported on his extensive study of conjugal bereavement in Connecticut. Surviving spouses in their twenties died seven times more frequently than the expected rate. In this group suicides were twelve times what was expected among widowers of all ages, and deaths due to liver cirrhosis and alcoholism increased up to seven times the expected.[9]

Jackson provides this clinical case of unbearable grief:

> John and Mary had been married for more than 50 years. . . . Their major emotional investment was in each other. Mary died rather suddenly from a heart failure. John was so overwrought that he had great

difficulty moving through the funeral process. A week later he was admitted to the hospital with no specific ailment but a generalized state of debilitation. His will to live seemed to have evaporated. Before the month was over he was dead of unspecified ailments. Heart failure was listed on the death certificate but it was merely the last event in a process of rapid disintegration of organic function.[10]

Arnold Toynbee thinks that the survivor of an intense involvement with another human takes the brunt of the suffering inflicted by death. At age seventy-nine, he wrote, "If, one day, I am told by my doctor that I am going to die before my wife, I shall receive the news not only with equanimity but with relief. . . . The sting of death is less sharp for the person who dies than it is for the bereaved survivor."[11]

Survivors of happy marriages frequently describe hallucinations in which the deceased is seen and heard. Psychiatrist Murray Parkes, a world authority on bereavement, has examined widows' illusions. A widow is sometimes impelled to identify with her husband someone who happens to be passing by. Or she may report a dream such as this: "He was in the coffin with the lid off and all of a sudden he came to life and got out. . . . I looked at him and he opened his mouth. I said, 'He's alive. He's alive.' I thought, 'Thank God, I'll have him to talk to.' "[12]

Parkes also comments on anticipatory grief, after tracing the phenomenon in a study of young Boston widows. He found that wives who nursed husbands during a terminal illness were significantly less disturbed a year later than those whose husbands had died suddenly.[13] Those who were with their husbands during a lingering illness began at that time to come to terms with the reality of death, accepting the inevitable. Anticipatory grief is found among all who are involved with the slow death of a loved one. Having braced themselves for the impact, they feel somewhat in control of the future. They may rehearse funeral plans and reflect on strategies for making the best of the bad situation. Exposure to the ravages of some diseases causes recognition that to continue with the illness is worse than death.

The classic example of anticipatory grief is King David with his infant son. During the period of terminal illness David wept, abstained from food, had sleepless nights, and disregarded his own grooming. After the infant's death, some in the ancient royal court feared that his mourning would become a more severe threat to his health. However, David discontinued his solitary lamentations. He bathed, changed from his mourning clothes, and went "to the house of the LORD, and worshiped" (2 Sam. 12:20). The shepherd who became king of Israel was strengthened by recognizing the presence of a divine shepherd while walking "through the valley of the shadow of death" (Ps. 23:4). By the time the infant died, David had calmly accepted that the separation was irreversible.

A contemporary example of anticipatory grief is found in Richard Kalish's *Death, Grief, and Caring Relationships*. A nurse reported that she was shattered by grief when she was told her father had cancer and a prognosis of six months to live. She decided to care for him in her home, and there they shared one another's company until he became comatose. A year after her father died, she said: "I never cried when he died—I think I'd finished with crying by that time." [14]

Some death educators have attempted to plot neat stages of bereavement, similar to Kübler-Ross' stages of dying. One text discusses five stages: denial, awareness, restitution, resolution, and idealization; another one, three stages: shock, despair, recovery. There is no general agreement as to what the grief phases are or even that there is a universal sequential pattern. Although normal grief leads to eventual recovery, different individuals attain this recovery in a wide variety of ways. It is dangerous to presume a single correct order in the grief process. Bereaved persons, for example, should not be deemed backsliders if they exhibit more tearfulness and restlessness one week than in a previous week.

The duration of the grief experience can best be compared with nature's slow process of healing after a person sustains a deep gash or the loss of a bodily limb. On receiving wounds people may be "all shook up" and unaware of what hit them. Due to the stunning effect of the initial impact, the pain may not be intense at first, but the wounded soon become aware that they need treatment in order to regain a normal life. They may attempt to use some self-cure medication, but more likely they will seek professional assistance. There may be times of excruciating pain—as, for example, when stitches are removed. After some time, the wound hurts only when it is in-advertently hit by the person or by others who brush against it. Gradually healthy tissue replaces the inflamed and damaged flesh. Eventually there is no more localized pain, but the person is reminded of the traumatic experience on looking at the scar. The wounded can talk about the experience without acute distress.

In some particular ways a high grief situation is like being cut deeply in an accident, or, in the case of a spouse loss, is like having an amputation. After the initial numbing shock, there is a lengthy period when the pain flares up. Sedatives may be used to treat the grief symptoms, but compassionate friends provide the best therapy. Pangs stab when acquaintances hit against the wound in an unsympathetic way. Months and even years later grief may surge up again when special objects or dates prompt recollections of the past loss. Birthdays, anniversaries of the wedding or death of the deceased, and new bereavements are often poignant times of remembrance. Normally healing is eventually effected, but the scar tissue of grief is never eradicated.

If a physical wound is not properly treated, infection can destroy other tissue and the result can be fatal. Correspondingly, abnormal grief can leave a personality diseased with morbidity. Rather than decreasing with the passage of time, the grief intensifies, and grievers become more isolated and may destroy themselves.

Children and Death

Parents often protect their children from the sight of death on the assumption that they are assisting in human development. Buddha's father had such a viewpoint. The story of Buddha's maturation has had international appeal over the past twenty-five centuries because many have found in his upbringing a reflection of their own. The wealthy Hindu father shielded his son from these disturbing experiences: old age, disease, and death. Only after beginning a family of his own did Buddha gain independence from his parents and venture out into the actual suffering world. He was distressed to see an elderly person degenerating, a sick person racked with pain, and a putrefying corpse. After those excruciating but enlightening sights,

Buddha rebelled against the cloistered conditioning his father had imposed on him and rejected his father's religion. He left the artificial milieu of his affluence-stricken extended family, and from then onward he comforted suffering mortals wherever he found them along the dusty roads of India. (Appendix C.1 illustrates how Buddha assisted a grieving mother.)

Few people have the genius of Buddha to enable them to rise above their parents' thanatophobia and face realistically the tragic facts of human existence. Many of today's young American parents were excluded from meaningful family communication about death as they were growing up and have not broken out of the cocoon in which they were nurtured. The unresolved fears of the older generation have been subtly transmitted to the younger generation, compounding their own phobias and developing cumulative death anxiety.

Contemporary young adults also are the first generation of parents whose ideas on death have been substantially influenced by television. With this background for parenting, the next generation may grow up with the most distorted outlook on death ever. Each year the average American child looks at more than a thousand deaths on television, yet has no personal exposure to the actual death of someone close by. When children are asked about death these days, they are more likely to retell a Dracula-type story of sadistic demise than they are to relate ideas generated by a frank discussion of real events with parents.

Television makes death seem reversible. A cartoon character is shot full of holes but after a temporary death is involved in another perilous situation. Having been desensitized by video death, a child may express little surprise in being told of a death in the family. When one mother announced her father's death, her son responded, "Who shot him?" Robert Kastenbaum tells of another child who reassured his sad sister, " 'Grandma will come back when she's through being dead.' " [15] The child presumed that the grandparent would reappear in another family life episode. When a dog was given a backyard burial, another child expressed confidence that the pet would come up and play with her again when the tulips came up. Some games that children play simulate television scenes. "Bang, you're dead," the cowboy or the cop shouts gleefully. The Indian or the robber drops dead for a short time in this customary pattern of fun. In school, children learn about assassinations of national leaders in the nineteen-sixties, but they appear to be as alive as ever when their speeches are rerun on television.

At least one parental guidance book recommends, in effect, that children's illusions be kept alive. Frances Ilg and Louise Ames, in *Parents Ask,* suggest that in some cases a child's dead or dying pet be quickly replaced so that the child can transfer affection to a new one. She writes that parents may want to send the child away for a visit elsewhere when an old pet is "put away" and thereby prevent the child's involvement in the death of a household member. Or the child might be told that the pet has "taken a turn for the worse" at a veterinary hospital. Apparently Ilg and Ames regard deception as sometimes preferable to mentioning the unmentionable.[16]

Often a person's earliest experience of death involves a pet cat or dog with whom a mutual attachment has been established. In such situations parents should not deprive children of their first opportunity to grieve. The death of a pet can provide a valuable training ground for mourning and can enable a child to move toward emotional maturity.

Parents are also unhelpful if they confuse their children into thinking that the dead are asleep. "Put to sleep" is a euphemism often used for the veterinarian's gassing method of killing old or unwanted pets. Children tend to think in a literalistic manner when, for example, they are told to speak only in whispers in a funeral home because "Grandmommy is sleeping." They will expect her to reenter the scene of the living after napping in her best clothes.

Other fears may be stimulated by a prayer which originated in the Middle Ages when a child was more likely to die than survive to adulthood. Many children are still taught to pray,

> Now I lay me down to sleep,
> I pray the Lord my soul to keep;
> If I should die before I wake,
> I pray the Lord my soul to take.
> *(New England Primer)*

The association of death with sleep at night can cause neurotic fright over what might happen during the dark hours. One child had difficulty falling asleep from wondering if the Lord would give back in the morning the soul that had been left in God's safekeeping. The child recalled once asking Mother to keep a frog, but the mother lost it. Would the Lord be more trustworthy?

Another way in which children's literalism hinders communication is illustrated by the misunderstanding of hyperbole. When an exasperated old person says to an irritating child, "You'll be the death of me yet," the child may believe, after the death of that person, that bad conduct by the child had a lethal effect. Rabbi Earl Grollman has observed that children project the causal relationship they have experienced, namely that bad things often result from naughty behavior. Hence the death of a parent may be interpreted as "retribution" for some terrible wrong the child has done.[17]

It is healthy when children weep to express grief. Since it is difficult for them to articulate how they feel, tears become their wordless messages. Wise parents recognize tears as a necessary safety valve, whereas foolish parents say to a child, "You musn't cry." Bottled-up grief will come out, so the longer it is postponed, the more explosive it is. After a study of deviant juveniles Mervyn Shoor concludes: "Delinquent behavior by children and adolescents is sometimes a substitute grief reaction. These children were unable to release their feelings in socially acceptable ways when confronted with the impact of loss and death." Shoor, along with some other social scientists, maintains that some destructive behavior is a grieving child's acting out his or her feelings.[18]

Unresolved childhood grief may not surface until adulthood. Psychiatrist Felix Brown found that forty-one percent of his large sampling of adults who had received treatment for depressive illness lost a parent through death before age fifteen.[19] Also, studies have shown a significant correlation between the death of a parent and suicide among college students. Those who have not been able to come to terms with parental death are unable to handle subsequent loss.[20] Thus it is evident that a child's grief over the death of a family member may be repressed but not eliminated. The child who is encouraged to act with passionless bravery when a loved one dies may replace normal grief with devastating pathological grief much later.

Coping with Bereavement

Authentic emotional expression is the first step in dealing with bereavement. *Bereave* has a graphic root meaning split or rip and is related to an ancient custom. Israelite men and women tore their clothes and wept in order to display openly the torn-up state within. In token of the traditional Jewish way of mourning, the *shivah,* a piece of shredded cloth, is still worn by relatives of the deceased for a week after the death. In Jerusalem there has long been the "wailing wall" for public lamentation. Physician Samuel Klagsbrun recommends that the newly bereaved be given a sheet to tear, thereby venting their raging emotions in physical action.[21] Kübler-Ross thinks that there is more need in hospitals for screaming rooms to express turbulent grief than for drugs to suppress it.

A basic difference between Christianity and Stoicism—one of Christianity's principal rivals in the Roman era—was in how they responded to death. Christians followed the Jewish mourning custom of commiserating with one another by profuse emotional outpouring. The Apostle Paul wrote about good grief that brings about the restoration of godly conduct (2 Cor. 7:10). In contrast with compassionate Christianity, dispassionate Stoicism attempted to eliminate emotions. The Stoic Seneca, for example, regarded grief as a sin to be shunned and believed it was unworthy of a wise person to shed tears over any misfortune.[22] Some latter-day "Stoics" in modern culture presume that strength is best displayed by a dauntless composure. However, psychotherapists generally agree that heavily suppressed grief remains as a poison in the bereaved personality and delays recovery.

Corpse contact has therapeutic value for some mourners. Parents who privately hold the body of their child in their arms after death has been pronounced may be helped by that act to overcome denial and accept the grim reality. When death occurs at any age, those who have been intimately associated with the deceased—both adults and children—may be assisted in coming to terms with what has happened if they gather around the deathbed to look at the lifeless body and/or embrace it. If dying has been painful, it may be a relief to witness the relaxed expression of the deceased and know that suffering has been erased. Some hospitals and nursing homes assist in confirming the fact of death by encouraging the bereaved family to visit the loved one's room with the body present and the institutional staff absent for an hour or so after death.

When serving as a parish minister in Scotland, I found that "coffining" times were a meaningful way of coping with bereavement. Shortly after death occurred, close relatives of the deceased invited their pastor to join with them in their home as they gathered around to prepare the body for burial. On one occasion I recall being present after unsuccessful efforts were made to revive a person who had drowned. The unembalmed body was enshrouded and placed in a coffin obtained from an undertaker. After good-bye kisses to the deceased and prayers for the living assembled there, the mourners screwed down the lid. No attempt was made to disguise the tragic loss of the young man.

Another reason for corpse viewing is advocated by the American funeral industry. An NFDA brochure states, "The restoration and cosmetizing aspects of embalming are . . . to provide for an acceptable recall image of the deceased." Morticians rightly claim that people wish to have a pleasant remembrance of the deceased before he or she wasted away with disease or was scarred by violence. However, for those with faint mental memories, photographs are a simpler means of stimulating a recall picture. At some European and Asian funerals enlarged color portraits are effectively used. Occasionally at American funerals a bulletin will contain a photograph or several snapshots taken at different stages of life. Photographs evoke a better recollection of a robust period of the deceased's life than the mortuary mannequin. Mortuary cosmeticians usually use photographs of the deceased to create a copy of a copy.

It is unlikely that there would be much interest in public viewing of so-called "restored" bodies were it not for aggressive promotion by morticians. There are even some drive-in morturaries where encased bodies are displayed for all who pass by. This convenience enables people to witness the spectacle and sign the visitation book, placed outside the viewing window and alongside the lane for vehicles, without speaking to the bereaved family. When Edwin Shneidman surveyed the young, well-educated readers of *Psychology Today,* he found that seventy percent disapproved of public viewings at funeral homes.[23] In 1978 the funeral industry conducted its own study and reported that a majority of their representative sample did not agree that a funeral viewing or a "lying-in-state" was beneficial.[24]

Participation in planning for a funeral service is an important means of coping with bereavement. Psychologist Robert Kastenbaum writes, "The opportunity to be involved in details of leave-taking ceremonies, although painful in many ways . . . provides a relevant activity for the bereaved."[25] The skilled minister plans the funeral service with those who have been closest to the deceased. After they discuss significant experiences involving their loved one, the minister can select examples to remind the congregation what the deceased stood for. The service can be further personalized by using, if appropriate, some readings, music, and prayers favored by the family. Presiding clergy have sometimes resorted to intoning words from a manual with little variation from funeral to funeral because they have not been made aware of the deceased's personal interests. Understandably the bereaved may regard such an impersonal ceremony as an empty formality. The tendency toward very brief services may reflect a growing disdain for rituals which are not adapted to the mourners' particular needs.

Rites of passage should reflect lifestyles. The traditional New Orleans Black funeral is a good example of the integration of death style with lifestyle. The spontaneity of the entire service echoes the congregational involvement characteristic of Black churches. A jazz band playing a subdued "O for a Closer Walk with Thee" heads the procession to the cemetery. After the words of committal, trumpeters lead off with "When the Saints Go Marching In" for the triumphant return march. A guitar-playing vocalist singing "Bridge over Troubled Waters" at the funeral of a folk-rock enthusiast would be another way of effecting individuality at a funeral. A fitting tribute to persons who loved to garden might be a display of flowers or a wreath from foliage they had nurtured. A lover of poetry might well be honored by a reading of verses which convey some personal insights and aspirations.

Funeral services show that mourning is a community as well as a family matter. Since most homes are not large enough to accommodate all the members of the community who would like to express their support of the bereaved family, a funeral home is a convenient place for the nonreligious to meet, and a synagogue or church is an appropriate gathering place for the religiously oriented. A survey published in a 1981 issue of the death education journal *Omega* shows that "support from the community, religious atmosphere, and choice of degree of personal involvement" are the most helpful aspects of a conventional funeral, while the presence of the corpse and lavish displays are among the least helpful features.[26]

At a funeral the most acutely grieving are sometimes treated like those suffering from a contagious disease. Many funeral "chapels" are structured so as to encourage the grieving family to isolate themselves from others. Here is a newspaper advertisement, entitled "Always Desired," that is not atypical: "We know from experience that the family invariably wishes seclusion during the services—a most trying period, when privacy is absolutely priceless. To provide such privacy, we have a family room which completely protects those within from contact with others in attendance." Of course, there will be private shedding of tears by the immediate family and by other friends, but it may add to the dread to recommend withdrawal at a public service. It is universally recognized that one of the most effective ways of lessening and managing grief is to share it with those who can see, hear, and touch one another in the gathered community. Grief is diminished when others are seen genuinely sorrowing for the loss of the same person.

A funeral is not only a time for releasing pent-up emotions, but is also a time for values clarification. If a family believes that material stuff is all that exists, then it is appropriate to give central attention to the flesh. The Russian and Chinese governments officially champion atheistic materialism, and their state rites harmonize practice with philosophy. At the funeral of an official, Russian citizens parade by the open coffin while dirges are played. Also, the tomb of Lenin in Moscow's Red Square is Russia's most honored monument. The glass-enclosed embalmed body of the founder of the Marxist state has been on exhibit longer than the fifty-four years Lenin lived. Pilgrims by the thousands wait in line every day in order to give adoration to his corpse. At the Square of Heavenly Peace in Beijing another Marxist is similarly enshrined. Chairman Mao's body lies in a crystal sarcophagus that functions as the central relic in an enormous mausoleum devoted to Chinese nationalism. His tomb is a kind of royal audience chamber for receiving perpetual homage from a continual stream of subjects.

World religious philosophies stand in bold relief to metaphysical materialism, yet funeral practices of various religions often bear much resemblance to those of the Communists. What practices are consistent with professed theologies? As a case in point, consider the dominant religion in American culture and reflect on ways it could be expressed in funeral ceremonies. The Apostle Paul was the earliest and remains the most authoritative Christian theologian. He affirmed that the living body was of great value and should be venerated as "a temple of the Holy Spirit" (1 Cor. 6:19), but he did not find the dead body of sacred value. Like the assemblage of materials used in a temple's construction, the building might as well be leveled or disassembled and used in other structures if there is no more divine worship going on within. Paul affirms that at death persons are not bound to the flesh any longer; they are "at home with the Lord" and "away from the body" (2 Cor. 5:8). A funeral in line with Paul's theology focuses attention on the intangible qualities of the deceased and reflects on the God of the Bible who is spirit and not flesh (Isa. 31:3). "The peace of God, which passes all understanding" (Phil. 4:7) to which Paul alludes, has nothing in common with seeing a bloodless carcass with lips glued together in a secure casket. *Shalom* comes from spiritual confidence in God's faithfulness amid forces threatening destruction. Without deception, a Christian can joyfully express the conviction that the essential self survives in spite of "dust to dust." As Paul says, Christians need not "grieve as others do who have no hope" (1 Thess. 4:13). The Apostle believes that the immortal existence is radically different from the material and perishable realm. Funeral practices based on Paul's gospel do not suggest that the life after death is an extension and improvement of material life.[27]

A funeral service inspired by Christian theology should be conducted in a church where life is commonly celebrated rather than in a house of death. The most fitting place is where children have been baptized, where youth have sung, where adults have married, and where families have commemorated Easter. Congregations think of themselves as participants in worship, not as spectators of a dead object—even if the body of the deceased is present.

During the early centuries of Christianity the characteristic black robes of pagan Roman funerals were forbidden, and white garments were worn as a witness to the radiant Christian hope.[28] During later times, when the body of the deceased was brought into the sanctuary, a common pall was placed over it to symbolize the equality of each before God. Such traditions are now being revived in some Christian denominations. The Presbyterian Church (U.S.A.), for example, now asserts in its *Book of Order*, "The casket, if it be present during the service, shall be closed at all times and should be covered with a white pall in order that the attention of those assembled may be directed to the Author and Finisher of their salvation."[29]

A growing number of Christians are opting for the memorial service, the designation given to a funeral without the corpse present. The body of the deceased is disposed of as soon after death as a grave can be dug or a cremation can be arranged, often with a committal service in the presence of the immediate family. Then, at a convenient time—perhaps an evening or a Sunday when most people are free from work—a memorial service is conducted. When the corpse is absent there can be more flexibility of place as well as time. If the deceased left numerous friends in widely separated communities, more than one memorial service for the same person might be appropriate. Memorial services stress the ongoing ideas and deeds of the esteemed person. Those attending a worship service with no distracting corpse present do not muse vulgarly on whether a polished box and its contents look good but rather reflect on whether the deceased was good and ponder whether God is good.

Monetary giving in memory of the deceased is another way of coping with bereavement. Depth of love can in some small but significant way be expressed by the worth and appropriateness of the gift. Morticians and florists rightly urge that mourning is not a time for cheapness, but the large expenditure need not be for funeral merchandise or floral arrangements. Americans spend approximately one billion dollars annually for funeral flowers. This averages about $450 per funeral.[30] Some Americans are beginning to realize that while beautiful flowers are a lovely symbol at any ceremony, a single cut rose may say as much as dozens of sprays. The popularity of floral tributes is waning, and people are beginning to shift attention to more lasting gifts related to the interests of the deceased. Adding to a library's collection, contributing to an agency or church with whom the deceased was identified, or endowing a scholarship fund to educate others in the profession of the deceased are among the more popular causes mourners have supported.

Jackson points out that support of pressing community needs is a constructive way of responding to grief. He tells of Russell H. Conwell whose life had been saved by the self-sacrificial act of a young man in the Civil War. Because of this, Conwell in turn gave his energies to helping others. The result of his dedicated effort produced Temple University and the Good Samaritan Hospital in Philadelphia. Jackson concludes, "The power of his life seemed doubled because he was determined to live not only for himself but for another."[31] Americans coped with their grief over the death of President Kennedy by carrying out what he had promoted in life. Passing the landmark civil rights legislation in the months after his death was viewed by many members of Congress as a way of honoring Kennedy's memory. The early Christian disciples responded to their grief over the death of Jesus by devoting themselves to spreading the gospel their leader had declared.

The most difficult period for the bereaved family is often after the funeral is over and the wave of thoughtful tributes and gifts from friends subsides. According to sociologist Geoffrey Gorer, the period of intense grief has a median range of about two months. He characterizes it in this way: "the mourner is in more need of social support and assistance than at any time since infancy and early childhood; and at the moment our society is signally failing to give this support and assistance. The cost of this failure in misery, lone-liness, despair and maladaptive behavior is very high."[32]

In order to save the grieving from a feeling of abandonment, a real need exists for nonjudgmental listeners who have an abiding concern. After making a study of bereavement, psychiatrist Alfred Weiner concluded that conversation about the deceased is the best therapy for bereaved persons.[33] They need to give details of the ac-cident or illness which brought on the death. Repetition of this story helps to reinforce the awareness that it really happened. When mourners are grappling with the more distant past, feelings of guilt as well as delight pertaining to the deceased are often verbalized. Unfortunately well-meaning friends often avoid the subject, wrongly believing that it would be too upsetting. The words of friends who chirp optimistically may sound hollow to those who need to dredge up deep feelings about the deceased.

The tightly knit support groups that were a built-in feature of traditional American culture have loosened. Individuals in urban America are often left to flounder privately in their grief; the care-giver network which is a part of small town and rural life may not be present. Some urbanites have not established personal communal bonds by means of churches, clubs, or neighbors living down the street. A priest, pastor, or rabbi is often not available to visit a wid-owed person who lives alone. In busy America few people are avail-able to "bear one another's burdens" (Gal. 6:2).

Psychiatrist Phyllis Silverman of Harvard Medical School has de-veloped a "widow-to-widow" program to counter the major isolation problem of some urban Americans. She arranges for those in acute grief to receive assistance from those who are recovering from simi-lar bereavement. By means of telephone calls and personal visits, the bereaved are involved with others who can be of genuine help. Vol-unteer programs of this type are being duplicated elsewhere and are providing the extra support needed by the bereaved.[34]

"The work of grief," to use a phrase from Freud, is the intense struggle involved in withdrawing emotional capital from the de-ceased and reinvesting it in other ventures. After a spouse's death, for example, former activities designed for couples may need to be replaced. A home arranged for the convenience of the deceased may need renovating, and personal belongings may need to be discarded. The survivor may be better off living in a different place and working with different people. Much energy may be consumed in developing new interests and in making new attachments to humans—or even to pets and plants.

Preplanning one's own funeral is a constructive way for a survivor to cope with bereavement. At the time of a death, weighty decisions need to be made hastily with respect to options such as embalming, cremation, and memorial service. Having realized that some choices made previously were wise and others had unsatisfactory results, the mourner can base future personal plans on that evaluation. This is a matter of doing for one's surviving loved ones what one wishes had been done by a deceased loved one who expressed little or no preference pertaining to body disposal or final rites. A Federal Trade Commission requirement that became operative in 1984 assists in preplanning. Morticians are now required to disclose in advance price information on goods and services. It is possible to "let your fingers do the walking," comparing by telephone what various funeral homes offer. A life insurance policy or a special trust fund can be set up to finance the desired type of funeral. Clergy can also be consulted regarding funeral service variations, and the anatomy department of a regional medical school can be contacted for body donation information. (Appendices B.3 and B.4 contain personal preplanning forms.)

The first memorial societies were formed in America in the nineteen-thirties for the purpose of funeral prearrangement. One of the oldest and now one of the largest memorial societies was established by some members of a congregation in Seattle who contracted with a local mortician for a funeral with simple dignity when the need would arise. Those becoming life members of the society by paying a few dollars were eligible for special body disposal rates that excluded embalming and corpse viewing. The membership of that Seattle society increases by thousands each year. In one decade the society saved consumers $18,000,000 by providing funerals at one-sixth the conventional cost.[35] The memorial society idea has spread nationwide, and in 1986 about 1,000,000 members are associated with 160 societies.

A few American congregations have decided to handle their own funerals without the use of morticians. In conservative Judaism a Society to Honor the Dead has been formed for building a wooden coffin, sewing a cotton shroud, providing cemetery transportation, and counseling the bereaved. The cost of these services is covered by voluntary contributions. Rabbi Arnold Goodman, who led in this development, points out that in Judaism the religious community has historically taken responsibility for burying the dead rather than leaving it to secular surrogates.[36]

In summary, healthy coping with bereavement involves full emotional expression, death-reality acknowledgment, public mourning rites, clarification of ultimate values, giving meaningful tributes, finding sympathetic listeners, developing new interests, and planning for one's own demise. In accomplishing this fatiguing grief work, the bereaved becomes a stronger person and more able to bear subsequent adversity.

9

LIFE AFTER DEATH

In religious literature, both *life* and *death* have double meaning. The creation account treasured by Jews, Christians, and Muslims well illustrates the dual connotation. The Garden of Eden story refers, first of all, to physical life and physical death which are a part of the immediate awareness of all—irreligious and religious alike. The opening chapters of Genesis affirm that living humans and animals are distinguished from inanimate clay figurines by breath. After respiring creatures expire (literally, "breathe out"), they return to "dust." When that dry earth is mixed with water, it can be reconstituted into some other organism in a "dust to dust" cycle.

In addition to an explanation of the start and finish of physical life, the Eden story holds a more subtle meaning of life and death, as is revealed in the announced punishment for eating forbidden fruit: "in the day that you eat of it you shall die" (Gen. 2:17). This first mention of death cannot refer to physical death because the humans who ate the forbidden fruit continued to breathe for many years afterwards. The writer of this simple but profound story is referring to a kind of spiritual suicide through which men and women cut themselves off from companionship with God. The mythological account concludes by asserting that had they not stolen fruit, they would have been permitted to partake of the "tree of life" fruit. This tree symbolized the life for "ever" (3:22) which would have resulted for Adam and Eve had they not been alienated from their Creator.

Making sense of that primeval story—and the literature of world religions which tells of life and death—requires recognition that each term has both a spiritual and a physical connotation. In the discussion to follow, a sampling will be given of the way humans across history have viewed a quality of life which extends and/or transcends physical life and death. (Study questions pertaining to what the Bible says about this subject are contained in Appendix A.3.)

Conditional Theories

The spectrum of beliefs about an everlasting life is broad. For purposes of discussion they can be divided into two major classifications: conditional and unconditional. The conditional theories have this form: if something is done by or for you, then you will attain life after death. Immortality is not guaranteed for everyone because humans—like all other organic species—are inherently mortal. Death is the final end *if* nothing is done to keep one's spirit alive.

Throughout history the most widespread form of conditional immortality has been rooted in reproduction. If one raises a family, one's genes are transmitted, and if there are everlasting generations of offspring, then portions of the biologically constituted person live forever. The transcontinental appeal of this type of immortality can be found in an African saying: "An ancestor lives on as long as there are children who remember." The sentiment expressed here sums up a main theme of Chinese Confucianism. Also, Abraham the Hebrew was strongly motivated to have offspring so that his name would be great in the future. A cultural as well as a physical inheritance is implanted in one's progeny. Living on through children and grandchildren is still a prominent reason for human procreation.

Both those who do and those who do not multiply also are entitled to an immortality of influence. A person who does something which has social impact will live on. It is said that Abraham Lincoln and

other national heroes are as alive as ever because they live in the
hearts of United States citizenry. The revolutionary ideas of Thomas
Jefferson, Susan B. Anthony, Martin Luther King, Jr., and other famous people affect us even as they did their contemporaries, so their
deaths remain in some sense unreal.

Social immortality has interested the irreligious at least as much
as the religious. Friedrich Engels concluded his funeral speech for
Karl Marx with this prophecy: "His name will live through the centuries and so will his work."[1] At the center of the capital of China is
a memorial to the Communist Revolution. On it is inscribed a slogan
of Mao Zedong: "The people's heroes are immortal."

Shakespeare was self-conscious of the way his poetry would
overcome his mortality. He boldly asserts:

> Nor marble, nor the gilded monuments
> Or princes, shall outlive this powerful rime. . . .
> (Sonnet 55, lines 1–2)
>
> . . . .
>
> Your monument shall be my gentle verse,
> Which eyes not yet created shall o'er-read.
> (Sonnet 81, lines 9–10)

Although Mary Ann Evans died more than a century ago in England, she continues to live by means of the acclaimed literary works
of her pseudonym George Eliot. She expressed her yearning in these
lines:

> O may I join the choir invisible
> Of those immortal dead who live again
> In minds made better by their presence
>
> . . . .
>
>   So to live is heaven:
> To make undying music in the world
>
> . . . .
>
>   May I reach
> That purest heaven, be to other souls
> The cup of strength in some great agony,
> Enkindle generous ardor, feed pure love,
> Beget the smiles that have no cruelty.
> ("O May I Join the Choir Invisible,"
lines 1–3, 10–11, 37–41)

The immortality of influence is not limited to those associated with government or those who have international notoriety. Someone who produces crafts or recipes which continue to be used or someone who originates ideas preserved in libraries will live on as long as the contribution is recognized as significant.

One need not have a good reputation to attain this type of immortality. For thousands of years Pontius Pilate's name has been and will continue to be remembered by millions every week because they recite from the Apostles' Creed that he was the ruler who permitted Jesus' crucifixion. Because of the atrocities for which he was responsible, Adolf Hitler's name will no doubt live in infamy longer than the thousand years he hoped the Third Reich would last.

A theological variety of conditional life after death recognizes that all organic things are mortal and presumes that God alone is naturally immortal, or deathless. Death is the natural final end of mice and humans. God, the possessor of infinite immortality, shares the divine quality with those found to be acceptable. Humans are immort-able inasmuch as each has a deathless potential which becomes actual if positive response is made to God's offer. For humans immortality is a privilege, not an inalienable right. Each has the option of "passing on" or of passing out of existence. Those who devote themselves to spiritual growth during their physical lives will be given the opportunity for further development after physical death. Life after death is seen as a continuance of the eternal or spiritual life which one began to enjoy during mortal life.

The corollary of this immortality theory is that self-destruction is the result of not being united with God. Those who do not become infused with the immortal Spirit of God and who do not accept the ensuing responsibilities of that relationship have nothing within them capable of surviving biological death. If they function on the sensate level of animals, they ultimately share the subhuman destiny of animals.

Some biblical writers accepted a conditional doctrine of everlasting life. The Garden of Eden story declares that humans lose spiritual life forever when they separate themselves from God. There is nothing in their future but dusty death. Paul, the writer of about half of the New Testament books, held a doctrine of conditional immortality. For him, as R. H. Charles comments, the immortal life "is the privilege only of those who are spiritually one with Christ."[2] Paul states that "the free gift of God is eternal life" (Rom. 6:23) and that death is the final end for those whom God finds unacceptable.

The biological, social, and theological types of conditional immortality are not mutually exclusive. It would not be inconsistent to think of someone achieving all varieties. For example, Abigail Adams, the mother of a United States president, a noted feminist writer, and a woman of religious devotion, would seem to fulfill the conditions for three kinds of conditional immortality. (Your response to the "Afterlife Survey" in Appendix A.2 may give a more personal dimension to the theories discussed in this chapter.)

Unconditional Theories

Theories of unconditional life after death affirm that all humans are endowed with permanently deathless spirits. The two main unconditional theories are commonly called reincarnation and everlasting life. In the global population today, approximately a billion people believe in reincarnation (also called transmigration). These people affirm that humans possess an eternal soul which is independent of physical birth and death. The concept can be grasped by means of this diagram:

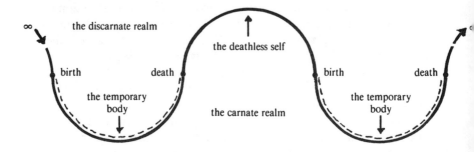

Fig. 4: Concept of Reincarnation

An individual self or soul oscillates between the immaterial and material realms. The self descends at birth to dwell in an earthly body for a comparatively brief time. After its release by physical death, it soars in an otherworldly sphere where it may receive rewards or punishments before returning to be attached to another body. This rhythm of the self can continue infinitely.

Reincarnation is basic to the predominant religions of East and South Asia. The Hindu viewpoint can best be seen in its most treasured Scripture, the *Bhagavad-gītā*. That epic tells of the dilemma of Arjuna, a warrior at the time of a civil war. He is unable to attack another human being on the battlefield until he can justify killing as beneficial. God Krishna reveals to Arjuna that the essential self is unkillable, so slaughtering bodies with the sword does not damage the victims' inmost personalities. Having resolved his qualms of conscience, Arjuna charges forth to separate souls from bodies. Hindus often chant at funerals this passage from the *Bhagavad-gītā:*

> Even as a person casts off worn-out clothes and puts on others that are new, so the embodied self casts off worn-out bodies and enters into others that are new. Weapons cut it not; fire burns it not; water wets it not; the wind does not wither it. This self cannot be cut nor burnt nor wetted nor withered. Eternal, all-pervading, unchanging, immovable, the self is said to be unmanifest, incomprehensible, and unchangeable. Therefore, knowing it to be so, you should not grieve. (2.22–25)

In Hinduism the cycle of rebirth is governed by the law of *karma* which declares that behavior in one's lifetime is inevitably recompensed in the subsequent cycling of the self. Hindu Scripture describes how people reap what they sow: "Those whose conduct here has been good will quickly attain a good womb. . . . But those whose conduct here has been evil will attain an evil womb—the womb of a dog, a pig, or [an outcaste]" (*Chāndogya Upanishad*, 5.10.7). Involved here is a cosmic bookkeeping system whereby each good attitude or act is entered on the credit side of the ledger while each bad attitude or act is entered on the debit side. For example, a lower-caste person who dutifully performs what has been traditionally expected of those in that status can reasonably hope to become a prince or a priest in one of the higher castes in the next incarnation. Or again, a glutton's punishment might be hellish torment in the discarnate realm and assignment to the body of a buzzard in the next enfleshment.

Reincarnation can be viewed as a doctrine with moral significance. Individuals start out in life in unequal circumstances with respect to intellectual potential, healthy organs, economic wealth, and political freedom. If reincarnation is true, then persons need not blame God for their having been born in situations which make success unlikely. Also, reincarnation believers have a moral imperative as they look to the future. If they regulate their lives by high principles, their self-development will be less constricted in subsequent lives.

It should not be overlooked, however, that Hindu priestcraft may partially explain the reincarnation doctrine of traditional India. Brahmans, who have designated themselves as the highest caste, can more easily keep their subjects following the rules they have established if wonderful rewards in an afterlife are promised to the compliant and horrible punishments are threatened for the noncompliant. Also, the priests can rationalize that they deserve their exalted position as a payoff for goodness in past lives and that the untouchables are receiving what they deserve because of viciousness in past lives. Reincarnation can be seen as a pragmatic but cruel doctrine for maintaining the status quo.

When Sakyamuni the Buddha taught in India some twenty-five centuries ago, he advocated, in a modified form, some aspects of the Hindu religion in which he was reared. Although he was not interested in upholding the caste system of the Brahmans, he did believe that one's future existence was remorselessly fixed by one's past character. He thought it was possible to break the weary cycle of endless rebirths by removing the deficits from one's *karma* account. If selfish passions are extinguished, a purified state of Nirvana will be reached. At that point, liberation from the chain of reincarnations is accomplished. These doctrines of reincarnation and *karma* became embedded in the cultures of East Asia when Buddhism became an international religion.

Outside Asia reincarnation doctrines are occasionally found in Europe, North America, and Africa. Plato, the most influential of the ancient Western philosophers, accepted reincarnation. In order to explain why humans can talk about absolute beauty, true equality, the whole truth, and other perfect ideas never experienced in this realm, he speculated that there is a perpetual cycling of what the Greeks called *psyche*. In an immaterial realm the psyche first comes to know those ideals. Plato reasons that learning of these ideals on earth is really a recollection of the transcendent archetypes our preexistent psyches have assimilated.

In his myth of Er, Plato tells of the psyche selecting the role it wants to play during its next incarceration on earth. What it decides to become is dependent on the character formed in the previous life. Psyches then drink from the river of forgetfulness. Those who drink in moderation will be able to recall in the postnatal existence some abstract ideas which they knew while in the discarnate realm. Those who overimbibe will find it difficult to remember any of the ideals to which they were exposed for a thousand years before their fall into the mundane realm. Earthlings who forget the concepts of art, religion, and philosophy they once knew will ignorantly claim that reality is limited to what they perceive and that only matter matters.[3]

William Wordsworth's *Ode: Intimations of Immortality* is permeated with Plato's outlook on the psyche. Especially apropos are these lines from that tantalizing ode:

> Our birth is but a sleep and a forgetting:
> The Soul that rises with us, our life's Star,
>   Hath had elsewhere its setting,
>   And cometh from afar:
>   Not in entire forgetfulness,
>   And not in utter nakedness,
> But trailing clouds of glory do we come
>   From God, who is our home.
> Heaven lies about us in our infancy!
> Shades of the prison-house begin to close
>   Upon the growing Boy,
> But he beholds the light, and whence it flows,
>   He sees it in his joy;
> . . . .
>
>   The homely Nurse [Earth] doth all she can
> To make her Foster-child, her Inmate Man,
>   Forget the glories he hath known,
> And that imperial palace whence he came.
>   (lines 58–70, 81–84)

Although reincarnation has not been widely accepted in American culture, occasionally the theory receives considerable public attention. One such time was a generation ago when *The Search for Bridey Murphy* became a bestseller and was made into a movie. It portrayed the alleged revelations, while under hypnosis, of Ruth Simmons of Colorado. She told of growing up in Ireland in the nineteenth century with the name Bridey Murphy. Although Simmons had never been to Ireland, she spoke in an Irish brogue as she related her experiences in that culture. Historical verification was found in Ireland for the descriptions Simmons had given. It was then hypothesized that the Irish data could only have been obtained when her soul dwelt in Murphy's body and that in 1923, decades after Murphy's death, her soul was reincarnated in an embryo to be named Ruth. The interest in this case subsided after it was learned that as a child in Chicago, Simmons had close contact with an Irishwoman named Bridie Murphy Corkell, who probably conveyed knowledge of Ireland to Simmons.[4] Hypnosis later uncovered what was hidden away in her subconscious. Since humans have a predisposition to accept stories that reinforce shaky belief in a never-dying soul, the first uncritical acceptance of fantasy as fact is understandable.

A recent experiment reveals that remembering an alleged past life is dependent to a large extent on a hypnotist's suggestion. Using students who had been found to be susceptible to hypnosis, psychologist Robert Baker exposed one group to a tape recording about "past lives therapy" which would enable them to "take a fascinating journey back in time." Afterward eighty-five percent of this control group told of at least one previous life during their hypnosis sessions. Another group was exposed to a derogatory message about reincarnation: "You might accidentally . . . drift back and imagine you're living in another lifetime . . . but most normal individuals haven't been able to see anything." In this group only ten percent reported having had a past incarnation.[5]

In recent years America's death and dying guru, Elisabeth Kübler-Ross, has come to believe that people "are reborn again in order to complete the tasks they have not been willing or able to complete in this life." She testifies that out-of-body experiences have led her to believe that immortality and reincarnation are scientifically true.

One of her soul's previous incarnations, she claims, was in a woman named Isabel who taught Jesus.[6] If there were a general acceptance of such claims in our culture, think of the advantage in personal résumé writing for a political science major, for example, if she or he could insert that she or he once taught Thomas Jefferson or actually was Jefferson!

Reincarnation is rooted in the belief structure of different peoples in Black Africa more strongly than in Western culture. In West Africa a baby may be given a name which means that the soul of some particular ancestor has returned.[7] Reincarnation is there compared with a vine which winds around a trunk and reappears at another level. According to a Zulu tale from South Africa,

> within the body is a soul, and within the soul is a spark of the Itongo, the Universal Spirit. After the death of the body, the soul hovers for a while near the body and then departs. . . . It sleeps till a time comes when it dreams that something to do and learn awaits it on earth, and is born again as a child. Again and again does the soul travel thus, till at last the [person] becomes true [human], and [the] soul, when the body dies, becomes one with the Itongo, whence it came.

One reason for the persistent worldwide belief in reincarnation is the resemblance of a child to a deceased relative. A mother, for example, may find in her child striking similarities to her father or grandfather, mother or grandmother. Both may have the same smile, the same mechanical ability, the same name, and the like. Though a consideration of genetic and cultural inheritance can explain the similarities, it is far more dramatic to affirm reincarnation in cultures where that doctrine is deeply rooted.

About a billion people today accept an everlasting life theory of unconditional immortality. In contrast to reincarnation doctrine, the everlasting life theory posits a unique soul for each individual. This soul, given to each person by the Creator, is believed to continue forever in a spiritual realm after death. The idea of unconditional everlasting life can be traced to the Parsees, whose homeland is now called Iran. The doctrine spread sequentially during twelve centuries to Judaism, Christianity, and Islam—other monotheistic religions originating in western Asia.

Zoroaster founded the Parsee (meaning Persian) religion in the sixth century before the Christian era. He stressed a personal afterlife in his eschatology, his theory of last things. In describing the joys of heaven Zoroaster introduced the term *paradise*, meaning Persian game park, into religious vocabulary. The sensuousness of that cool, colorful, and fragrant garden, he believed, largely replicates earthly experiences. Food is consumed not to satisfy hunger, but for the pleasures of tasting and smelling while dining. Sex is engaged in not for producing children, but for the tactile sensations of intercourse. The paradisal destiny is only for those who have been judged worthy by the God of light, called Ahura Mazda. The Parsees tell of a narrow bridge spanning an abyss leading to paradise, over which all the deceased must travel. The bridge is precarious; it is made of a sword blade. As a wicked person crosses, the sharp edge of the sword is turned up, causing him to drop into a purgatory governed by a prince of darkness. The inhabitants of the dark, infernal place experience the opposite sensations from the righteous. Its stench is overwhelming, and its frigidity and loneliness are agonizing. The inmates have appetites, but they are fed only nauseating food. Those who repent of their earthly sins are eventually purified and restored to the paradise they lost.[8]

Prior to their contact with the Persian culture, the Jews had no developed idea of individuals surviving death. The earlier books of their Scriptures occasionally refer to an abode of the dead called Sheol. It was a terminal grave for good and bad alike. Any shadowy existence that might be there was presumed to be discontinuous with life on earth (see Gen. 37:35; Job 10:21–22; Ps. 88:3–6).

Parsee eschatology profoundly influenced the Jews during the era of Persian domination. The Jews, who had been uprooted from their homeland by Babylonian invaders, had a comparatively positive relationship with the Persians. After a generation of exile in the Mesopotamian valley, the Jews were given liberty to return to Judah by a Parsee called Cyrus the Great. The Jews introduced into their religion during the Persian era such notions as a postmortem judgment, a bodily resurrection, paradisal archangels, and devilish spirits.

The Jews suffered heavy persecution from Greek rulers after the destruction of the Persian Empire. During this time they developed a doctrine to explain better the success of the immoral and the suffering of the ethical. An apocalyptic movement which sprang up maintained that God Yahweh will correct in an individual's afterlife injustices for which there was no compensation before death. The apocalyptic book of Daniel contains this forecast: "many of those who sleep in the dust of the earth shall awake, some to everlasting life, and some to shame and everlasting contempt" (12:2). This verse is the only one in the entire Jewish Bible which states clearly the individual life-after-death doctrine which was to become normative in Judaism for many centuries. A number of other apocalyptic Jewish books written during the Greco-Roman era elaborate on Parsee ideas about the condition of those who have received the judgment of God immediately after death. Second Esdras 7:36 depicts a "paradise of delight" and a "pit of torment" for those whose works deserve one type of recompense or the other.

Early Christianity was even more inspired by apocalyptic Judaism than Judaism had been by Parsee eschatology. Jesus told a parable in which the afterlife situations of a poor man and a rich man reverse what they were accustomed to before death. Lazarus, the poor man, went to a paradisal banquet while the rich man, who had expressed no concern for sick Lazarus during his lifetime, watched him enviously from a place of torment. The rich man cried out, "I am in anguish in this flame" (Luke 16:19–24). In contrast to the Parsee's dark and cold pit, Jesus pictured a brightly burning place of punishment.

Elsewhere in his teaching Jesus referred to the eschatological place of fiery punishment with the term *Gehenna* (Matt. 5:22, 29–30). That word, translated into English as *hell*, originally had references to a "valley of the son of Hinnom" (Jer. 7:31; 32:35) near Jerusalem which the Jews in Jesus' day considered defiled because children had been sacrificed there to the god Molech in an earlier era. After the Jews conquered Jerusalem, the valley became a trash dump where rubbish was incinerated. It is unlikely that Jesus intended to describe in his parable a literal spot on earth, beneath the earth, or separate from the earth, where the damned are fried and where the elect are refreshed. He used picturesque imagery from Jewish lore to teach the affluent to help the needy.

As is reported in one of the Gospels, Jesus borrowed from Parsee eschatology as he was being crucified. To the repentant thief on another cross, he said, "Truly, I say to you, today you will be with me in Paradise" (Luke 23:43). Jesus was probably speaking about a spiritual condition in which God and humans are at one, not about a physical place in the cosmos. (Appendix C.2 provides a further exposition of what Jesus said about an afterlife.)

The paradise motif is prominent in the last book of the New Testament, entitled The Revelation or The Apocalypse. To Christians suffering intense persecution, this assurance is given: "To him who conquers I will grant to eat of the tree of life, which is in the paradise of God" (2:7). The final chapters of Revelation enlarge on those traditional symbols. There will be a renewal of all creation which, like the uncorrupted original Garden of Eden, will be a place for close fellowship between God and those who have remained faithful. Paradise is pictured as a "new Jerusalem, coming down out of heaven from God, prepared as a bride adorned for her husband" (21:2). The final earthly paradise will abound in precious metals and stones. The pearly gates, jasper walls, and golden streets suggest everlastingness as well as dazzling beauty. Neither moth nor rust consumes these materials. The vegetation suggests abundance for all: "On either side of the river stood a tree of life, which yields twelve crops of fruit, one for each month of the year. The leaves of the trees serve for the healing of the nations" (22:2 NEB). God's people partake of the fruit and drink "the water of life."

The influence of Parsee eschatology is later found in Christianity when the medieval church added a purgatory doctrine to the concept of an eternal hell for the very wicked. Thomas Aquinas described the three-tiered eschatology in this way: ". . . since a place is assigned to souls in keeping with their reward or punishment, as soon as the soul is set free from the body it is either plunged into hell or soars to heaven, unless it be held back by some debt, for which its flight must needs be delayed until the soul is first of all cleansed."[9] Over the centuries most Roman Catholics have presumed that they belong in the middle category; consequently purgatory has been for them the center of afterlife concerns. A 1983 survey by *U.S. Catholic* of its readers showed that ninety-seven percent of those responding believed in heaven but only thirty-three percent expected to go straight there when they die. Fifty percent said they hoped to go to heaven after being purged of sin. Due perhaps to American optimism, only one percent of those responding said they expected to go to hell, even though eighty-six percent expressed belief in hell.[10]

Islam is the last major religion to be influenced by the eschatology of earlier religions from Western Asia. However, it is unlikely that Muhammad, any more than the apocalyptic Jews—including Jesus—was aware of adopting ideas originating with the alien Parsees. Only as the historian of religions looks back does the pattern of cultural influence emerge. Each religion founder assumed that his ideas came in large part by a hot line to heaven, and none was conscious of adapting mythology from other cultures. Muhammad, six centuries after Christ, believed he was inspired to recite the exact words Al-lah, the God, had written in a heavenly book. His graphic description of paradise and hell is similar to the earlier pictures we have examined. Muhammad viewed paradise as a lush Garden of Eden, but without forbidden fruit. Even intoxicants, which the holy *Quran* forbids for mortals, are permitted. The delights in the passage which follows were apparently designed to cater principally to males:

> Oh, how happy shall be the people on the right hand! . . . In gardens of delight they will recline on decorated couches. Ever-blooming maidens wait on them with goblets of flowing wine. No headache will they feel, nor will their wits be dimmed! There are such fruits as they choose and such flesh of fowls as they desire. For them there will be the fair ones with large dark eyes, like pearls hidden in their shells—a reward for their past labors. No vain talk shall they hear, no charge of sin, but only the assurance, "Peace! Peace! . . . There will be tall trees with abundant fruits, neither out of reach nor forbidden, in extended shade, by flowing waters. The fair ones, who lie face to face on couches, are created anew as spotless virgins. These lovers and friends are for those on the right hand. (56:8–37, paraphrase Phipps)

Muhammad may have been influenced in his description by his Arabian landscape. Paradise is envisioned as an oasis, while its opposite is an inferno with torturing winds.

> Oh, how wretched shall be the people on the left hand! They will be found amid scorching wind and scalding water, and in the shadow of black smoke, hot and horrid to behold. They were previously effete with luxury and persisted in terrible sin. They were prone to say,

"What, after we have died, and become dust and bones, shall we or our forefathers be raised?" . . . On the Day of Judgment the erring and the deniers . . . will drink boiling water and be roasted in the fire of hell. (56:41–47, 93–94, paraphrase Phipps)

Should these revelations to Muhammad be interpreted only figuratively, or should they be accorded a literal as well as a symbolic meaning? The descriptions of carnal pleasures and pains seem to imply that a carnal interpretation is meant. At least one passage in the *Quran* confirms that an actual resurrection of the flesh is intended. It is found in this question and answer: "Does man think that we shall not re-unite his bones? Allah is able to restore even his fingers" (75:3–4).

Some Muslims have expressed skepticism toward the afterlife doctrine of their orthodox tradition and have preferred to emphasize a this-worldly paradise. Omar Khayyám, a twelfth-century Persian, was intrigued by Muhammad's promise of intoxicating drinks and maidens. However, he opted for present fun posthaste, fearing posthumous relations might never transpire. Edward Fitzgerald has provided a poetic adaptation of Khayyám's *Rubáiyát*:

A Book of Verses underneath the Bough,
A Jug of Wine, a Loaf of Bread—and Thou
Beside me singing in the Wilderness—
Oh, Wilderness were Paradise enow!

Some for the Glories of This World; and some
Sigh for the Prophet's Paradise to come;
Ah, take the Cash, and let the Credit go,
Nor heed the rumble of a distant Drum! (lines 45–52)

When eschatological symbols are interpreted literally, they often stimulate more doubt than conviction among the educated. Some significant meanings are lost when mythopoetic language is treated as prosaic description of the afterlife. To illustrate the psychological insights which emerge with demythologizing, consider the following comments by both religious and irreligious writers:

(1) The leading medieval poet Dante depicts hell as total despair and claims that above the entrance to hell is this inscription, "Abandon all hope, ye who enter here" (3. line 9). Dante translator John

Ciardi notes, "Hell is not *where* the damned are; it is *what* the damned are" (*Inferno,* p. XIV).

(2) The Puritan poet John Milton writes, "The mind . . . can make a Heaven of Hell, a Hell of Heaven" (*Paradise Lost,* I, 254– 255).

(3) A Russian priest in Feodor Dostoyevsky's *The Brothers Karamazov* ponders: " 'What is hell?' I maintain that it is the suffering of being unable to love. . . . In the parable of the rich man and Lazarus . . . that is just [the rich man's] torment. . . . They talk of hell fire in the material sense. I don't go into that mystery and I shun it. But I think if there were fire in material sense, they would be glad of it, for I imagine that in material agony, their still greater spiritual agony would be forgotten for a moment" (6.3).

(4) Existentialist Jean-Paul Sartre, in his play *No Exit,* presents a shabby hotel room in which several people with opposing temperaments are confined. It is void of windows, books, music, pictures, radio, and television. Each character is doomed to sit in silence or talk to others. All project their own emptiness, their selfishness and cruelty. When the mutual resentfulness becomes unbearable torment, one prisoner screams before the final curtain: "So this is hell. I'd never have believed it. You remember all we were told about the torture-chambers, the fire and brimstone. . . . There's no need for red-hot pokers. Hell is—other people!"(*No Exit and Three Other Plays,* trans. Stuart Gilbert, p. 47).

(5) In T. S. Eliot's *The Cocktail Party* a hollow socialite cries out: "Hell is oneself, / Hell is alone, the other figures in it / merely projections" (Act I, scene 3).

Across the centuries interpreters have shown that the polar opposite images of hell and paradise have meaning when describing a quality of life rather than a postmortem place. Theologian Kenneth Foreman asserts: "Hell is within. A person does not discover he is in hell; he discovers hell is in him. . . . Away-from-God is a synonym for hell. It is only half a truth that 'myself am hell' or that 'hell is other people.' Neither I nor others would be hell unless we were running away from God."[11] Paul Tillich holds that a genuine symbol, whether artistic, political, or religious, unlocks depths of our selves and reveals the human situation.[12] Although the Apostle Paul uses a variety of images to point to the existential relationships of humans, he readily admits that things beyond imagining have been prepared for those who love God (1 Cor. 2:9). A similar insight regarding "lovers" is found in this testimony of psychiatrist and philosopher Karl Jaspers: "I achieve immortality to the extent that I love. . . . I dissipate into nothingness as long as I live without love, and therefore in chaos. As a lover I can see the immortality of those who are united to me in love."[13]

What Proof?

Can life after death be convincingly proven to exist? Shortly before his execution Socrates offered reasons for his affirmative answer to this question. His defense of the immortal psyche, the most famous in world philosophy, is found in the dialogue *Phaedo*, written by his disciple Plato. In English there is no one-word equivalent for Socrates' and Plato's term *psyche*. It means both mind and soul: mind in reference to its rational aspect, and soul in reference to its spiritual aspect.

In the dialogue Simmias confronts Socrates with a harp analogy to show that the psyche and the body terminate simultaneously. A harp is constructed to produce invisible, beautiful, and divine harmony. The material instrument has little value apart from the melodies which fill the air when it is being played. If the strings and frame are destroyed, the precious invisible music is also destroyed. In the same way, Simmias reasons, the psyche is dependent on the physical body. When the tangible parts can no longer be "plucked," the intangible psyche will be annihilated.

Socrates offers a personal example to show Simmias the faultiness of his analogy. If the psyche is dependent on the body, why has the condemned man refused to heed his body's cravings? The basic striving of an organism is biological preservation. Following Simmias' analogy, Socrates' psyche should be subordinate to his bones and muscles, which want to stay alive at any price. If controlled by physical impulses, the psyche would take the easy escape route friends had arranged and go to another Greek city to avoid the death penalty. However, Socrates demonstrates that his psyche is free from physical determinism by not running away and by courageously drinking the poisonous hemlock. He observes that while his body decays with age, his psyche is growing stronger in a resolve to face death with integrity. Socrates laughs at his relatively worthless body, asserting that when shackles are cast off by death he will be off to engage in exciting conversation with the disembodied psyches of various Greek heroes.

Socrates argues for immortality from the nature of deity as well as from the nature of the psyche. He lived in a culture where it was generally agreed that gods exist and possess immortal psyches. Socrates argues that the gods, being good, want to share their eternal psychic substance. Hence the divine and the human both have imperishable psyches.

The psyche's immortality is also implied, Socrates says, by the nature of justice. Justice is recognized as a divine quality basic to government. However, many evil people go to their graves unpunished, and many innocent people are punished. If psyches are extinguished rather than extended at death, there is no way to avoid concluding that life is unfair and that we do not live in a moral universe.

Other ancient philosophers sometimes held positions opposed to that of Socrates on the immortality of the psyche. Epicurus, another Athenian, agrees that the gods could be called immortals but believes they do not share their nature with humans. All that is above as well as below the neck in humans is reducible to matter in motion. What we call psychic activity is actually the rapid movement in the skull of atomic particles too small to be seen. Epicurus, like Simmias, argues that the existence of rational process and spiritual awareness is totally dependent on the life of the physical body. Epicurean ideas were later championed in the Roman culture by a poet named Lucretius. "When the body has died," he argues, "we must admit that the soul has perished." For both Epicurus and Lucretius, the conscious self cannot survive when physical processes terminate.[14] The immortality of the soul continues to be argued, but the reasons advanced now are not strikingly different from those expressed by the ancient Greco-Roman philosophers.

Empirically oriented persons find philosophical deductions less convincing than extrapolations from personal experience. If they have not themselves had primary experiences of communicating with the physically dead, they rely on the testimony of others.

In the course of history mediums occasionally have claimed power to communicate with the dead in the spirit realm. In Jewish Scriptures there is an account of the medium (called "witch" in older translations) of Endor who was sought after by King Saul. The desperate monarch, who had a history of mental illness, wanted to establish contact with the dead prophet Samuel. He hoped his former religious advisor might be able to foretell who would win the battle the next day against the Philistines. According to the record the medium saw an old man wrapped in a robe coming up out of the earth. The temporarily revived Samuel first complained about being disturbed. He then carried on a conversation with Saul, from which the king learned that he would join Samuel in the realm of the dead the next day (1 Sam. 28:14–19).

It is peculiar that this Endor story should be in the Scriptures of a religion rejecting mediums who claim power to establish contact with the dead. Indeed, the Endor medium was initially fearful of Saul, assuming he had come to enforce the law of Moses which prohibited corpse communication. Prior to the Palestinian invasion, Moses designated mediums, wizards, and necromancers as abhorrent because "these nations, which you are about to dispossess, give heed to soothsayers and to diviners" (Deut. 18:14). Even though necromancy was a feature of paganism which was rejected by the biblical culture, the Endor story set a pattern for medium conduct in subsequent eras.

The French word *séance,* meaning a session, is now used to refer to a meeting with spirits of the dead which is presided over by a psychic, also called spiritualist or medium. The psychic goes into a self-hypnotic trance in an attempt to establish contact with people presumed to be in the spirit realm and to obtain from them assurances for clients.

Earlier this century a renowned medium named Arthur Ford lived in Philadelphia. Episcopal Bishop James Pike, distressed over the suicide of his son, made an appointment with Ford in hopes of getting in touch with his son's departed spirit. Pike left the séance satisfied that he had obtained messages from his son. After consultations were made with additional psychics, Pike wrote *The Other Side* about his experiences.[15] That book, coupled with a television program in 1967 based on Ford's séance with Pike, gave spiritualism its biggest American boost since the Bridey Murphy affair.

Shortly after Ford's death in 1971 his biographer disclosed that the psychic engaged in careful research before conducting a séance, learning numerous tidbits of information from newspapers and *Who's Who* on his famous clients. Then, at the séance, he duped the gullible into believing that personal information extracted from library resources was descending from his contact person in the spirit world.[16]

Unscrupulous psychics have always been ready to exploit the insatiable desire of humans for proof that the dead are still alive and conscious. For example, the medium of Endor who reported that she "saw" Samuel rise up may have used ventriloquism to assure her panicky client that Samuel could prophesy. Some people can be at least temporarily persuaded by tricksters that deceased loved ones live on. Believing such to be the case provides a ray of hope to psychic clients that they also will live blissfully forevermore. But an abiding conviction that the self has a potential for, or has achieved, everlasting life must rest on a careful individual and corporate evaluation of the afterlife testimonies of the parties involved. To be fully convincing, the testimonies must bring new meaning and value into the lives of the participants.

The Christian church was established on the affirmation by certain of Jesus' contemporaries that their leader was raised from the dead a short time after his crucifixion and burial. Christianity continues to be perpetuated on the basis of this good news. According to the New Testament, Jesus was seen on different occasions by certain men and women in his home country. Those who were called Apostles were convinced of the happening and believed that Jesus was a model human. Therefore, if God resurrected Jesus physically and/or spiritually, everlasting life was assured for those who possessed the apostolic faith.

The record of the alleged resurrection of Jesus has been scrutinized and weighed more thoroughly than any writing in world history. Some investigators have pointed out that some who saw visions may have been hallucinating, for hallucinations are sometimes triggered by acute grief. But even if a fraction of those resurrection witnesses are accepted as creditable, then an Easter happening of momentous significance occurred. On the basis of painstaking research, some open-minded scholars with impeccably rational credentials have judged the fundamental Christian claim to be true and have patterned their lives on that conviction. They have found the New Testament account categorically different from the reports of ancient witches or modern psychics.[17]

In our modern era some people are intensely curious about the possibility of souls living on after death, but they trust only what can be concluded from laboratory observations. In the past generation James Kidd was among those who had unbounded confidence in what could be submitted to the scientific method. Kidd left in his estate a generous bequest to stimulate research which would provide, in the words of his will, "some scientific proof of a soul of the human body." He believed it should be possible to photograph the soul as it left the body at death. Following Kidd's death, dozens of individuals and organizations filed petitions with a court in Arizona to obtain funding, but no plausible evidence has been presented.[18]

Thus far the results on experimental soul research have not been encouraging. In the nineteen-thirties Russian engineer Semyon Kirlian found that a dazzling photographic record could be obtained after introducing a small amount of high-frequency current into subjects. Some parapsychologists have interpreted the resulting "energy body" as an "aura" containing the subtle psychic essence which emanates from each person. However, Kirlian's photography, which shows white translucent vapor trailing off from subjects, may be nothing more than a phenomenon obtainable from any object that has been charged in a particular electrical manner.[19]

Patrick O'Donnell, an X-ray specialist in Chicago, claimed to have viewed "the flight of the vital spark" by watching a dying person through a glass which had been coated with certain chemicals. O'Donnell states:

> I tried the experiment on a dying man. He was rapidly sinking. Suddenly the attending physician announced that the man was dead.

The aura began to spread from the body and presently disappeared. Further observations of the corpse revealed no sign of the aura. We do not claim that the light is the soul or the spirit. In fact, no one seems to know what it is. In my opinion, however, it is some sort of radioactivity made visible by the use of the chemical screen. My experiments, however, seem to prove that it is the animating power or current of life of human beings."[20]

The assumption that the soul is a filmy matter which flies away at death also has been suggested by Western art. The Greeks and Romans sometimes portrayed heroes with light radiating from their heads. Following that adoration style, Christian artists depicted saints with halos. The Greeks also carried forward the Egyptian tradition of representing the soul as a small human-headed bird in flight. One Greek tomb object shows the psyche as a woman winging heavenward. Angels and fairies are still so represented in folk art. Thus it is understandable that some people envision the soul as a cherub.

Some experimenters have attempted to ascertain whether the soul is a measurable physical substance. Ernst Haeckel, a noted nineteenth-century scientist, assumed that anything real has mass. Hence, if there were a soul it should be a gas which can be caught in a test tube when it is "breathed out" at the moment of death. Then, by lowering the temperature of the gaseous stuff, "soul-snow" crystals should precipitate. After obtaining no results, Haeckel concluded that there is no immortality of the soul.[21]

Other scientists have claimed more success in finding soul mass. In Massachusetts, early in this century, five physicians constructed a delicate weighing device on which dying patients were placed. As soon as a patient's heart stopped beating, any change of weight was noted. They established to their satisfaction that the soul was a material thing because body weight decreased "from a half-ounce to an ounce when it flew away."[22]

Today no reputable scientist would be caught dead performing such experiments on the soul, possibly because a consensus has been reached that the soul is a nonentity and is no more worthy of serious study than the tooth fairy. Or scientists may have decided that the methods appropriate for examining physical substances are not germane for spiritual substances. Science can validly make judgments about objects with physical properties measurable by laboratory instruments. However, if the soul, like God, is an intangible reality, science is unable to perform any experiments either affirming or denying its existence.

Our earthbound imaginations pale at intuiting the nonsensory, thus limiting our understanding of both science and religion. Astronomer Carl Sagan observes that when scientists try to imagine extraterrestrial life, they often rely, quite mundanely, on forms already known.[23] In a parallel manner, we are often no more able to envisage what is beyond space and time than fetuses, living in fluid with closed eyelids, are able to imagine what it is like to smell stimulating aromas, see colorful sights, and savor tasty foods. Imagining antimatter in the nucleus of an atom or conceiving of fleshless selves among whom there is personal communication requires a radically different mode of thinking. The nature of the life after death, like the nature of the holy, suffering, loving God, transcends all conceptualizing.

NOTES

CHAPTER 1: FACING UP TO DEATH

1. Robert E. Kavanaugh, *Facing Death* (Los Angeles: Nash, 1972), p. 15.
2. Robert Fulton, "On the Dying of Death," in *Death and Dying: Challenge and Change*, ed. Robert Fulton (San Francisco: Boyd & Fraser, 1981), p. 13.
3. Geoffrey Gorer, *Death, Grief, and Mourning* (New York: Doubleday, 1965), pp. 195–196.
4. Lynne Anne DeSpelder and Albert Lee Strickland, *The Last Dance: Encountering Death and Dying* (Palo Alto: Mayfield, 1983), p. 19.
5. Judith Stillion and Hannelore Wass, "Children and Death," in *Dying: Facing the Facts*, ed. Hannelore Wass (New York: Hemisphere, 1979), p. 210.
6. Richard A. Kalish, "Dying and Preparing for Death: A View of Families," in *New Meanings of Death*, ed. Herman Feifel (New York: McGraw-Hill, 1977), p. 222.
7. David Hendin, *Death as a Fact of Life* (New York: Norton, 1974), p. 100.
8. Alan Harrington, *The Immortalist: An Approach to the Engineering of Man's Divinity* (New York: Random House, 1969), p. 3.
9. Kalish, "Dying and Preparing for Death," p. 217.

10. Dag Hammarskjöld, *Markings*, trans. Leif Sjöberg and W. H. Auden (New York: Knopf, 1965), p. 160.
11. George Santayana, "War Shrines," in *Soliloquies in England* (New York: Scribner's, 1924), pp. 98–99.

CHAPTER 2: DEFINING DEATH AND LIFE

1. Philostratus *Apollonius* (trans. Conybeare) 4.45.
2. David Wallechinsky and Amy Wallace, *The Book of Lists #3* (New York: Morrow, 1983), p. 427.
3. Philippe Ariès, *The Hour of Our Death*, trans. Helen Weaver (New York: Knopf, 1981), pp. 377–378.
4. "Real and Apparent Death," *The Lancet* 1 (29 Jan. 1887):233.
5. Hendin, *Death as a Fact of Life*, p. 23.
6. United Press International, *The Intermountain*, 5 Mar. 1966; 23 May 1980; 18 Apr. 1983.
7. John D. Arnold, Thomas Zimmerman, and Daniel Martin, "Public Attitudes and the Diagnosis of Death," *The Journal of the American Medical Association* 206(25 Nov. 1968):1954.
8. United Press International, *The Intermountain*, 10 Feb. 1984; 16 Dec. 1980.
9. Task Force on Death and Dying of the Institute of Society, Ethics, and the Life Sciences, "Refinements in Criteria for the Determination of Death: An Appraisal," *The Journal of the American Medical Association* 221(3 July 1972):46, 50–51.
10. "Defining Death," *Time*, 10 Mar. 1975, 76.
11. President's Commission for the Study of Ethical Problems in Medicine and Biomedical and Behavioral Research, *Defining Death: A Report on the Medical, Legal, and Ethical Issues in the Determination of Death* (Washington: Government Printing Office, 1980), p. 73.
12. United Press International, *The Charleston Gazette*, 6 Oct. 1985, sec. E.
13. Robert E. Field and Raymond J. Romanus, "A Patient's Story: The Struggle to Save a Life Already Lost," *The New York Times*, 23 Sept. 1984, sec. E.
14. Robert M. Veatch, *Death, Dying, and the Biological Revolution* (New Haven: Yale University, 1976), p. 76.
15. Claudia Wallis, "To Feed or Not to Feed," *Time*, 31 Mar. 1986, 60.
16. Raymond A. Moody, Jr., *Life After Life* (New York: Bantam, 1976), pp. 21–23.
17. Kenneth Ring, *Life at Death* (New York: Coward, McCann, and Geoghegan, 1980), pp. 45, 50.
18. United Press International, *The Charleston Gazette*, 6 Oct. 1985, sec. E.

19. Michael E. Sabom, *Recollections of Death: A Medical Investigation* (New York: Harper & Row, 1982), p. 57.
20. George Gallup, *Adventures in Immortality* (New York: McGraw-Hill, 1982), p. 32.
21. Charles Panati, "Is There Life After Death?" *Family Circle*, Nov. 1976, 84.
22. Sigmund Freud, "Thoughts for the Times on War and Death," in *The Complete Psychological Works of Sigmund Freud*, ed. James Strachey (London: Hogarth, 1952), 14. 289.
23. Dina Ingber, "Vision of an Afterlife," *Science Digest*, Jan. 1981, 95–97, 142.
24. Sabom, *Recollections of Death*, pp. 168–178.
25. Mark Silk, "How Different Religions View Abortion," *The Boston Globe*, 21 Oct. 1984.
26. Presbyterian Church in the U.S., *Minutes of the 113th General Assembly* (June 1973), p. 138.
27. Aquinas *On the Sentences* 3.3.5; *Summa Theologica* (trans. Fathers of the English Dominican Province; rev. Daniel J. Sullivan) 1.118.2; cf. Aristotle, *Politics* 1335b.24.
28. Joseph Donceel, "A Liberal Catholic's View," in *Death and Society*, ed. James Carse and Arlene Dallery (New York: Harcourt Brace Jovanovich, 1977), pp. 28, 30.
29. Testimony before the Judiciary Subcommittee, 20 May 1981, quoted in *The Intermountain*, 2 Sept. 1981.
30. Roe v. Wade, 410 U.S. 113 (1973).
31. Aeschylus *Eumenides*, lines 661–663.
32. Vern L. Bullough, *Sexual Variance in Society and History* (New York: Wiley, 1976), pp. 498, 545–548.
33. Martial *Epigrams* (trans. Ker) 9.41.
34. Richard Capel, *Tentations*, 2nd ed. (London: R.B. for John Bartlet, 1635), p. 355; see also William E. Phipps, "Masturbation: Vice or Virtue?" *Journal of Religion and Health* 16(1977):185.
35. Otto Friedrich, "A Legal, Moral, Social Nightmare," *Time*, 10 Sept. 1984, 55.
36. John J. Paris and Ronald E. Cranford, "Definition of Brain Death," *Theology Today* 40(Apr. 1983):9.
37. *The Charleston Gazette*, 5 July 1981.
38. Roe v. Wade, 410 U.S. 113 (1973).
39. Angela Roddey Holder, *Legal Issues in Pediatrics and Adolescent Medicine* (New York: Wiley, 1977), p. 113.

CHAPTER 3: LIFE EXPECTANCY AND AGING

1. Leonard Hayflick, "The Cell Biology of Human Aging," *Scientific American* 242(Jan. 1980):60.
2. Associated Press, *Daily News-Record*, Harrisonburg, Virginia, 21 June 1984.
3. Monroe Lerner, "When, Why, and Where People Die," in *Death and Society*, p. 444.
4. James B. Pritchard, ed., *Ancient Near Eastern Texts* (Princeton: Princeton University, 1955), p. 265.
5. DeSpelder and Strickland, *The Last Dance*, p. 9.
6. Lewis R. Aiken, *Dying, Death, and Bereavement* (Boston: Allyn & Bacon, 1984), pp. 10–15.
7. Ibid., pp. 42–43.
8. J. Lawrence Angel, "Ecology and Population in the Eastern Mediterranean," *World Archaeology* 4(June 1972):94–95.
9. "Life and Death," *The Washington Post*, 19 Jan. 1986, sec. A.
10. Estelle R. Ramey, "The Natural Capacity for Health in Women," in *Women: A Developmental Perspective*, ed. Phyllis W. Berman and Estelle R. Ramey (Bethesda: U.S. Dept. of Health and Human Services, 1982), p. 4.
11. *The Boston Globe*, 11 Apr. 1985.
12. Boston Women's Health Book Collective, *Our Bodies, Ourselves*, 2nd ed. (New York: Simon and Schuster, 1976), p. 335.
13. U.S. Bureau of the Census, *Statistical Abstract of the United States: 1985*, 105th ed. (Washington, D.C.: Government Printing Office, 1984), p. 75.
14. H. L. P. Resnik and L. H. Dizmang, "Suicidal Behavior Among American Indians," in *Death and Society*, p. 216.
15. "Sixty Minutes," 2 Feb. 1975.
16. "High Hoax," *Time*, 27 Mar. 1978, 87–88.
17. Durk Pearson and Sandy Shaw for the Laboratory for the Advancement of Bio-medical Research, *Life Extension: A Practical Scientific Approach* (New York: Warner, 1982), p. 615.
18. Alex Comfort, "The Life Span of Animals, *Scientific American* 205 (Aug. 1961):114.
19. *The New Encyclopaedia Britannica*, 15th ed., s.v. "life-span."
20. John Langone, *Death Is a Noun: A View of the End of Life* (Boston: Little, Brown, 1972), pp. 182–183.
21. Anastasia Toufexis, "Report from the Surgeon General," *Time*, 8 Mar. 1982, 72.
22. "Smoking: Bad News," *Newsweek*, 8 Mar. 1982, 89; United Press International report on The World Watch Institute, *The Charleston Gazette*, 12 Jan. 1986, sec. A.

23. Toufexis, "Report from the Surgeon General," p. 72.
24. *Parade*, 15 Apr. 1984.
25. Claudia Wallis, "Hold the Eggs and Butter," *Time*, 26 Mar. 1984, 56–58.
26. Philip Elmer-DeWitt, "Extra Years for Extra Effort," *Time*, 17 Mar. 1986, 66.
27. Pat Levak, "The Seat Belt—Why Aren't You Wearing It?" *The Motorist*, Mar./Apr. 1984, 14.
28. *The Boston Globe*, 16 Apr. 1985.
29. *Accident Facts* (Chicago: National Safety Council, 1985), p. 53.
30. Associated Press, *The Charleston Gazette*, 2 Mar. 1986, sec. A.
31. "Child-seat laws start to pay off," *Consumer Reports*, Apr. 1986, 210.
32. Editorial, *The Journal of the American Medical Association* 252(9 Nov. 1984):2613.
33. United Press International, *The Intermountain*, 12 Jan. 1983; Langone, *Death Is a Noun*, pp. 76–77.
34. "Socio-Feedback," *Time*, 16 Jan. 1978, 15.
35. *Inspiration and Wisdom from the Writings of Thomas Paine*, ed. Joseph Lewis (New York: Freethought Press, 1954), p. 103.
36. Harvey C. Lehman, "Optimum Ages for Eminent Leadership," *Scientific Monthly* 54(Feb. 1942):173–174.
37. Wilder Penfield, "Where Is Science Taking Us?" *Saturday Review*, 2 Sept. 1961, 44.
38. Ibid., p. 45.
39. Sylvia Porter, "Mandatory Retirement Costly in Resources," *The Atlanta Journal*, 9 Sept. 1961, sec. C.
40. Frank Trippett, "Looking Askance at Ageism," *Time*, 24 Mar. 1980, 88.

CHAPTER 4: THE DYING PATIENT

1. Elisabeth Kübler-Ross, *On Death and Dying* (New York: Macmillan, 1969), p. 34.
2. Elisabeth Kübler-Ross, "What Is It Like to Be Dying?" *American Journal of Nursing* 71(Jan. 1971):57.
3. Kübler-Ross, *On Death and Dying*, p. 74.
4. Ibid., p. 100.
5. Edwin S. Shneidman, *Deaths of Man* (New York: Quadrangle, 1973), pp. 6–7.
6. Edwin S. Shneidman, "Malignancy: Dialogues with Life-Threatening Illnesses," in *Death: Current Perspectives*, ed. Edwin S. Shneidman, 3rd ed. (Palo Alto: Mayfield, 1984), p. 199.
7. Robert Kastenbaum, "Do We Die in Stages?" in *Understanding Death*

and Dying: An Interdisciplinary Approach, ed. Sandra Galdier-Wilcox and Marilyn Sutton, 3rd ed.(Palo Alto: Mayfield, 1984), p. 131.

8. Elisabeth Kübler-Ross, "Facing Up to Death," *Today's Education* 61(Jan. 1972):31.

9. Liston O. Mills, "Pastoral Care of the Dying and Bereaved," in *Perspectives on Death,* ed. Liston O. Mills (Nashville: Abingdon, 1969), p. 256.

10. Elisabeth Kübler-Ross, *Questions and Answers on Death and Dying* (New York: Macmillan, 1974), pp. 136–137.

11. Dennis H. Novack et al., "Changes in Physicians' Attitudes Toward Telling the Cancer Patient," *The Journal of the American Medical Association* 241(2 Mar. 1979):898.

12. Robert Kastenbaum and Ruth Aisenberg, *The Psychology of Death* (New York: Springer, 1972), p. 216.

13. Ibid., p. 222.

14. Kavanaugh, *Facing Death,* p. 6.

15. Glen W. Davidson, "Hospice Care for the Dying," in *Dying,* p. 170.

16. The $250,000 award was made in London.

17. Claire F. Ryder and Diane M. Ross, "Terminal Care: Issues and Alternatives," in *Death and Dying,* p. 170.

18. Ibid., p. 171.

19. Cicely Saunders, "St. Christopher's Hospice," in *Death: Current Perspectives,* pp. 270–271.

20. Virginia H. Hine, "Dying at Home: Can Families Cope?" *Omega* 10(1979–1980):175.

21. Donald McCarthy, "The Hospice Movement," *Theology Today* 38(Apr. 1981):76–77.

22. Ibid., p. 74.

23. David Dempsey, *The Way We Die* (New York: Macmillan, 1975), pp. 110–111; *USA Today,* 3 Jan. 1984.

24. Ernest Jones, *The Life and Work of Sigmund Freud,* vol. 3 (New York: Basic, 1957), p. 245.

25. Andrew H. Malcolm, "A.M.A. Rule: Step Toward a Social Policy on Dying," *The New York Times,* 17 Mar. 1986, sec. B.

26. *Concern for Dying Newsletter* (Fall 1984):6.

27. William A. Nolen, *The Making of a Surgeon* (New York: Random House, 1968), pp. 256–257.

28. Holder, *Legal Issues in Pediatrics and Adolescent Medicine,* p. 108.

29. *Concern for Dying Newsletter* (Spring 1985):2.

30. John Paul II, "Declaration on Euthanasia," 5 May 1980.

31. S. H. Imbus and B. E. Zawacki, "Autonomy for Burned Patients When Survival Is Unprecedented," *New England Journal of Medicine* 297 (11 Aug. 1977): 308–311.

32. John Sherrill, "A Whisper of Eternity," *Creative Help for Daily Living,*

July 1983, pp. 27–35. Excerpted from John Sherrill, *Mother's Song* (Old Tappan: Revell, 1982). Used by permission.

33. Langone, *Death Is a Noun,* p. 82.

CHAPTER 5: SUICIDE

1. Shneidman, *Deaths of Man,* pp. 33, 91, 123.
2. Modification by James M. Eddy and Wesley F. Alles, *Death Education* (St. Louis: Mosby, 1983), p. 164.
3. John Leo, "Could Suicide Be Contagious?" *Time,* 24 Feb. 1986, 59.
4. Herbert Hendin, *Suicide in America* (New York: Norton, 1982), pp. 59–60.
5. Langone, *Death Is a Noun,* p. 157.
6. *Statistical Abstracts of the United States: 1985,* p. 79.
7. Jack C. Horn, "Dignified Leap," *Psychology Today,* Apr. 1983, 88.
8. Robert J. Kastenbaum, *Death, Society, and Human Experience* (St. Louis: Mosby, 1977), p. 294.
9. Frederick Lemere, "What Happens to Alcoholics," *American Journal of Psychiatry* 109(1953):5; Herbert Hendin, *Suicide in America,* p. 125.
10. "Suicide Belt," *Time,* 1 Sept. 1980, 56.
11. Mathew Ross, "Suicide Among Physicians," in *Death and Society,* pp. 203–213.
12. *Encyclopaedia of Religion and Ethics,* 1st ed., s.v. "suicide (Muhammadan)."
13. "Suicide—International Comparisons," in *Death and Society,* p. 198.
14. Augustine *City of God* (trans. Dods) 1.25–26.
15. Aquinas *Summa Theologica* 2.2.64.5.
16. A. Alvarez, "The Background," in *Suicide: The Philosophical Issues,* ed. M. Pabst Battin and David Mayo (New York: St. Martin's, 1980), p. 12.
17. Emile Durkheim, *Suicide,* trans. John A. Spaulding and George Simpson (New York: Free Press of Glencoe, 1951), p. 16.
18. *The National Observer,* 21 Dec. 1974.
19. Plato *Phaedo* (trans. Jowett) 68.
20. Kastenbaum, *Death, Society, and Human Experience,* p. 279.
21. *Parade,* 15 Apr. 1985.
22. A. E. Hotchner, *Papa Hemingway* (New York: Random House, 1966), p. 228.
23. Herbert Hendin, *Suicide in America,* pp. 50–51.
24. Sigmund Freud, *The Ego and the Id,* in *The Complete Works,* 19. 53.
25. Karl Menninger, *Man Against Himself* (New York: Harcourt Brace Jovanovich, 1981), pp. 35–36.
26. Michael R. Leming and George E. Dickinson, *Understanding Death,*

   Dying, and Bereavement (New York: Holt, Rinehart and Winston, 1985), p. 290.
27. "Campus Concern," *Time*, 29 Oct. 1984, 78.
28. *Encyclopaedia Britannica*, 14th ed., s.v. "Suicide."
29. Durkheim, *Suicide*, pp. 21–22.
30. A. Venkoba Rao, "Suicide in India," in *Suicide in Different Cultures*, ed. Norman L. Farberow (Baltimore: University Park, 1975), p. 233.
31. Mamoru Iga and Kichinosuke Tatai, "Characteristics of Suicides and Attitudes Toward Suicide in Japan," in *Suicide in Different Cultures*, pp. 258–259.
32. Russell Spurr, *A Glorious Way to Die*, quotation taken from Clay Blair, "Sink the Yamato!" a review of *A Glorious Way to Die*. *The Washington Post*, 22 Nov. 1981, *Book World*.
33. Durkheim, *Suicide*, p. 131.
34. "'Hurry, My Children, Hurry,'" *Time*, 26 Mar. 1979, 27–28.
35. *Encyclopaedia Britannica*, 14th ed., s.v. "suicide."
36. Kastenbaum, *Death, Society, and Human Experience*, pp. 288–290.
37. DeSpelder and Strickland, *The Last Dance*, p. 206.
38. Friedrich Nietzsche *Beyond Good and Evil* (trans. Kaufman) 4.157.
39. Friedrich Nietzsche *Twilight of the Gods* (trans. Kaufman) 36.
40. Donahue Transcript No. 5200, 20 May 1980, p. 4.
41. Jacques Choron, *Suicide* (New York: Scribner's, 1972), p. 96.
42. Max Delbrück, "Education for Suicide," *Prism* 2(Nov. 1974):19, 50.
43. "Suicide for the Terminally Ill: A Need for New Thinking," *Concern for Dying Newsletter* (Fall 1980):4.
44. Lawrence Maloney, "A New Understanding About Death," *U.S. News & World Report*, 11 July 1983, 63.
45. M. Pabst Battin, "Suicide: A Fundamental Human Right?" in *Suicide: The Philosophical Issues*, p. 268.
46. Alvarez, "The Background," p. 27.
47. Eusebius, *Church History* 8.12; William E. Phipps, "Christian Perspectives on Suicide," *The Christian Century* 102(30 Oct. 1985):970.
48. "Suicide: Is It an Acceptable Alternative for the Terminally Ill?" *Concern for Dying Newsletter* (Fall 1981):4.
49. John Donne, *Biathanatos* [1608?], in *The Complete Poetry and Selected Prose of John Donne*, ed. Charles M. Coffin (New York: Modern Library, 1952), p. 303.
50. Dietrich Bonhoeffer, *Ethics,* trans. Neville Horton Smith (New York: Macmillan, 1965), pp. 168, 170.
51. William F. Buckley, Jr., "Death of a Christian," *The Reader's Digest*, Sept. 1976, 32. Condensed from *Execution Eye—and other Contemporary Ballads* (New York: Putnam,1976).
52. Linnea Pearson and Ruth Purtilo, *Separate Paths: Why People End*

Their Lives (New York: Harper & Row, 1977), pp. 134–135. "Good Death," *Time*, 10 Mar. 1975, 83–84.

53. The Presbytery of New York City, "Pastoral Letter on Euthanasia and Suicide," 9 Mar. 1976, p. 3.

CHAPTER 6: VIOLENCE AND DEATH

1. Nikki Meredith, "The Murder Epidemic," *Science 84*, Dec. 1984, 43.
2. Ibid., p. 44.
3. Joseph Henry Jackson, Preface to *The San Francisco Murders*, ed. Joseph Henry Jackson (New York: Duell, Sloan and Pearce, 1947), pp. 2–3.
4. "Drunk Driving," *Facts on File 1984* (New York: Facts on File, 1985), p. 524B.
5. Bob Haeseler, "Mother's Rage at Killer in Oakland Court," *The San Francisco Chronicle*, 17 Aug. 1984, sec. A.
6. Ibid.
7. "Dear TIME: A Look at 1983 Letters," *Time*, 12 Mar. 1984, 13.
8. Associated Press Survey, *The Boston Globe*, 30 Jan. 1985.
9. "Effective Warnings," *Time*, 30 Jan. 1984, 24.
10. *The Boston Globe*, 13 Apr. 1985; *The Charleston Gazette*, 23 Feb. 1986, sec. A.
11. Hugo Adam Bedau, "Recidivism, Parole, and Deterrence," in *The Death Penalty in America*, ed. Hugo Adam Bedau, 3rd ed.(New York: Oxford University, 1982), p. 177.
12. Reported from the *Congressional Record*, 8 Feb. 1984, in "Mistakes and the Death Penalty," *Harper's Magazine*, July 1984, 18.
13. U.S. Department of Justice, *Capital Punishment* (Washington: Government Printing Office, 1981), p. 9.
14. "Arguing About Death for Rape," *Time*, 11 Apr. 1977, 80; Karl Anderson, "An Eye for an Eye," *Time*, 24 Jan. 1983, 30.
15. Associated Press, *The Boston Globe*, 29 Jan. 1985.
16. James Webb, "What We Can Learn from Japan's Prisons," *Parade*, 15 Jan. 1984, 7.
17. Meredith, "The Murder Epidemic," p. 45.
18. Ibid., p. 47.
19. Gay Pauley, "Drawing a Bead on Gun Control," *The Charleston Gazette*, 27 June 1982.
20. United Press International, *The Intermountain*, 12 Apr. 1980; see also L. Harold DeWolf, "The Death Penalty: Not a Remedy but a Symptom," *The Christian Century* 97(30 Jan. 1980):93.
21. Edward S. Corwin and J. W. Peltason, *Understanding the Constitution*, 4th ed.(New York: Holt, Rinehart & Winston, 1967), p. 115; Irving

Brant, *The Bill of Rights: Its Origin and Meaning* (New York: Bobbs-Merrill, 1965), p. 486.

22. *The Charleston Gazette,* 27 Jun. 1982.
23. Pete Shields with John Greenya, *Guns Don't Die—People Do* (New York: Arbor House, 1981), pp. 73–76.
24. "NRA Leadership Battle Divides Membership," *Washington Reports on Medicine and Health* 37(June 1983):5–6.
25. Sigmund Freud, *The Interpretation of Dreams,* in *The Complete Works,* 5. 356.
26. U.S. Department of Justice, *Uniform Crime Reports: Crime in the United States* (Washington: Government Printing Office, 1984), p. 10.
27. Pete Earley, "The Gun Dealer," *The Washington Post,* 8 Mar. 1981, sec. A.
28. *USA Today,* 4 Apr. 1984.
29. Shields, *Guns Don't Die,* p. 88.
30. Arnold Toynbee, "Death in War," in *Death and Dying,* p. 366.
31. Roland H. Bainton, *Christian Attitudes Toward War and Peace* (Nashville: Abingdon, 1960), pp. 66–68.
32. "Acts of Martyrs," *Bulletin of Fordham University* (July 1968):24–25.
33. "Augustine," in *War and Christian Ethics,* ed. Arthur F. Holmes (Grand Rapids: Baker Book House, 1975), pp. 61–83; Ralph B. Potter, Jr., "The Moral Logic of War," *McCormick Quarterly* 23(May 1970):209–210.
34. Encyclical Letter of John XXIII, "Pacem in Terris" (London: Catholic Truth Society, 1963), pp. 3, 46.
35. "Reagan Adamant on Space Defense Even After Talks," *The New York Times,* 12 Feb. 1985, sec. A.
36. William James, "The Moral Equivalent of War," in *Essays on Faith and Morals* (1910; New York: Longmans, Green, 1949), pp. 311–328.
37. Ibid.
38. George Santayana, *Reason in Common Sense,* vol. 1 of *The Life of Reason,* 2nd. ed. (New York: Scribner's, 1932), p. 284.

CHAPTER 7: BODY DISPOSAL

1. Ann Warren Turner, *Houses for the Dead* (New York: David McKay, 1976), pp. 8–9.
2. Herodotus *Histories* (trans. deSelincourt) 2.85–90.
3. James Hamilton-Paterson and Carol Andrews, *Mummies: Death and Life in Ancient Egypt* (New York: Viking, 1979), pp. 36, 47–53.
4. Christiane Desroches-Noblecourt, *Tutankhamen* (London: George Rainbird, 1963), p. 221.
5. Michael Davison, *The Splendors of Egypt* (New York: Crown, 1979), p. 92.

6. Pliny *Natural History* (trans. Eichholz) 36.27.
7. Athanasius *Life of Antony* 90–91.
8. Thomas Greenhill, *The Art of Embalming* (London: Privately printed, 1705), pp. 4–5.
9. James J. Farrell, *Inventing the American Way of Death, 1830–1920* (Philadelphia: Temple University, 1980), pp. 157–158.
10. Henry Tuckerman, "The Law of Burial and the Sentiment of the Dead," *The Christian Examiner and Religious Miscellany* 61(Nov. 1856):345.
11. Robert W. Habenstein and William M. Lamers, *The History of American Funeral Directing* (Milwaukee: Bulfin Printers for the National Funeral Directors Association of the United States, Inc., 1962), pp. 323–325.
12. Charles Hamilton and Lloyd Ostendorf, *Lincoln in Photographs: An Album of Every Known Pose* (Norman: University of Oklahoma, 1963), p. 234.
13. Farrell, *Inventing the American Way of Death*, p. 148.
14. Ibid., p. 174.
15. Ibid., p. 161.
16. Ruth Mulvey Harmer, *The High Cost of Dying* (New York: Crowell-Collier, 1963), pp. 110–116, 134.
17. Jessica Mitford, *The American Way of Death* (New York: Simon & Schuster, 1963), p. 128.
18. Harmer, *The High Cost of Dying*, pp. 111–112.
19. Thomas Jefferson, Letter to John W. Eppes, 24 June 1813, in *The Writings of Thomas Jefferson*, vol. 13, ed. Andrew A. Lipscomb and A. E. Bergh (Washington: Under the auspices of the Thomas Jefferson Memorial Association, 1904), p. 272.
20. David Hendin, *Death as a Fact of Life*, p. 209.
21. Ibid., pp. 213–215.
22. Michelle Slatalla, "Finding Room for the Dead," *Newsday*, 6 Aug. 1984, sec. B.
23. Thorstein Veblen, *The Theory of the Leisure Class* (New York: Huebsch, 1899), p. 74.
24. *The Pittsburgh Press*, 24 June 1984.
25. Vanderlyn R. Pine, *Caretaker of the Dead* (New York: Irvington, 1975), p. 94.
26. "New Light on Jewish Catacombs," *Time*, 23 May 1977, 75.
27. Tacitus *Histories* (trans. Jackson) 5.5.
28. *Corpus Juris Canonici* 1203. 1.
29. *Instructio: De cadaverum crematione*, 5 July 1963.
30. Hannelore Wass et al., "Similarities and Dissimilarities in Attitudes Toward Death in a Population of Older Persons," *Omega* 9(1978–1979):337–354.

31. "Cremation Changing the Burial Industry," *The Washington Post*, 24 June 1984, sec. A.
32. Turner, *Houses for the Dead*, pp. 57–63.
33. Ibid., pp. 80–84.
34. Richard E. Leakey and Roger Lewin, *Origins* (New York: E. P. Dutton, 1977), pp. 220–221.
35. R. C. Ettinger, *Man into Superman* (New York: St. Martin's, 1972), p. 257; Pearson and Shaw, *Life Extension*, p. 609.
36. United Press International, *The Intermountain*, 4 Feb. 1985.
37. "The Rip Van Winkle Wrinkle," *Time*, 22 June 1981, 71.
38. United Press International, *The Intermountain*, 14 Feb. 1985.
39. The Living Bank, Box 6725, Houston, TX 77265.
40. "Dear Abby," *The Intermountain*, 23 July 1980.
41. Habenstein and Lamers, *The History of American Funeral Directing*, pp. 3–50.

CHAPTER 8: GRIEF AND BEREAVEMENT

1. Edgar N. Jackson, "Grief," in *Concerning Death: A Practical Guide for the Living*, ed. Earl A. Grollman (Boston: Beacon, 1974), pp. 5–6.
2. Erich Lindemann, "Symptomatology and Management of Acute Grief," in *Understanding Death and Dying*, p. 178.
3. Robert Fulton, "Death and the Funeral in Contemporary Society," in *Dying*, p. 241.
4. C. S. Lewis, *A Grief Observed* (New York: Seabury, 1961), pp. 7–14.
5. Lily Pincus, "The Process of Mourning and Grief," in *Death*, p. 406.
6. Eddy and Alles, *Death Education*, p. 94.
7. Colin Murray Parkes, *Bereavement* (New York: International Universities, 1972), pp. 16–17.
8. W. Dewi Dees and Sylvia G. Lutkins, "Mortality of Bereavement," *British Medical Journal* 4(7 Oct. 1967):15.
9. Ralph H. Redding, "Physiology of Dying," in *Dying*, p. 99.
10. Edgar N. Jackson, "Bereavement and Grief," in *Dying*, p. 267.
11. Arnold Toynbee et al., *Man's Concern with Death* (New York: McGraw-Hill, 1969), p. 271.
12. Parkes, *Bereavement*, p. 62.
13. Ibid., p. 130.
14. Richard A. Kalish, *Death, Grief, and Caring Relationships* (Monterey: Brooks/Cole, 1981), p. 246.
15. Kastenbaum, *Death, Society, and Human Experience*, p. 2.
16. Frances Ilg and Louise Bates Ames, *Parents Ask* (New York: Harper & Brothers, 1962), pp. 362–363.
17. Earl A. Grollman, "Children and Death," in *Concerning Death*, p. 76.

18. Mervyn Shoor quoted in Edgar N. Jackson, "Bereavement and Grief," in *Dying*, p. 262.
19. Felix Brown, "Depression and Childhood Bereavement," *The Journal of Mental Science* 107(1961):769.
20. Herbert Hendin, *Suicide in America*, p. 40.
21. Dempsey, *The Way We Die*, p. 160.
22. Seneca "On the Happy Life " in *Epistulae* (trans. Gummere) 92.
23. Edwin Shneidman, "You and Death," *Psychology Today*, June 1971, 79–80.
24. "California Attitude Toward Death and Funerals," *American Funeral Director* (Nov. 1978):27.
25. Kastenbaum, *Death, Society, and Human Experience*, p. 249.
26. M. Betsy Bergen and Robert R. Williams, "Alternative Funerals: An Exploratory Study," *Omega* 12(1981–1982):75.
27. William E. Phipps, *Paul Against Supernaturalism* (New York: Philosophical Library, 1986), pp. 74–83.
28. Geoffrey Rowell, *The Liturgy of Christian Burial* (London: Alcuin Club Collections/S.P.C.K., 1977), pp. 9, 23.
29. *The Book of Order*, 1983–1985 (New York: The Offices of the General Assembly of the Presbyterian Church (U.S.A.), 1981), S.5.0500.
30. Eddy and Alles, *Death Education*, p. 214.
31. Edgar N. Jackson, "Bereavement and Grief," p. 272.
32. Gorer, *Death, Grief, and Mourning*, pp. 134–135.
33. David Hendin, *Death as a Fact of Life*, p. 179.
34. Ibid., p. 178.
35. "Funerals: The memorial-society alternative," *Consumer Reports*, Aug. 1979, 490.
36. Leming and Dickinson, *Understanding Death*, p. 247.

CHAPTER 9: LIFE AFTER DEATH

1. John Lewis, *The Life and Teachings of Karl Marx* (New York: International, 1965), p. 273.
2. R. H. Charles, *Eschatology* (1899; New York: Schocken, 1963), p. 444.
3. Plato *Republic* 10.614–621; *Phaedrus* 248–249.
4. C. J. Ducasse, *A Critical Examination of Belief in a Life After Death* (New York: Charles C. Thomas, 1961), pp. 276–299.
5. Robert A. Baker, "The Effect of Suggestion on Past-Lives Regression," *American Journal of Clinical Hypnosis* 25(July 1982):74.
6. George Kuykendall, "Care for the Dying: A Kübler-Ross Critique," *Theology Today* 38(Apr. 1981):44.
7. Geoffrey Parrinder, *African Traditional Religion* (London: Hutchinson House, 1954) pp. 138–139.

8. R. C. Zaehner, *The Dawn and Twilight of Zoroastrianism* (New York: George Putnam's, 1961), pp. 302–308; and *Zurvan: A Zoroastrian Dilemma* (Oxford: Clarendon, 1955), p. 199.

9. Aquinas *Summa Theologica* 3.69.2.

10. James Breig, "Beyond the Pearly Gates: What *U.S. Catholic* readers believe about the afterlife," *U.S. Catholic* 48(May 1983):14–15.

11. Kenneth J. Foreman, "Which Way Is Hell? Satan, Sartre, and the Scriptures," *The Presbyterian Outlook* (29 Sept. 1958):9.

12. Paul Tillich, *The Dynamics of Faith* (New York: Harper & Row, 1957), pp. 42–43.

13. Karl Jaspers, *Death to Life* (Chicago: Argus Communications, 1963), p. 34.

14. Laertius, *Lives of the Philosophers* 10.24; Lucretius, *On the Nature of Things* 3.805.

15. James A. Pike, *The Other Side* (New York: Doubleday, 1968).

16. Allen Spraggett, *Arthur Ford: The Man Who Talked with the Dead* (New York: New American Library, 1974), pp. 255–262.

17. See, for example, G. Ernest Wright and Reginald H. Fuller, *The Book of the Acts of God* (New York: Doubleday, 1957), pp. 305, 359; Hans Küng, *On Being a Christian*, trans. Edward Quinn (New York: Doubleday, 1984), pp. 381–382.

18. James Lee Christian, *Philosophy: An Introduction to the Art of Wondering* (New York: Holt, Rinehart & Winston, 1986), p. 545.

19. "Boom Times on the Psychic Frontier," *Time*, 4 Mar. 1974, 70.

20. Langone, *Death Is a Noun*, p. 213.

21. Ernst Haeckel, *The Riddle of the Universe* (New York: Harper & Brothers, 1900), pp. 201, 210.

22. Langone, *Death Is a Noun*, pp. 208–209.

23. Carl Sagan, *Cosmos* (New York: Random House, 1980), p. 40.

APPENDICES

A.1: DEATH PROBE

The study of death is more meaningful if information about dying is related to your own perceptions and dilemmas. The inquiries that follow should assist you in uncovering viewpoints that you may have suppressed. After thinking through the various death-related issues, it would be cathartic to share your responses with others.

1. What is death? Is it a bad thing or a good thing? Why?
2. With several fresh similes, complete the following: "Dying is like. . . ."
3. At what age were you first aware of death? Describe that first experience.
4. Have you ever experienced a "brush with death"? If so, what stands out from that event?

5. Can you imagine your own death? If you had a choice, what kind of death would you prefer and at what age?
6. Have you thought of a particular illness or accident in connection with your own death? If so, why?
7. Have you discussed dying and death with your family? With others? Tell about some views they have shared with you.
8. If you have ever been in a funeral home or at a funeral elsewhere, describe what you saw, heard, smelled, and touched.
9. Have you ever had the urge to kill yourself or someone else? If so, what motivated the urge(s)?
10. Should one have the right to take his or her own life? If so, specify the circumstances.
11. Do you fear dying? Discuss.
12. Under what circumstances, if any, would you be willing to give up your life?
13. To what extent do you think psychological factors can influence, or even cause, death?
14. Do you think science can one day make humans immortal or nearly so? What problems might arise if the human life span were extended for centuries?
15. Would you want your physician to tell you if you had a terminal illness? Why or why not?
16. Under what conditions, if any, should a person not be kept alive?
17. If you were told you were terminally ill with less than a year to live, how would you want to spend your time?
18. Do you plan to write a will for yourself? Why, or why not?
19. What writings, films, or music have influenced your thoughts about death?
20. What are qualities that make life worth living?
21. Some think a person's last words contain sentiments that give valuable clues to understanding the person. What would you like your last words to be if you were to die in the near future?
22. Write your own eulogy as you would like it to be.
23. What guidance does your religion, if you have any, give on how you should face death? If you are not religious, what guidance is available?
24. What do you think the word *soul* means? Do you think you have one?

25. What do you believe happens to your "self" at death?
26. Do you hope for life after death? What do you think that life might be like?
27. Do you think you are punished for your sins either in this life or in a life after death? If so, by what means?
28. What bearing does your religious belief, or lack thereof, have on your outlook on life after death?
29. What do you think of reincarnation, that is, of the notion that persons return to this physical life in another form after death?
30. Have you ever had evidence of immortality in visions or in out-of-body experiences? If so, specify.
31. Under what conditions, if any, would you favor courts giving the death penalty?
32. Under what conditions, if any, would you favor your nation declaring war?
33. Under what conditions, if any, would you favor abortion?
34. Do you think most people are honest in their statements about death? Discuss.
35. If you have grieved over the loss of a person or a pet, did the experience make you weaker or stronger? Explain.
36. Death can be approached personally or impersonally and emotionally or intellectually. What approach or combination of approaches do you think is best for a study of death? Why?
37. What question about death would you most like to have answered?
38. Add any other remarks regarding dying and death which you feel may be interesting or informative.

A.2: AFTERLIFE SURVEY

Here are a variety of ideas that people have had on life after death. How likely do you feel each possibility is? Circle one X for each phrase.

	Very likely	Some-what likely	Not likely
1. A perpetual, peaceful sleep	X	X	X
2. An opportunity for moral development	X	X	X
3. A life like the one now, only better	X	X	X
4. A life without many things which make our present life enjoyable	X	X	X
5. A life without troubles	X	X	X
6. A shadowy form of life, hardly life at all	X	X	X
7. A spiritual life, involving mind but not body	X	X	X
8. A paradise of pleasures and delights	X	X	X
9. A place of intellectual stimulation	X	X	X
10. Communion with God	X	X	X
11. Absorption into divine reality	X	X	X
12. Reunion with loved ones	X	X	X
13. A spirit roaming the earth	X	X	X
14. A spirit reincarnation in another body	X	X	X
15. A consciousness without communication	X	X	X
16. A place of reward or punishment	X	X	X
17. A higher level of consciousness	X	X	X
18. An angel in heaven	X	X	X
19. No life at all, nothing	X	X	X
20. (other) _____			

A.3: DEATH IN THE BIBLE

1. What did the writer of the second and third chapters of Genesis believe about the origin of death? Judging from 3:4–6 and 5:5, what meaning does death have in 2:17? Explain why the human is called "dust" (2:7; 3:19).

2. What idea found in Genesis 4:8–11 is also contained in ghost tales?

3. What strange death data are contained in Genesis 5? How does Enoch differ from the others (see Heb. 11:5)? How does the life span of the pre-flood people differ from what is stated in Genesis 6:3 and in Psalm 90:10?

4. How and why did Joseph have his daddy made into a mummy (Gen. 50:1–6)? Compare that Egyptian practice with the customary Jewish practice described in John 19:38–41.

5. What is stated regarding the deaths of Moses and Elijah (Deut. 34:1–6; 2 Kings 2:4–14)? Do you know any songs that are based on these legends?

6. Regarding the story of Samson's self-inflicted death in Judges 16:23–30, what case can you make that the writer thought it to be one or more of the following: a) heroic; b) cowardly; c) appropriate for the situation; d) disapproved by God; e) morally neutral. Make the same analysis for two more suicides: Saul (1 Sam. 31:1–7) and Judas (Matt. 27:1–5).

7. Judging from 1 Samuel 28:3–20 and Deuteronomy 18:9–14, what was the general biblical outlook on attempting to consult with the dead, a practice called necromancy?

8. Read Job 14:1–14 and Ecclesiastes 3:19–22 to discover the view of death contained there.

9. To what extent do you agree with the poem on time in Ecclesiastes 3:1–8?

10. In Ezekiel 37:1–14, what is portrayed in a dramatic way? Was the prophet referring to individuals in another realm or to his nation Israel which had been destroyed?

11. Examine the usage of the term *hell* in Matthew 5:22–30 and try

to determine its meaning. Get a definition of *Gehenna* and relate it to Jeremiah 7:31 and 32:35.

12. What did Jesus say about death observances (Matt. 8:22; 23:29–31)?

13. What view of the hereafter is found in Luke 16:19–31? Did Jesus think that witnessing a miraculous resurrection would cause a person to live in a more responsible manner?

14. How did Jesus respond in Luke 20:27–38 to the question of those who were skeptical of a hereafter? Compare his reply to 1 Corinthians 2:9.

15. What is meant by *life* and *death* in John 5:24 and 10:10; 11:25–26? What does the verbal tense indicate regarding when "eternal life" begins?

16. Study, in John 20, Mary Magdalene's experience some time after Jesus' crucifixion. Do you think this was entirely a subjective phenomenon, triggered by grief over the tragic death of the man she loved? Or do you think it was an objective phenomenon that could have been recorded with a camera, had such an instrument been available then? Or do you have some other explanation?

17. What view of death and life after death does Paul express in Romans 6:4–11, 2 Corinthians 4:16—5:1, and in Colossians 3:1–3?

18. What convictions did the writer of the last two chapters of the Christian Bible have regarding death and the hereafter? How does Revelation 22:2 relate to Genesis 2:9 and 3:22?

A.4: SUICIDE ISSUES

Your simple yes and no answers to the following questions can provide a personal dimension to the investigation of a complex topic. Before reading what suicidologists have written, jot down your present opinions on suicide. After your study, return to these questions to see if your mind has changed

1. Is suicide usually a sign of insanity?
2. Is there a moral difference between suicide to escape a miserable death and suicide to escape a miserable life?
3. Is suicide morally acceptable as a way to resolve great emotional problems?
4. If the taboo against thinking about suicide is replaced by rational consideration, will the suicide rate rise?
5. Is suicide morally acceptable as a way for the aged and the disabled to end their lives?
6. Should a terminally ill person be assisted in suicide, if requested?
7. Should a terminally ill person be criticized for attempting suicide?
8. Should a terminally ill person commit suicide if a family member objects?
9. Should our nation establish centers where people can obtain information on painless and reliable methods for committing suicide?
10. Should manuals be permitted to circulate freely which give directions on how to destroy one's life?
11. Should people be given access to lethal drugs if they choose to end their lives?
12. Should a terminally ill person be permitted to refuse food and medication?
13. Should persons be encouraged to sacrifice themselves to save the lives of other persons?

B. Death Preplanning

B.1: INDIVIDUAL LIFE EXPECTANCY

The following method for calculating longevity is similar to the ones some life insurance companies use. It not only points to the inevitability of dying but identifies specific ways of increasing one's chances for living longer.

The base number of years for computing life span in the United States: <u>75</u>

If you are male, subtract 4; if you are female, add 4:   ___

If you plan to live in an urban area for most of your life, subtract 2; if a town or a rural area is planned, add 2:   ___

If you anticipate having a desk job for most of your life, subtract 3; if the work requires regular physical labor, add 3; if you anticipate working after 65, add 3:   ___

If you anticipate earning over $50,000 or under $10,000 a year, subtract 2:   ___

If you exercise vigorously several times weekly, add 3:   ___

If you anticipate living with a spouse or friend for most of your life, add 4; if not, subtract 1 for every decade alone after reaching age 30:   ___

If you are an extrovert, enjoying the society of others, add 2; if you are an introvert, preferring to be by yourself, subtract 2:   ___

If you are intense, aggressive, and easily angered, subtract 3; if you are relaxed, easygoing, and worry little, add 3:   ___

If you have been given a ticket for speeding in recent years, subtract 2; if you regularly wear a seat belt while traveling, add 2:   ___

If you anticipate finishing, or have finished, college, add 1; for a graduate degree, add 2:   ___

If any grandparent lived to 85, add 2; if all four grandparents lived to 75, or are now living, add 3:   ___

If either parent died of heart failure before 50, subtract 5; if any parent, brother, or sister under 50 has (or had) a heart condition, or has diabetes, subtract 3:   —

If you get intoxicated at least once a month, subtract 2; if a chronic alcoholic, subtract 8:   —

If you are overweight by more than 50 lbs., subtract 8; by 30–50 lbs., subtract 4; by 10–30, subtract 2:   —

If you smoke more than 2 packs a day, subtract 8; 1 or 2 packs, subtract 6; ½ to 1, subtract 3:   —

If you are over 30 make this adjustment: 31–40, add 2; 41–50, add 3; 51–70, add 4; over 70, add 5.   —

B.2: A LIVING WILL

To My Family, My Physician, My Lawyer and All Others Whom It May Concern

Death is as much a reality as birth, growth, maturity and old age—it is the one certainty of life. If the time comes when I can no longer take part in decisions for my own future, let this statement stand as an expression of my wishes and directions, while I am still of sound mind.

If at such a time the situation should arise in which there is no reasonable expectation of my recovery from extreme physical or mental disability, I direct that I be allowed to die and not be kept alive by medications, artificial means or "heroic measures". I do, however, ask that medication be mercifully administered to me to alleviate suffering even though this may shorten my remaining life.

This statement is made after careful consideration and is in accordance with my strong convictions and beliefs. I want the wishes and directions here expressed carried out to the extent permitted by law. Insofar as they are not legally enforceable, I hope that those to whom this Will is addressed will regard themselves as morally bound by these provisions.

(Optional specific provisions to be made in this space)

DURABLE POWER OF ATTORNEY (optional)

I hereby designate _____ to serve as my attorney-in-fact for the purpose of making medical treatment decisions. This power of attorney shall remain effective in the event that I become incompetent or otherwise unable to make such decisions for myself.

Optional Notarization:	Signed _____
"Sworn and subscribed	Date _____
to before me this_____	Witness _____
day of _____, 19_____."	Witness _____

_____
    Notary Public
    (seal)

Copies of this request have been given to _____

_____ _____

(*Optional*) My Living Will is registered with Concern for Dying
(No. _____)
This form is reprinted with permission of Concern for Dying, 250 West
57th Street, Suite 831, New York, NY 10107 (212) 246-6962.

To make best use of your living will you may wish to add specific statements in the space provided for that purpose above your signature. Possible
additional provisions are:

1. "Measures of artificial life-support in the face of impending death that I
   specifically refuse are:
   a) Electrical or mechanical resuscitation of my heart when it has stopped
   beating.
   b) Nasogastric tube feeding when I am paralyzed or unable to take nourishment by mouth.
   c) Mechanical respiration when I am no longer able to sustain my own
   breathing.
   d) _____ "
2. "I would like to live out my last days at home rather than in a hospital if
   it does not jeopardize the chance of my recovery to a meaningful and
   sentient life or does not impose an undue burden on my family."
3. "If any of my tissues are sound and would be of value as transplants to
   other people, I freely give my permission for such donation."

B.3: LAST WILL AND TESTAMENT FORM*

I, _____, a resident of _____, state of _____, do hereby make and declare this to be my last will and testament, hereby revoking any and all former wills and codicils[†] previously made by me.

1. I direct that my just debts, including the expenses of my last illness and funeral, be paid as soon as may be practicable after my death.[‡]

2. I bequeath to my son (daughter), _____, the sum of _____ dollars and these specific gifts:[§] _____.

3. I bequeath to _____ this:[‖] _____.

4. All the rest of my estate, whether real, personal, or mixed, wheresoever situated, I bequeath to my wife (husband), _____, for her (his) own use and benefit forever.[#]

5. I appoint as executrix (executor) of my will my wife (husband, etc.).[**] I direct that no bond be required of her (him), and that she (he) shall consider proper, any or all of my real or personal estate, except those specific gifts mentioned above.

In testimony whereof, witness my hand this _____ day of _____, A.D. _____[††]

Signed: _____

The foregoing instrument, consisting of _____ typewritten pages,[‡‡] each page being identified by the signature of the willmaker, was subscribed and declared to be his (her) last will and testament. In his (her) presence, at his (her) request, and in the presence of each other, we have subscribed our names as witnesses;[§§] and we believe he (she) was of sound mind and memory and under no constraint.

Signed _____
Address _____
Signed _____
Address _____

---

*"Where there's a will there's a way" to express concerns and divide property among family, friends, and charities. When a person leaves no will (a condition called "intestate") the major beneficiaries are often the government and lawyers. It is wise to

study current federal and state estate laws before preparing a will. Consult a lawyer after drawing up a first draft.

†A codicil is a supplement later added to a will. It explains or alters current provisions. If important changes are necessary, it is better to write a new will and destroy the old one.

‡Some wills specify the type of funeral arrangements and state approximate costs. Since decisions about being kept alive by extraordinary life-support equipment and about body and/or organ donation need to be executed before or immediately after death, and since a will may be impossible to retrieve quickly, matters pertaining to such should be recorded elsewhere and a copy placed in the hands of one's physician.

§Each offspring should be specifically mentioned, or the will may be set aside. If there are minor children, a guardian whose values are acceptable should be appointed. Describe nonmonetary gifts in detail.

‖After designations for individual relatives (or others) are made, there often follows a provision for a percentage of the residual estate or money (tax-exempt) to be left to charities—to institutions such as churches, colleges, and libraries.

#A will can be contested in many states if a certain minimum proportion of the estate is not left to one's spouse. This may range from one-third to one-half.

**Often the trust department of a bank rather than an individual is named as executor. However, the fee for estate settlement can be reduced or eliminated by naming a relative to perform this function.

††Every few years a will should be reviewed and rewritten if it no longer expresses what the willmaker wants.

‡‡Fasten the pages firmly together, because a will may be voided if a page is lost or replaced. If insertions or corrections are needed, the whole document should be retyped before signing. Make several copies and place the original signed copy in a secure location. Give a copy to the executor.

§§The witnesses should know the willmaker well but should not be beneficiaries. They should be adults but younger than the willmaker. Thus they will more likely be living when the will is probated—that is, taken to court in order to certify it.

B.4: FUNERAL CONSIDERATIONS

The concerns expressed here should be discussed with your closest relatives and/or friends. One of them should be given a copy of this record. Requests should have clarity since there will be no way of finding out what you meant when your notes are used.

To assist those responsible for arrangements after my death, I make these requests:

1. These people should be notified as soon as possible:
   Name   Relationship   Address   Telephone

   _____

   _____

   _____

2. ( ) I would like to donate any organs or tissues that are needed to help others.

3. ( ) I would like to give my body for anatomical study, if needed. The medical school to be notified is: _____

   _____

4. ( ) I am willing to have my body made available for an autopsy if this can be of some value to society.

5. ( ) I would like to have my body embalmed for the purpose of open casket display.

6. Notice of my death should be published in these places: _____

   _____

   _____

7. ( ) I would like to have visitation hours for friends: ( ) at the funeral home; ( ) at my home.

8. ( ) I would prefer that, instead of sending flowers, my friends make memorial gifts, if they wish, to: _____

   _____

9. Specific preferences:
   as to body container: _____

as to vault, if such is desired: _____

as to disposal of ashes, if cremation is requested: _____

_____

as to pallbearers: _____

other directions: _____

10. Approximate cost of funeral (including body container):

_____

vault _____; cemetery lot _____; grave marker _____.
( ) I have prepaid my funeral expenses. The receipt can be
found: _____

_____

11. I wish to have a funeral service held:

( ) at my church, which is _____

( ) at a funeral home, namely _____

( ) at my home, located at _____

12. I wish to have:
( ) a service at which my body is present, followed by separate
( ) graveside rites; ( ) cremation.
( ) a graveyard service only
( ) a memorial service after private
( ) interment; ( ) cremation.

13. I would like to have my body ( ) buried in the ground; ( ) en-
tombed in a mausoleum in _____ Cemetery
located in _____.

( ) I own a lot or crypt certificate and this is located in _____

_____

I wish my grave to have this location on the lot: _____

14. ( ) I wish to have a memorial marker, made of _____ and
placed _____ with this inscription_____

_____

15. ( ) I have a safe deposit box, number _____, located in _____

_____

( ) I have these insurance policies: _____

_____

_____

( ) I have made out a will, dated _____ and located
in _____

My executor is: _____

16. ( ) I have written down on attached sheets suggestions regarding what would be appropriate for my service. There you will
find any preferences that I have with respect to: (a) readings; (b)
prayers; (c) music; (d) biographical statement; (e) other matters.

Date _____ Signature _____

S. S. Number _____

B.5: CEMETERY VISITATION

Visit the oldest cemetery you can find.

1. What do you take to be the plan by which this cemetery was developed? (Notice where the earlier burials are located, the way the roads are arranged, etc.)

2. Which memorial markers seem more durable: marble, granite, or bronze? Are all inscriptions still readable? What colors of granite can be found?

3. Examine inscriptions, looking for some which contain more than a name, dates, and a trite saying (such as "Rest in Peace"). What religious symbols can you find? What artistic motifs are found, and what does each mean to you? Make some sketches and record some epitaphs of interesting gravestones.

4. Record the age at death of a dozen women taken at random. Do the same for a dozen men. What is the average age at death for each gender? What significant difference, if any, is there in these averages?

5. Are there mausoleums in this cemetery? How do they differ from other burial places? Why do you think some people prefer them? How are the crypts arranged within a mausoleum?

6. If you see a caretaker or mortician around, ask such questions as: How are graves dug? What is the source of the money which pays for the upkeep? What is the difference in cost of a burial lot and a mausoleum crypt? Have there been any racial restrictions in the past? Do any racial prejudices appear to be operative now?

7. "Memorial Park" is usually the designation for cemeteries where all markers are flush with the ground. They appear to be vast lawns and are less expensive to maintain because the grass can easily be trimmed. Do you find them less objectionable than cemeteries with upright markers? Is relative anonymity and conformity more appropriate for the dead?

8. From your observations, what case can be made that death is, or is not, a leveler of economic classes?

9. In areas where there is an option, why do you think hillsides rather than valleys are usually chosen for cemeteries?

10. What considerations do you think are important in selecting a cemetery or a family plot within it? What do you think of cemeteries which attempt to sell plots only to those of one religious or ethnic group? Do you think it should be permissible for domestic pets to be buried in a family plot?

11. Compose an epitaph to be placed under your name. In it express significant qualities about yourself in a few words.

C. Ancient Views on Death

C.1: BUDDHA ON GRIEF

(This paraphrase of a mustard-seed legend is found in several ancient forms. The story expresses these central Buddhist doctrines: our human situation is miserable; selfish craving is the cause of this misery; and this craving can be eliminated by following the teachings of Buddha.)

Kisa Gotami had only one son, and he died. In her grief she carried the dead child to all her neighbors, asking them for medicine. The people said, "She has lost her senses; the boy is dead."

At length, Kisa met a man who replied, "I cannot give you medicine for your child, but I know a physician who can." The young mother said, "Please tell me, sir; who is it?" And the man replied, "Go to Sakyamuni, the Buddha."

Kisa went to the Buddha and cried, "Lord and Master, give me the medicine that will cure my boy." The Buddha answered, "I want a handful of mustard seed." When the mother in her joy promised to procure it, the Buddha added, "The seed must be taken from a house where no one has lost a child, spouse, parent, or friend."

Poor Kisa now went from house to house, and the people pitied her and said, "Here is mustard seed; take it!" But when she asked, "Did a son or daughter, husband or wife, father or mother, die in your family?" they answered her, "Alas! the living are few, but the dead are many. Do not remind us of our grief." And there was no home found where there had not been mourning.

Kisa became weary and hopeless and sat down beside the street, watching the lights of the city as they flickered up and were extinguished again. At last the darkness of the night reigned everywhere. She thought to herself, "How selfish am I in my grief! Death is common to all; yet in this valley of desolation there is a path that leads to deliverance those who have surrendered all selfishness."

The Buddha said, "The life of mortals is brief and combined with pain. There is not any means by which those that have been born can avoid dying. As all clay vessels made by a potter end in being broken, so is the life of mortals. Both young and adult, both those who are fools and those who are wise, all fall into the power of death; all are subject to death. Parents cannot save their children, nor kin their relations. The world is afflicted with death and decay, and so the wise do not despair, knowing the terms of the world.

"Not from weeping nor from grieving will people obtain peace of mind; on the contrary, their pain will be the greater and their bodies will suffer. They will make themselves sick and pale, yet the dead are not saved by their lamentation. Those who seek peace should draw out the arrow of lamentation, complaint, and grief. Those who have drawn out the arrow and have become composed will obtain peace of mind; those who have overcome all sorrow will become free from sorrow and be blessed."

C.2: JESUS ON DEATH AND AFTERLIFE

An examination of Jesus' earliest recorded sayings reveals that he apparently said little about life after death. This is surprising, since his life has had great impact on the conviction that billions of Christians have held on the subject. Jesus' most significant teaching on the afterlife is this: "When [humans] rise from the dead, they neither marry nor are given in marriage, but are like angels in heaven" (Mark 12:25). This explanation is given as to why there is no need for marriage: "For they cannot die any more" (Luke 20:36). Throughout church history interpreters have found these words to be both enigmatic and enlightening.

Jesus' assertion was given in response to a skeptical question raised by the Sadducaic priestly party during his last week in Jerusalem. They found no basis for a doctrine of resurrection in the "books of Moses," the only Scriptures they recognized as authoritative. Quite accurately, those party members recognized that the concept of an individual afterlife arose long after the earliest biblical books were written.

The idea of a postmortem revival of the body was introduced into apocalyptic Judaism around 200 B.C. The latest book of Jewish Scriptures prophesies that many of the dead shall arise and receive either everlasting life or everlasting contempt (Dan. 12:2). That late Hebrew outlook was influenced by religions surrounding Palestine. The Persian prophet Zoroaster taught that there would be a life after death and its nature would be similar to the pleasures and pains that had been experienced on this side of death (*Bundahism* 30, 25). An eternity of happy marriage and sensuous pleasures would reward the righteous. Judaism may also have been influenced by ideas from the opposite end of the Fertile Crescent. Egyptians believed in an afterlife in which wives and lands would bear abundantly (J. Hamilton-Patterson and C. Andrews, *Mummies* [New York: Viking, 1979], p.65).

The Syriac Apocalypse of Baruch provides a good example of the materialistic ideas about the afterlife that were popular during Jesus' time: "the earth will then assuredly restore the dead, which it now receives, in order to preserve them, making no change in their form" (50:2). Some rabbis assumed that marriage and propagation would continue unchanged in the life after death. The Pharisaic party to which they belonged tended to believe that there would be a reanimation of relics at the time of God's final judgment.

The conservative priests scorned the newfangled notions that liberal Jews had imported from alien cultures. To ridicule the doctrines of the Pharisees, they added a stinging question to an old Jewish tale. The book of Tobit tells of seven husbands dying in succession shortly after marrying the same bride (3:8). The Jerusalem priests asked Jesus which one of them would be married to the widow in an alleged resurrection. Rather than seeking information, they were trying to trap Jesus into advocating an idea that was both nontraditional and absurd. Enraged by his denunciation of temple commercialization in which they were engaged, these priests struck back in this and other ways.

Jesus' view of the afterlife differed from that of his Jewish adversaries. In contrast to the priests, Jesus held that there is a life after death which is based on the nature of God. The faithful and powerful God does not permit covenantal bonds to be severed by the physical death of "those who are accounted worthy" (Luke 20:35). Hence the present tense is used in reference to the Hebrew patriarchs in this revelation to Moses: "I am . . . the God of Abraham, the God of Isaac, and the God of Jacob" (Exod. 3:6; cf. Mark 12:26). Jesus chides the priests for not knowing their Scriptures fully enough to understand the implications of the character of God for a doctrine of human life continuance.

Over against the outlook of some Pharisees, Jesus believed that the afterlife is not a mere extension of physical life. Reproduction, for example, is only needed in a mortal society which must replace some of the dying to avert extinction. As it is generally institutionalized, marriage is the bonding of pairs from unrelated families in order to provide the genetic diversity and lengthy nurture needed by the anticipated offspring. In contrast to the exclusive sexual union, the ecstasy of marital coupling could be expanded in the resurrection.

The life of the earliest Christian community may afford a clue to this more inclusive life. Those Jerusalem Christians were able, at least temporarily, to widen the communal bond of ideal family life by sharing their possessions. Transcending a mine-thine individualism, they received from members according to their abilities and gave to them according to their needs (Acts 2:44–46). Similarly, in the resurrected community, the harmonious give-and-take of a happy family will be enlarged so that all will be in perfect concord.

The best way to gain insight into the afterlife is to extrapolate on the deepest earthly love. Marital love will become something wonderfully inclusive and intense as persons move from the provisional material sphere to the permanent spiritual one. In his *Bottom Line Catechism for Contemporary Catholics* Andrew Greely asserts: ". . . we will love one another in the resurrected life even more intensely, even more joyfully than we do in the present life. . . . It is utterly unthinkable that there would not be between those who work close to one another on earth an even more powerful and more rewarding intimacy in the life of the resurrection" (Chicago: Thomas More, 1982, pp. 105–106).

Early Christian theology affirms that the afterlife is not less than the happiest life of communal caring and sharing that we can now experience. In one of the earliest comments on Mark 12:25, Clement of Alexandria pointed out that Jesus had blessed the married state, so his words should not be read, as some monks then were prone to do, as a denigration of marriage (*Stromateis* 3, 12, 87). Clement discerned that Jesus was criticizing a carnal interpretation of human resurrection, not sexual intercourse. Jesus suggested that the afterlife would have a quality greater than the highest expression of love we can attain in the earthly life.

C.3: PAUL ON RESURRECTION

In a study of viewpoints on death in world cultures, sociologist Panos D. Bardis states, "One of the greatest Christian thinkers, Saint Paul, made the first profound statement regarding *resurrection*" (*History of Thanatology* [Washington: University Press of America, 1981], p. 47). An exposition of Paul's immortality ideas follows.

Will humans live again? This question, anxiously raised by Job (14:14), is as new as the freshest grave. The fullest New Testament discussion of this haunting question is contained in a letter of the Apostle Paul.

Some Greeks whom Paul addressed in 1 Corinthians 15 answered the question of human immortality in the negative (vs. 12). At that time many Greeks were followers of Epicurus, the founder of an Athenian school centuries earlier. That philosopher argued that the human soul is annihilated at death. A thoroughgoing materialist, Epicurus thought humans were no more than atoms which eventually would be recycled into other physical organisms. Since there is no court of judgment after death where gods can hold mortals accountable for crimes committed, Epicurus advised mortals to concern themselves exclusively with maximizing lasting personal pleasures here and now. Paul alludes to an Epicurean slogan when he quips, "If the dead are not raised, 'Let us eat and drink, for tomorrow we die'" (vs. 32).

The Acts of the Apostles tells of Paul's visit to Athens and of the reaction to his preaching by Epicureans and other members of the university city. As long as the Apostle delivered a polished oration to the cultured Greeks, they listened politely. But as soon as he asserted belief in "the resurrection of the dead" they began to ridicule. To most Athenians the notion of God's raising the dead was too fantastic to swallow (17:22–34).

In response to Greek skepticism about resurrection, Paul includes in his Corinthian letter a carefully reasoned statement of Christian doctrine. The Apostle first presents the evidence for Jesus' resurrection. Its certainty is based on the postmortem appearances of Jesus to various individuals separately and to more than five hundred people at one time. After transmitting the core tradition of what happened after Jesus' death and burial, Paul testifies from firsthand experience that Jesus appeared to him personally. The verb *appeared* which Paul uses to refer to these Easter events usually describes in the Greek New Testament revelations occurring within persons (see Matt. 17:3; Acts 16:9; 26:16). It is significant that Paul makes no mention of Jesus' corpse disappearing or of angels rolling away a stone from an empty tomb. Evidently, if Paul received from other Christians a tradition of Jesus' *physical* resurrection, he considered it to be either unconvincing or too trivial to relate.

After presenting the case for Jesus' spiritual resurrection, Paul goes on to consider its significance. Without the resurrection, he claims, there would be no good news to preach and no Christian church. The resurrection was the electrifying charge that sparked the Apostles' missionary efforts. The early Christians did not regard the resurrection as merely a nonessential postscript to the biography of their executed leader. They considered it to be the central theme of the gospel. According to Paul, Christians who reject this event have no bedrock foundation for their faith. To deny Jesus' resurrection leaves no hope that good and life will prevail over evil and death. Christians are left with a pessimistic, even tragic, view of life.

Paul then connects the special resurrection of Jesus to the general resurrection of Christians. As the Apostle defines elsewhere, Christians are those who have been "raised with Christ" (Col. 3:1). Being "with Christ" is for Paul the essence of the spiritual life, both before and after physical death (Phil. 1:23; 1 Thess. 4:17). Hence, the resurrection of those who are in union with Christ is as certain as was his resurrection. Christ is "the first fruits of those who have fallen asleep" (1 Cor. 15:20) and he "will change our lowly body to be like his glorious body" (Phil. 3:21). If Christ "the first fruits" did not return to the conditions of his earthly life, neither will the full crop of resurrected Christians.

Having established to his satisfaction the certainty and the significance of Jesus' resurrection, Paul moves forward in his discussion to deal with the tough questions: "how are the dead raised? In what kind of body?" (1 Cor. 15:35 NEB) He realistically accepts the biological fact that the fleshly organism decays when it dies. He frankly and plainly states that "flesh and blood cannot inherit the kingdom of

God, nor does the perishable inherit the imperishable" (vs. 50). He did not believe that the residual buried dust or cremated ash would be the substance of a new heavenly organism. When Paul writes about "the resurrection of the dead" he does not mean the reassembling and the reanimation of the corpse. The expression "spiritual body" (vs. 44) which he uses does not refer to the physical skeleton and the flesh that hangs on it. Rather, the spiritual body means, in modern terminology, the self or the personality.

By way of providing a commonplace analogy, Paul compares the process of a mortal putting on immortality with the growth process of seed. When a gardener sows seed, it disappears in the earth. It mingles with the soil in which it lies and will never again be seen in the form in which it was planted. If you were to ask a gardener why he or she plants seed that will quickly decompose in damp ground, the reply might be, "I am not throwing away the seed in vain. Although I do not fully understand the process of growth, I know that the seed, if it is any good, will come up in another form. Then, when it sprouts forth, it will produce a plant more valuable than the original seed."

Paul's picturesque seed illustration affirms both transformation and continuity as humans pass from the mortal to the immortal existence. When seed germinates, the outer husk becomes fertilizer while the inner core or nucleus becomes more alive than ever. There is a similar transformation when "the mortal puts on immortality" (vs. 54). "We shall be changed," Paul twice states (vss. 51–52). The corpse is the outer husk that disintegrates in the soil. But meanwhile, the essential kernel, the true self, lives on in a lovelier and more valuable way. What "is sown a physical body," explains Paul, "is raised a spiritual body" (vs. 44).

When plants grow there is continuity between the seed and the fruit it produces. The immortal person is connected with the old mortal existence as an ear of corn is connected with the seed which produced it. Paul posits that those attaining life after death will continue to be their particular selves and know one another. Separate individuals are not absorbed into the infinite Spirit of God after death like drops in an ocean. Thus the Apostle does not hold a pantheistic view of immortality. Rather, he believes there is no loss of the particular ego; each personality remains unique. Paul draws from the observable heavens an illustration of the continuity of distinct personality. He presumes that each of the celestial bodies—such as Jupiter and the North Star—has an individuality of its own. In a similar manner the heavenly self has a distinct individuality. Paul writes, that as "star differs from star in glory, so is it with the resurrection of the dead" (vss. 41–42).

After probing deeply into the religious significance of death, the Apostle breaks into poetry:

> O death, where is thy victory?
> O death, where is thy sting?
> (vs. 55)

Paul's confidence in the face of death does not mean that he felt he had unraveled all the mysteries of death or that he fully understood the nature of the life beyond physical existence. Earlier in this Corinthian letter Paul admits our partial knowledge: "Now we see only puzzling reflections in a mirror, but then we shall see face to face" (13:13 NEB). The Apostle recognized that we do not now have the details which can satisfy all our curiosity about life after death. However, he affirms in 1 Corinthians 2:10 that it will exceed the fondest imagining of those who love God.

Paul's final words on this subject in the Corinthian letter display concern lest Christians become carried away with otherworldly speculation on immortality and thereby shirk their responsibilities in the communities in which they are living. He did not want them to engage in idle contemplation about the raptures of the hereafter. The religiously oriented can become so heavenly minded that they are of no earthly use. Some become so engrossed in contemplating how they will meet with their friends in heaven and who will be there to meet that they fail to interact with friends on earth. Thus the Apostle ends his brilliant discussion of the resurrection with a challenge to activity. "Work without limit," he exhorts, "since you know that in the Lord your labor cannot be lost" (15:58 NEB).

INDEX